JOHN BROWN'S TRIAL

WITHDRAWN

JOHN BROWN'S TRIAL

Brian McGinty

HARVARD UNIVERSITY PRESS

Cambridge, Massachusetts

London, England

2009

Publication of this book has been supported through the generous provisions
of the Maurice and Lula Bradley Smith Memorial Fund.

Library of Congress Cataloging-in-Publication Data
McGinty, Brian.
John Brown's trial / Brian McGinty.
p. cm.
Includes bibliographical references and index.
ISBN 978-0-674-03517-1 (alk. paper)
1. Brown, John, 1800–1859—Trials, litigation, etc.   2. Trials (Treason)—
Virginia.   3. Brown, John, 1800–1859.   4. Abolitionists—United States—
Biography.   5. Harpers Ferry (W. Va.)—History—John Brown's Raid, 1859.
I. Title.
KF223.B765M34 2009
973.7'116—dc22   2009004724

To Jim Barnett

CONTENTS

Ilustrations follow page 130

JOHN BROWN'S TRIAL

INTRODUCTION

John Brown needs no introduction to students of American history. A century and a half after he died on a Virginia gallows, the famous abolitionist's turbulent life story remains fascinating—and enduringly controversial. It has inspired generations of historians, novelists, poets, playwrights, and screenwriters to examine and reexamine the strange mix of idealism and violence that fueled his self-declared war against American slavery. Over and over again, biographers of Brown have recalled his sternly Calvinist religious roots, his puzzling psychology, his long and spotty career as a farmer and businessman, and the role he played in the violent struggles in "Bleeding Kansas" in 1855–1858. They have told and retold the story of the bloody raid he led on the United States armory and arsenal at Harper's Ferry, Virginia, on October 16, 17, and 18, 1859;[1] quoted the famous refrain "John Brown's body lies a-mouldering in the grave"; and attempted to explain why "his soul goes marching on."[2] Few of these chroniclers, however, have paid more than cursory attention to the trial that followed so swiftly on the heels of Brown's Harper's Ferry raid.[3]

This neglect is not, perhaps, surprising. Historians are not usually trained in the law. Many are unaware of the truly remarkable history that can be made in a courtroom. Few know much of the dynamics of the adversary system, in which truth is pursued in a contest between opposing sides, each jousting with the other for advantage in the eyes of the judge, the jury, and, in very important cases, public opinion. If, at the end of a trial, there is a winner and a loser, it is not always clear which got the better of the contest, for a trial often bears more resemblance to a battle than a war, and seasoned warriors know only too well that battles may be won even while the war is being lost.

Brown came into Harper's Ferry in October 1859 believing that, armed with pistols, rifles, and pikes, he could help slaves rise up against their masters and then retreat into the adjoining mountains with great waves of slaves following behind. Two weeks later, he left the Jefferson County Courthouse in nearby Charlestown[4] with his dream of a slave insurrection shattered but convinced that, by dying on the scaffold, he could achieve an even greater victory. If he stood before the bar in Judge Richard Parker's courtroom a condemned murderer, traitor, and conspirator, he left the gallows a martyr for the cause of freedom. If he lost his fight before the bar of Virginia justice, he struck a great blow against slavery, for less than a year and a half after he was hanged—thanks in large part to his Charlestown trial—the Civil War began in all its horror; less than two years after that, Abraham Lincoln issued his Emancipation Proclamation, driving a knife deep into slavery's heart; and within three more years slavery met a final death with the ratification of the Thirteenth Amendment to the Constitution. If, in his trial, Brown lost his battle to retain his life, in death he achieved a stunning victory in the war against human bondage.

America's fascination with trials is long and complex. Drawing on roots in the common law, the English forms of the trial crossed the ocean with the first English settlers of the colonies where, modified by the needs and experiences of American life, they were stripped of much of their Old World formality. After the Revolution, spurred by a determination not to perpetuate the injustices imposed on the English people by their kings, Americans reshaped their trials into the disciplined, almost ritualistic judicial proceedings familiar to later generations. Although its form and requirements changed much in the nineteenth century, the trial remained a bulwark of the American legal system, and one of the key institutions of the American experiment in self-government.

Whether formal or informal, improvised or ritualized, trials in America have always been recognized as struggles between opposing forces. The trial is a contest, much like the clash of prize-fighters in a ring or opposing armies on a battlefield. At the outset, the strength of the conflicting forces can only be estimated, and the damage that will be inflicted on the combatants is the subject of speculation. As the contest continues, one side or the other may appear to have gained the upper hand, but the outcome must remain unknown until the last blow has been struck or the last gunshots fired. The elements of drama are present in every trial, though in some they are more vivid than in others. Little wonder, then, that Americans are attracted to trials as elemental conflicts, life-and-death struggles with portentous consequences. Unlike other contests, however, the ritual of a trial channels the violence into the peaceful forms of judicial procedure. In criminal trials, there are no jabs or body blows, no artillery salvos or cavalry charges, but indictments and pleas, opening statements, witnesses' testimonies, cross-examinations, closing arguments, jury deliberations, verdicts, and, ultimately, sentences. Trials do not eliminate the lust for violent confrontation that is basic to the human race, but they do moderate that lust with the knowledge that disputes can be settled in courtrooms, before judges and juries, according to rules laid down by lawmakers and enforced by the state.

When a trial is purely civil, private rights and privileges are asserted. When a trial is criminal, however, the collective rights of the public are at stake. In England and in the American colonies, criminal charges were filed in the name of the Crown, alleging that the accused had breached the duty of obedience to the king's laws. After independence, the states and the federal government assumed the authority previously held by British monarchs to enforce the law and punish violators, and crimes were no longer affronts to the head of state but violations of the social contract. The injured party was not the Crown, but the "people" who (in constitutional theory if not always in practice) held the ultimate sovereignty at both the state and federal levels. If loyal British subjects were interested in the conduct and outcome of criminal trials as examples of the fate that might befall them if they fell afoul of the king's or queen's law, American citizens were interested in how justice was meted out not only *to them* but also *in their name*. Trials thus assumed a more central role in the body politic.[5] They were not only demonstrations of power and authority but expressions of the society's collective concepts of fairness and justice. It was on this level that John Brown was brought to trial—an accused lawbreaker arraigned for a basic violation of the social contract and made to answer for his offense to the people of Virginia.

The trial is particularly important in a self-governing society—critically so in a society that claims to be based on the rule of law. Laws are made by legislatures but applied by courts after the parties have been summoned to the bar of justice, the facts examined, and guilt or innocence determined. The trial has been called the "keystone of our system of personal liberties."[6] It is in the trial that accusations are made, rights enforced, and liberties guarded. In America, the trial is almost always open to public scrutiny—and rightly so, for the Constitution enshrines the right to "a speedy and public trial" as one of the basic guarantees of the Bill of Rights.[7]

The requirement that trials be public is designed to ensure, among other things, that trials are fair. It may surprise many readers to learn that a fair trial, as such, is not one of the rights guaranteed by the U.S. Constitution, and that the word "fair" does not appear even once in that fundamental charter or in either of its predecessors, the Articles of Confederation or the Declaration of Independence. In fact, studies of American legal procedures—even some that explicitly refer to judicial fairness—are notable for their inability to define the term "fair trial."[8] This does not mean that fairness is not one of the basic values of American liberty or that trials that fall short of that standard are not vulnerable to reversal on appeal. If it means anything at all, it is that fairness is an elusive concept and is tied, in the context of trials, to the observance of many different rights: the right to be informed of the nature and cause of the accusation, for example; the right to be confronted with the accusing witnesses; the right to have compulsory process for obtaining favorable witnesses; the right to the assistance of counsel; and the right to be tried by an impartial jury.[9] The Fifth and the Fourteenth Amendments to the Constitution include guarantees of due process of law, and through a long series of judicial decisions these guarantees have been interpreted to mean something equivalent to fair trial—but not exactly.[10]

It is important to observe at the outset that when Brown was tried, the guarantees enumerated in the Bill of Rights (including due process of law) were not binding on the states. By their own terms, they constrained the federal courts but not the state courts.[11] They were later applied to the states, but only through the mechanism of the Fourteenth Amendment, which became a part of the Constitution in 1868, and only after the U.S. Supreme Court, in a series of controversial decisions, determined that the amendment had "incorporated" those guarantees—or at least most of them.[12] In 1859, in Charlestown, Virginia, the contours of a fair trial were thus governed by the statutes, court decisions, and constitution of the Commonwealth of Virginia, operating independently of federal mandates.

Notwithstanding all this, the concept of fairness was very much alive and often invoked during Brown's trial. Brown himself frequently spoke of it when he addressed the judge. At the outset, he reminded the court that he had been promised a "fair trial" by the governor of Virginia, Henry Alexander Wise. During the trial, when objecting to some of the judge's rulings, he complained that he was being given a mere "mockery of a trial." In the end, however, he announced that he was "entirely satisfied" with the treatment he received in his trial, and one of his own attorneys stated in open court that the trial had been fair. But this was not the end of the subject, for both Brown and his attorneys had been too intimately involved in the trial to appraise it objectively. And Brown was not a lawyer. He did not know the procedural requirements of Virginia law, the rules of evidence that prevailed in Virginia courts, or the rights of accused felons.

Whether or not the trial was in fact fair, it was important to Virginia authorities that it be seen as fair, for to them the perception of fairness was as important as the reality. They knew only too well that the eyes of the country—North and South alike—were on the courtroom in Charlestown. Brown's was the first trial to be extensively reported, not just by state and local newspapers, but also by regional and national media. Reporters converged on the courthouse in Charlestown from all parts of the country, and news magazines with national circulation sent artists to record visual images of the trial.[13] A special telegraph line was extended from Harper's Ferry to Charlestown for the specific purpose of covering the trial, connecting the proceedings there to national telegraph lines and allowing dispatches from the trial to be wired to editorial desks in eastern cities with a speed that would have been unimaginable a few years before.[14] Major newspapers combined their reports through the telegraph services of the Associated Press, making detailed reports of the trial available to newspapers all over the country.[15]

John Brown's trial has been called the "first modern courtroom event" and "a milestone in the development of American journalism."[16] Because it was subject to intense media coverage, Virginia was put on notice that the state's institutions would be subject to intense scrutiny and that Southern fairness as well as Northern "treachery" would be on trial in Charlestown. As important as it was for Virginians to bring Brown to justice, it was almost equally important that they show outsiders that they adhered to civilized standards of trial. For too long, they believed, they had been derided by Northerners for their toleration of slavery in a world that increasingly condemned it as a relic of barbarism. They defended slavery as just and necessary, even as sanctioned by the Bible, and they rightly regarded Brown's trial as an opportunity to demonstrate their respect for basic rights (disregarding, of course, the embarrassing fact that those rights were denied to blacks).

But if Virginia authorities recognized that the world was watching them in Charlestown, Brown was aware that the trial presented him with a unique opportunity to attack slavery. Southerners—and Northern critics of abolitionism—were quick to condemn him as a madman and fanatic who had defiled the peace of a Virginia town. But Brown realized that Virginia and slavery were also on trial in Charlestown. He had invaded Harper's Ferry to incite a slave insurrection. His intent was to maim and, if possible, kill slavery, but not, he protested, to take innocent life. If his life was in the hands of a jury of Virginians, the future of slavery itself was now in the hands of public opinion.

It would have been difficult for an ordinary man to argue the case against slavery in Charlestown, in a great state that was committed to perpetuation of the institution. But Brown was not an ordinary man. He used the opportunities the trial presented to level his own accusations against Virginia, even as Virginia leveled its accusations against him. And he did so with an eloquence that excited admiration throughout the country—even in the South, where he was personally held in contempt and his antislavery aims were subject to passionate loathing.

Brown was not an orator, at least not in the usual sense of that term. He had received only a rudimentary formal education—a few years in country schools and a few months in an academy at which he had hoped to train for the ministry. But when an eye inflammation and lack of money forced him to give up his dream, he contented himself with self-education, studying the Bible (even attempting to commit all of it to memory) and reading popular books that taught moral lessons. As he grew to manhood, he developed a forceful manner of speaking and writing. In his Calvinist worldview, there were two great forces in the world: good and evil. Men who loved God pursued good with all their strength; men who did not were evil and were subject to God's holy wrath. In Charlestown, he spent most of his time in the courtroom lying on a cot, nursing the wounds he sustained when he was captured but rising on occasion to address the judge, the attorneys, and the jury. "If we are to be forced with a mere form—a trial for execution—you might spare yourselves that trouble," he said at one point. "I am ready for my fate."[17] Later, he turned the spotlight on his accusers, saying: "I see a book kissed, which I suppose to be the Bible, or at least the New Testament, which teaches me that all things whatsoever I would that men should do to me, I should do even so to them. . . . Now, if it is deemed necessary that I should forfeit my life for the furtherance of the ends of justice, and mingle my blood further with the blood of my children and with the blood of millions in this slave country, whose rights are disregarded by wicked, cruel, and unjust enactments, I say let it be done."[18]

It seemed to most spectators that Brown's situation in Charlestown was hopeless. There were, after all, hundreds of witnesses who saw him in Harper's Ferry during his raid and who stood ready to testify against him. If his cause was hopeless, however, he did not seem to know it. He spoke with confidence and made his points deliberately and clearly. He believed that slavery was an offense against God and that it was the duty of God-fearing Christians to do everything in their power to end it. Virginians were not persuaded by his logic. They regarded slavery not as a moral evil but as one of the essential institutions of a civilized society. They were, however, impressed by Brown's courage. It was clear that he was a man of principle, not a mere thug or cutthroat. However much Southerners might disagree with his principles, they could not readily deny his sincerity in expressing them. And Brown himself felt empowered by his words. When he went from the courtroom to his jail cell, and from the jail to the gallows erected outside Charlestown, he was convinced that the case he made against slavery in the courtroom was stronger than the case the prosecutors had made against him and that, in God's eyes, Virginia's guilt was by far the more egregious. Many in the North, following reports of his trial in the newspapers, agreed.

Criminal trials often result from unforeseen events, which imbue them with something of the character of accidents: If the accused's bullet missed its intended victim, he would be tried not for murder but for attempted murder or aggravated assault. If the victim was shot, but not fatally, the accused would face a long prison sentence but not execution. If the accused himself was gunned down by one of his intended victims or killed by a police officer, his name would be recorded in a crime report but not immortalized in a public trial. The same can be said of

Brown. If he had been shot dead during his raid or if he had bled to death from the sword wounds inflicted on him when marines stormed his last refuge in the U.S. armory and arsenal, he would have died without a trial, been condemned as a madman, and been relegated to a footnote of history.[19] Because he survived, however, and because the townspeople were unable to stop him on their own but had to wait for federal troops to come to their rescue, and because the sword wielded by marine Lieutenant Israel Green was a ceremonial weapon too dull to inflict fatal wounds, Brown survived to stand trial and win a place in history.[20] He became the principal actor in his own trial by virtue of a series of events quite unanticipated when the drama began. He lived to speak his piece, accuse his accusers, and become a martyr to the cause of racial justice in the United States.[21]

Brown's ability to speak so forcefully in his trial is attributable to another curious accident of history. For centuries in both England and America, parties to litigation, criminal or civil, were disqualified from testifying in their own behalf. Only "disinterested" witnesses were permitted to testify, for it was believed that a person who had a personal interest in a case would inevitably lie.[22] Personal interest was thought to be so strong that it would trump even the obligations of an oath, and swearing to tell the truth would not remove the disqualification. Ordinary witnesses were sworn to tell the truth, of course, but they were also subject to cross-examination. If a trial court today denied an accused criminal's request to give sworn testimony in his own behalf, the denial would quickly be overturned by an appellate court. Not so in Brown's time. Most discussion about the testimony of criminal defendants today centers on the privilege against self-incrimination guaranteed by the Fifth Amendment to the Constitution.[23] This discussion concedes that every criminal defendant has a right to testify *if he chooses,* but it also makes clear that he may not be *compelled to do so.* When Brown was brought to trial in Charlestown, no one suggested that he might have a right to take the witness stand. So far as the record reveals, no criminal defendant had ever advanced such a novel claim in any American court, and none would do so until sometime after the Civil War, when the right to testify would gain recognition, mainly as a result of legislation.[24] Though Brown had no right to give sworn testimony, he did have the right to make an unsworn statement in open court. This statement—sometimes called an allocution—had long been traditional in criminal prosecutions in both England and America and was customarily given after the judge (or clerk, depending on the court's practice) asked the defendant if he had anything to say before sentence was pronounced.[25] It was given in the defendant's own words and was not subject to cross-examination. Brown took advantage of this right, delivering an oration so moving that Emerson later ranked it with Lincoln's Gettysburg Address as one of "the two best specimens of eloquence we have had in this country."[26] More recently, legal scholar Robert A. Ferguson has called it "one of the great set speeches in nineteenth century oratory," and Civil War historian James M. McPherson has praised its "surpassing eloquence."[27] It was printed in newspapers all over the country and reprinted countless times—sometimes even as a separate publication. In his statement, Brown showed himself to be a man of conviction and principle. He enunciated words that inspired the enemies of slavery. He indicted slavery as an offense against the "law of God" and expressed the firm belief that by seeking to interfere with slavery, he himself had done "no wrong, but right."[28]

If Brown had given sworn testimony, his freedom to make his own case would have been severely hampered. He would have had to answer questions propounded by the attorneys. He would have been subject to cross-examination, which could have been searing. He would have been constrained by the rules

of evidence, which exclude matters that are immaterial or irrele-
vant to the strict proof of guilt or innocence. He almost certainly would have sought to invoke a "higher law" to defend his
actions, but the judge would just as certainly have limited him to
the laws of Virginia. The formal legal process would have interfered with his presentation and made it difficult, if not impossible, for him to expound as movingly as he did. Had he testified
and submitted himself to cross-examination, he could still have
made a statement before sentence was passed—his right to an
allocution would not have been waived. But its value would
have been seriously impaired, for whatever he said at the close of
the trial would be compared to the testimony he gave on the
witness stand; inconsistencies would be pointed out; admissions,
if any, made under the stress of cross-examination would be emphasized. If the statement was eloquent, the eloquence would
be diluted by the earlier statements made in answer to questions
from the lawyers. But such was not to be the case with John
Brown, for he had no right to testify, he did not have to answer
questions, and he was not subject to cross-examination. But he
could—and did—deliver a statement in his own words. Thus did
an ancient rule of judicial procedure, abolished only a few years
later—a then-uncontroversial rule prohibiting an accused criminal from giving sworn testimony in his own case—enable John
Brown to take his place with Lincoln in the pantheon of great
orators.

Before Brown could make his stirring courtroom statement
in Charlestown, however, two important legal obstacles had to
be overcome, and the way in which they were dealt with contributed in their own ways to the ensuing drama. At the outset
was the question of the legal jurisdiction to try John Brown. He
had, after all, invaded a U.S. armory and arsenal in Harper's
Ferry, taken forcible possession of federal property, captured
federal employees, and shattered the peace and security of a fed-

eral enclave. When President James Buchanan learned of the attack on Harper's Ferry, he ordered federal troops (marines under the command of Army Lieutenant Colonel Robert E. Lee) to the scene. Lee and the marines promptly quelled Brown's insurrection and took him into custody, all on federal territory. Governor Wise and President Buchanan both had to confront fundamental questions about how Brown should be dealt with. Had he offended federal law or the laws of the Commonwealth of Virginia—or perhaps both? Buchanan was a Northerner with Southern sympathies—a "doughface" in the political slang of the day—and was almost always willing to accommodate Southern demands. He could have ordered Lee to turn Brown and his accomplices over to the United States marshal to be charged with federal crimes and tried in the U.S. District Court for the Western District of Virginia, soon to convene in Wytheville. But Wise wanted Brown to be tried in a Virginia court for crimes against Virginia, and Buchanan acceded to the governor's demand.[29]

The Virginia prosecutor assigned to Brown's case decided to charge Brown with treason—perhaps the most serious criminal charge that can be leveled against any man.[30] This raised another problem, however. Treason is an offense against allegiance, which is the duty of loyalty and obedience that citizens (and legal residents) owe to a nation or state.[31] John Brown owed allegiance to the United States, of course, because he was a U.S. citizen. But he was neither a citizen nor a resident of Virginia, and the question arose whether he owed any allegiance to Virginia. His attorneys argued that he did not and thus could not be tried for treason against it. They pointed out that he had come into the state from Maryland, traversed a short strip of Virginia land, and then launched his raid against federal property. Before his arrest, he had been on Virginia territory only a few minutes. The armory and arsenal at Harper's Ferry, the immediate targets of his raid, were as much subject to the exclusive control of the federal government as the District of Columbia.[32] But Brown's prosecutor argued that because Brown enjoyed the privileges and immunities of a U.S. citizen when he came into Virginia, he had a duty of allegiance to Virginia even though he was neither a citizen nor a resident; that he would have owed the same allegiance to any state he entered; and that this duty was sufficient to subject him to prosecution for treason against Virginia. The prosecutors won this argument in the court in Charlestown, but the judge's ruling on the issue was never clearly explained, and it was not clarified on appeal. It was one of the most troubling of all the legal questions raised by the trial, for it lay at the heart of the federal system erected by the Constitution. In a nation of individual states joined together in a federal union, one in which the national government's sovereignty is supreme but states retain sovereignty in their own spheres, where is allegiance owed? If a series of acts can be construed as treason against both a state and the United States, can the state prosecute the perpetrator and disregard the jurisdiction of the federal courts? The answer provided in 1859 was more political than legal. The president of the United States and the governor of Virginia decided that Brown would be tried in Virginia for treason against the Commonwealth of Virginia, and that is where he was tried. This decision thrust Virginia rather than the United States into the role of the offended sovereign and contributed incalculably to the widening abyss between North and South. John Brown was condemned not as an enemy of the American people but as an enemy of Virginia and, by logical extension, of Southern slaveholders.

Despite all the years that have passed since it concluded, John Brown's trial still commands the attention of history—and with reason. It is not just that it was the first trial in American history to receive massive attention from national media, the first trial in which an accused defendant appealed to a "higher law" to justify violent crimes, the first trial in American history in which a defendant was executed for treason against a state.[33] It was all of these things, but more. It was a high drama played out on a national stage, and it pitted two starkly different moral visions against each other. One of those visions condemned slavery as an affront to human rights, a violation of God's law, and an embarrassment to a nation that claimed to be founded on the "self-evident truth" that "all men are created equal." The other defended slavery as traditional, necessary, just, and worthy of protection from "outside interference."[34] The drama reflected the troubling issues of a troubled time and the increasingly desperate efforts of Americans to deal with them.

As Brown's body was carried from Charlestown, Virginia, to North Elba, New York, and laid in his grave, there to "moulder" into an unforeseen future, Northerners extolled him—hesitantly at first, but later more enthusiastically—as a modern-day saint and savior, and Southerners condemned him more and more bitterly as an "outlaw," a "marauder," a "Yankee meddler" in Southern affairs. Slaveholders regarded Brown as evidence that they could protect slavery only by severing their ties with the North. Southerners had been talking for years of the possibility of secession, but the talk now became louder and more intense, and it took on a deadly serious tone. A wave of secessionist fervor spread across the South, reaching its crescendo after Abraham Lincoln was elected president of the United States, pledged to preserve the Union but morally and politically committed to policies that would put slavery on the road to "ultimate extinction."

Trials that attract enormous media attention have been encountered with some regularity in American history. It is not strange that it should be so in a nation that claims to be governed by laws, not men, in which guilt or innocence is determined according to legal formalities and with respect for basic rights, and in which freedom of speech and of the press are enshrined as basic values. Trials that attract unusual journalistic attention have often been described as trials "of the century"—or, more precisely, a particular trial will be labeled "The Trial of the Century" and will hold that distinction until another seems more deserving of the designation. In the twentieth century alone, dozens of trials were so labeled, among them the 1925 "Monkey Trial" of John T. Scopes, the 1935 "Lindberg Baby Kidnapping Trial," the 1954 murder trial of Dr. Sam Sheppard, and the 1995 murder trial of O. J. Simpson. The common denominator of all these trials is the extraordinary public excitement that they generated, either because celebrated names were associated with them, the charges against the defendants were particularly lurid or heinous, or the trials themselves were conducted in a theatrical atmosphere with lawyers, clients, and sometimes even judges "playing to the gallery." Although Brown's trial attracted great attention, although he was a noted actor in the abolitionist movement before the trial began, and although he comported himself during his trial in such a way as to command attention, the real importance of his trial does not rest on any of these characteristics. The trial was important because of the effect it had on American history, the forces it unleashed, and the very real consequences that flowed from it.

It would be absurd to argue that John Brown *caused* the Civil War. Many forces contributed to that conflict; some were deeply rooted in American history, and others were more immediately related to the outbreak of hostilities. Secession, of course, was the immediate precursor to the bombardment of Fort Sumter, and Lincoln's decision to protect Washington, D.C., against

Confederate attack followed quickly on the bombardment. But what *caused* secession? Historians generally agree, with Lincoln, that slavery was at the root of it.[35] Brown's conduct during his trial in Charlestown—his resistance to the slaveholding powers that prosecuted him, his eloquent argument against slavery and in favor of abolition—intensified feelings on both sides of the divide. Abolitionists were inspired by his eloquence and by his willingness to lay down his life for his convictions. Slaveholders grudgingly admired his courage even as they condemned his resort to violence and deplored the apparent willingness of so many Northerners to condone or even celebrate it.

It has long been understood that John Brown's campaign against slavery was closely bound up with the Civil War. Longfellow noted the connection when he wrote that Brown's execution was a harbinger of the "whirlwind" that soon swept over the country.[36] Melville affirmed it when he called Brown both the "portent" and the "meteor of the war."[37] Modern historians, appropriately reluctant to generalize about causes and effects, have noted that Brown and Harper's Ferry were "sparks" for the war, a "trigger" for the great conflict, and that they "did much to bring on that war."[38] All of these comments, however, assume that it was the violence at Harper's Ferry that unleashed the forces that led to war. I am convinced that these forces were set in motion by the trial that followed the raid, not by the raid itself, and that it was the eloquence and courage that Brown exhibited during his trial, much more than the recklessness he displayed in the raid, that transformed his public image from that of a violent fanatic into one of a public hero. Without the trial, the violence at Harper's Ferry would have been dismissed (and generally condemned) as an aberrant exercise in criminality. The trial elevated the violence to a new level of purpose. In the courtroom, Brown exhibited bravery and selflessness, an ideal-

ism and altruism that excited admiration and convinced many
Americans that he was probably more right than wrong about
the future of slavery in the United States. Perhaps, as he argued,
it would take action rather than mere words to erase the stain
from the nation's honor.

If importance is measured by consequences, John Brown's
trial was arguably the most important criminal trial in the history
of the United States, for it was intimately related to the war
that followed so quickly, and it was in large measure responsible for the fact that slavery died during the war. In the trial,
we see Brown's real legacy: the force of his courtroom words
and demeanor and the strength of the argument he made in his
final speech. And these things, in the end, were more powerful
than all the rifles and pistols and pikes that Brown brought to
Harper's Ferry.[39]

For all the attention focused on it, John Brown's crusade
against slavery will always be controversial. Is it ever justifiable to
resort to violence to correct injustices? When there are peaceful means of redressing moral wrongs, can any man who re-
jects those means earn the approval of a just society? In Brown's
own time, he was frequently condemned as a madman (or "monomaniac," in mid-nineteenth-century parlance). No man "in his
right mind," his critics argued, would have attacked Harper's
Ferry with so little likelihood of success and with such casual disregard for his own life and the lives of others. It was "insanity"
to do what he did, where he did it, and when he did it. Was his
attack on Harper's Ferry, as these critics averred, attributable
to mental derangement? Was his conduct during the trial in
Charlestown the product of a mind so troubled that it could
not conform to normal standards of civilized behavior? Brown's
trial touched on all these great questions, though it did not exhaust any of them. A careful, objective study of the trial and all

its implications holds some useful—and perhaps unexpected—
answers to these questions.

This book is a narrative history. It tells a story of real events in
the lives of real people. For the most part, it follows the chronol-
ogy of the real events, but not rigidly. There are excursions here
and there to set scenes, explain backgrounds, and explore legal
issues that help us understand the story of the trial. But these excursions do not intrude on the story line, at least not unduly so.
When a law or set of laws that affects the course of the trial is
first introduced, I describe it, discuss it, and set it in perspective.
Although this book is a *legal history*, it is not a *legal treatise*, and
it makes no effort to exhaust any of the legal issues it explores. It
is my hope that scholarly readers will profit from its insights and
revelations and that general readers will find enough human interest in the story to keep the pages turning until the last word
of the last chapter has been read.

If the story of John Brown's trial includes some improbable
surprises, it is because life itself is often improbable and because
history, like the life it purports to record, is neither neat nor pre-
dictable. But history needs neither neatness nor predictability to
win our attention. It needs only authenticity. If it has any quality
at all, the story that unfolds in this book is authentic, for it is
drawn from contemporary records of the trial: surviving court
documents, contemporary newspaper reports, diaries and letters
written by participants in the drama, and the recollections of
those who witnessed it. The testimony of the witnesses is taken
from the transcripts published in the newspapers of the day. (No
official transcript was prepared, for there were no court reporters in the courtroom during the proceedings.) The newspaper
reports were sometimes long and detailed transcriptions of the
actual words used by the witnesses, attorneys and judge, and

sometimes shorter summaries or paraphrases. In recording these reports, I have adhered as closely as possible to the newspaper texts, shortening them when necessary to avoid repetition, occasionally adding commentary to explain the thrust or import of a particular question or statement. Nothing has been added to these original texts, however. Not a single statement made in the courtroom has been manufactured; not a word of dialogue has been invented.

After all the years, the story drawn from the contemporary record of John Brown's trial is still compelling. It is to that record that we turn for the facts of the story and the lessons it can teach us.

1

TO FREE THE SLAVES

The little procession moved quietly along the country road, two men on foot in front, a horse-drawn wagon following, and sixteen others walking behind. The wagon was driven by a gray-haired man with a short beard who bent low over the reins. The wagons carried an assortment of tools and weapons: some Sharps rifles; several long, wooden pikes (or spears) with iron blades at the end; a sledgehammer; a crowbar; and some pine torches. Each of the men on foot carried a pistol and had a rifle slung over his shoulder, with a long gray shawl drawn over the rifle to conceal it from prying eyes. The night was dark, with no moon to illuminate the road, and a drizzle filled the air with mist.

The five-mile route from the farmhouse in the Maryland hills to the town at the confluence of the Potomac and the Shenandoah Rivers was familiar enough. Some of the men had been over it many times in the preceding days and weeks, and the others had been tutored in its twists and turns. From the banks of the Potomac, rocky cliffs interspersed with grassy ledges and thickets of trees and bushes rose more than thirteen hundred feet to the summit of the Maryland Heights. Across the confluence to the south and west, another wall of cliffs rose to the lofty crest of the Loudon Heights in Virginia. It was a magnificent meeting of land and water, a narrow opening in the Blue Ridge Mountains through which two of the most powerful rivers in Virginia thundered over boulder-strewn beds on their route to the nation's capital fifty-five miles to the southeast. Visiting the spot in 1783, Thomas Jefferson proclaimed it "one of the most stupendous scenes in nature," and "worth a voyage across the Atlantic" to see.[1] But this Sunday night, October 16, 1859, the men who tramped along the road to Harper's Ferry were bent not on enjoying the scenery but on crossing the bridge that connected the Maryland shore with the town as quietly and unobtrusively as possible.

Harper's Ferry was not a large town—its total population was about three thousand in 1859—but its peculiar location on a narrow neck of land at the confluence of two important rivers, with Maryland on one side, Virginia on the other, and the Pennsylvania state line just twenty-five miles to the north, gave it strategic significance. The presence in the town of the U.S. armory and arsenal, located there in the 1790s by George Washington himself, added to its significance. There was one other U.S. armory, located in Springfield, Massachusetts. The Harper's Ferry armory produced about ten thousand rifles annually, and the arsenal provided storage for about two hundred thousand weapons. The arsenal and armory were much on the minds of the silent men making their way toward the bridge that wet October night. But the blacks who lived in and about the town—some slaves and others free—were even more in their thoughts.

With its arsenal and armory, Harper's Ferry was not a typical Southern town. Its population was mostly white, made up largely of Virginians who had forsaken the plantations of the tidewater region for the bustle of town life, with a good number of Northern artisans and immigrant craftsmen (mostly Germans and Irish) thrown in. The streets that lined the riverbanks and climbed the steep slopes above them were lined with stores, shops, restaurants, hotels, churches, boardinghouses, and private homes. The armory complex itself included twenty workshops and offices, arrayed in two lines that stretched for six hun-

"School of adversity."[3] But if there was resignation in his stooped posture and a hint of fatigue in his lined face, there was determination in his blue-gray eyes, and it was the determination that persuaded the band of men who now followed him to go wherever he led them.

The last leg of the country road led along the north bank of the Potomac to its intersection with the Baltimore and Ohio Railroad and the eastern end of the Potomac bridge. The rail road was one of the most important in the nation, leading from Baltimore in the east through Harper's Ferry and thence westward to Wheeling on the Ohio River. Branch lines connected the road to Philadelphia, Washington, and Richmond. The bridge over the Potomac, a short distance upstream from its confluence with the Shenandoah, was nine hundred feet long and covered with a tin roof. It was wide enough to accommodate not only the railroad tracks but also a wooden deck for wagons, horses, and pedestrians. Before the men reached the bridge, however, John Brown ordered two of his men to go down the bank toward the river, climb a pole, and cut the telegraph lines that connected the town with the rest of the country. He had business in Harper's Ferry, and when he got there he did not want the whole world to know of it. Then Brown ordered two more of his men to walk ahead of the wagon and onto the bridge. The party quickly encountered the night watchman, an old man named William Williams. Raising his lantern in the darkness, Williams recognized them as men who had recently taken up residence at the Kennedy Farm. He was astonished when they brandished weapons, told him that he was their prisoner, and ordered him across the bridge. As they crossed the bridge, the men also crossed the invisible line that separated Maryland from Virginia, with the Potomac rushing in its bed forty feet below.[4] The line had more legal than practical impor-

dred yards along the Potomac, and the arsenal was housed
two large brick buildings closer to the Shenandoah. Abou
mile up the Shenandoah shore stood the workshops of Ha
Rifle Works, originally a private arms factory but since the 18
a part of the government's manufacturing complex at Harp
Ferry. There were two hundred or three hundred blacks in H
per's Ferry, and fully half of those were "free coloreds" (r
and women who had been given or bought their freedom
then set out to make their own livelihoods in the town).[2] T
were farms beyond the town, but they were mostly small op
tions with a few slaves to help their masters with tilling and
vesting; there were no large plantations like those farther s
and east.

The man who drove his wagon toward the Potomac b
called himself Isaac Smith. It was a name he assumed whe
took up residence at the Kennedy Farm in the Maryland hil
previous summer, and the name by which his neighbors
knew him. The young men who followed him were awar
his real name was John Brown, though some preferred t
him "The Captain" or "The Old Man," and people outsi
circle often referred to him as "Osawatomie Brown." H
earned the military title and the sobriquet of "Osawatom
commanding a company of antislavery volunteers in O
tomie, Kansas, in August 1856. He came to be known as
Old Man" only gradually, and by dint of patience and
verance.

He was not really very old—he had celebrated his fift
birthday less than six months earlier—but he gave the a
ance of greater age, for his once-ramrod-straight back w
and stooped, his thick hair was streaked with gray, and th
he had grown to assist his transformation from John
to Isaac Smith was white. More important, he seemed o
perience, a world-weary graduate of what he liked to

tance, for traffic across the bridge flowed freely, and Brown may not have thought much about it as he crossed.

On the Harper's Ferry side of the river, the bridge and the railroad branched in two directions, forming a large Y. One section, called the Curved Span, supported tracks that gently turned to the north and west and came out in front of a hotel called the Wager House. From that point, the railroad continued along an elevated trestle that followed the Harper's Ferry bank of the Potomac, and two short streets led toward the pillared gates that marked the entrance to the armory grounds. Another section of the bridge, called the Winchester Span, ran southwesterly along the Harper's Ferry bank of the Shenandoah River. From the Wager House, the armory gate was about sixty yards away.[5] Brown and his men emerged from the Curved Span, quietly passed in front of the Wager House, and proceeded straight to the gate. Just inside it was a small brick building partitioned into two rooms, one of which was used as a guardhouse and the other as an engine house for the armory's firefighting equipment. When a guard came out to greet them, Brown ordered him to unlock the gate. He refused, so one of Brown's men took the crowbar from the wagon and quickly broke the chain that bound the gate. As the wagon and men entered the compound, Brown ordered his men to spread out through the government buildings. Then he returned to the gate and told the guard: "I came here from Kansas, and this is a slave State; I want to free all the negroes in this State; I have possession now of the United States armory, and if the citizens interfere with me, I must only burn the town and have blood."[6] It was an astonishing thing to say—it seemed as if it might have been rehearsed, perhaps as part of a strange ruse—but the guard could not regard it as anything other than a terrifying ultimatum when he saw the pistols and rifles that each man carried, and the long-handled, iron-tipped pikes that lay in the wagon. If the man with the white beard did not truly mean what he had just said, perhaps he was a madman. Madman or revolutionary, the guard would obey him.

With his entry into the armory compound, Brown had once again moved across a sovereign boundary, this one separating the commonwealth of Virginia from territory belonging to the United States. Since 1796, this part of Harper's Ferry had been owned and administered by the national government, pursuant to statutes enacted by Congress and the General Assembly of Virginia.[7] Brown was an intelligent man and must have understood the jurisdictional significance of passing through the armory gate, though there is no evidence that he gave it much thought. His mind was focused on other matters, his heart and brain devoted to the attainment of a goal that depended not one whit on jurisdictional lines plotted out on maps or recorded in statute books.

The road that took John Brown to Harper's Ferry that wet October night in 1859 had its start much farther away than the Maryland Heights or the Kennedy Farm. It began in Torrington, Connecticut, where John Brown was born in May 1800, the third child of Owen Brown and his wife, Ruth Mills Brown. In the years that followed, the road crossed and recrossed much of the northeastern United States, passed several times through the Midwest, included a short but bloody sojourn in "Bleeding Kansas," and paused for several months in the mountains of western Virginia. Along the way, Brown came into contact with some of the most divisive social issues of the mid-nineteenth century—slavery, race relations, and the steadily increasing animosities between Northern and Southern states—all of which helped to shape the personality and character of one of the most unusual men to ever call himself an American.

The family into which John Brown was born was descended from old New England stock (they claimed that one ancestor had come to America on the Mayflower, although later research put the claim in doubt). They were honorable and industrious people and pillars of their Congregational church, but they had little money and lived a modest lifestyle. When John was five years old, they left Connecticut for Ohio, where they settled in the town of Hudson, about twenty-five miles south of Cleveland. Brown's father was a shoemaker and tanner by profession, and although never affluent he commanded respect in his new town, where he acquired some farmland, served as justice of the peace and county commissioner, and came to be called the "Squire." The boy was devastated when his mother died in 1808 and feared for a long time that he would never recover from the loss. Since money was never in abundance, he began at an early age to work on his father's farm and in his tannery. Owen Brown was a devout Calvinist and a bitter foe of slavery, and he imbued the same feelings in his son; he taught his children that the Golden Rule applied to all people, regardless of their race. During the war of 1812, the senior Brown supplied American troops near Detroit with cattle and horses. He made several long drives from Ohio north into Michigan, taking his twelve-year-old son along to help him tend the animals, and at least once he sent John alone to drive a herd north. On one such trip, John stayed for a while with a white family, and there he became friendly with a slave boy about his same age. The slave boy was intelligent and friendly and showered John with "numerous little acts of kindness." But the master of the house treated the slave boy more like an animal than a human being, denying him proper food and clothing, forcing him to sleep outside in cold weather, and even beating him before John's eyes with iron shovels "or any other thing that came first to hand." This brutality led John "to reflect on the wretched, hopeless condition" of slaves and to "declare, *or Swear: Eternal war* with Slavery." After his experience in Michigan, Brown became "a most determined Abolitionist."[8]

Back in Ohio, Brown continued to work in his father's tannery, where he dressed animal skins and learned to make buckskin breeches, shoes, whips, and other leather items. Although he had been taught since earliest childhood to "fear God & keep his commandments," he did not develop strong religious feelings until he was about fifteen, when, as he later recalled, he "became to some extent a convert to Christianity & ever after a firm believer in the divine authenticity of the Bible." He attended the Congregational church in Hudson, read the Bible avidly, and even taught Sunday school classes. In the Sunday school, he delighted in revealing his almost encyclopedic knowledge of the holy scriptures. One of his daughters later recalled that his knowledge of the Bible was so "perfect" that "when any person was reading it, he would correct the least mistake."[9]

He was a hard worker and got along well with other boys and men in the town. He became his father's foreman and later started his own tanning business. He claimed that he was "bashful" around others but still relished the opportunity to give them orders. He admitted that "the habit so early formed of being obeyed" made him "too much disposed to speak in an imperious or dictating way."[10] Years later and many miles away from Hudson, he would become noted for his commanding manner and for his ability to inspire other men to "obey" him.

In 1820, when Brown was twenty years old, he married Dianthe Lusk, the nineteen-year-old daughter of a widow who lived nearby. Although he thought Dianthe "remarkably plain," he liked her industrious ways and "earnest piety." Dianthe shared his religious values and commitment to family life and, before her death twelve years later, presented him with seven children, five of whom survived to adulthood. After a year of bitter mourning, Brown married Mary Ann Day, the seventeen-year-old daughter of a blacksmith, who had come to do the spinning in his house. She was strong, healthy, and unusually quiet, but he found in her a dependable source of emotional and physical support. In the twenty-one years that followed, Mary Ann presented Brown with thirteen more children, six of whom survived to adulthood.

Brown and his two wives loved their children dearly, and the children reciprocated the feelings, though Brown seemed to outsiders an unusually severe father. He was determined that his children should not form the "habit of lying" and imposed corporal punishment on them when he thought they were not rigorously truthful. But he could also be tender and attentive, staying up all night to nurse a child through an illness. The Sabbath was strictly enforced in the Brown house, with visitors discouraged, and a gloomy atmosphere pervaded the day. Brown never danced or played cards and, after 1829, never imbibed alcohol, although he said that "a free use of pure wines in the country would do away with a great deal of intemperance, and that it was a good temperance work to make pure wine and use it."[11]

Always willing to work hard at whatever task presented itself, Brown involved himself in dozens of business and farming ventures, none of which were notably successful. Some of his failures were attributable to the unpredictable business cycles of the young Republic, which brought periodic panics and saw the value of money fluctuate wildly. Other failures, however, were attributable in part to his rigid personality. He was distrustful of men who exalted material wealth over spiritual values and, even when he had money, never forgot that it could all disappear quite quickly. In Brown's case, it often did.

He continued his early career as a tanner after he moved to the town of Richmond, Pennsylvania, where he took on the additional duties of postmaster and schoolteacher. In 1835 he returned to Ohio, this time to the town of Franklin Mills, where he formed a partnership to operate yet another tannery and secured a contract to construct a part of the Ohio and Pennsylvania Canal. He planned to develop an ambitious town site on the canal, but the project came to grief when the canal company diverted the water away from the town site. In 1840, he crossed the Ohio River to survey an undeveloped tract of twenty-one thousand acres in western Virginia owned by Oberlin College. Founded by abolitionists in 1833, Oberlin was the first college in the United States to admit black students and was one of the first to be coeducational. The New York philanthropist Gerrit Smith, a social reformer and abolitionist whose vast land holdings included more than a million acres in New York, Pennsylvania, and Virginia, had given the college the land to further its founding goals. Brown's father was one of Oberlin's trustees, and it was at his suggestion that John contracted to survey the tract for the trustees. Impressed by the terrain and its potential for the development of a sheep farm, Brown wrote his family back in Ohio that he had found "the spot where if it be the will of providence, I hope one day to live with my family." The trustees offered him a deed for a thousand acres at a very attractive price, but he waited so long to accept that they withdrew the offer.[12] Disappointed, he took up the business of sheep herding on a farm he owned in Ohio, but that property was subject to a large mortgage, and he could not keep up the payments. When the mortgage holder foreclosed, Brown and two of his sons took up guns to try to keep possession of the property. They were briefly jailed but were released when the sheriff took pity on them. In 1842, as Brown's creditors fought over his remaining assets, he filed bankruptcy.

Now in his forties, Brown tried to start his business career over. He found a partner in Richfield, Ohio, who financed another sheep farm, which Brown and his sons managed energetically. He won prizes at fairs and soon developed a reputation as an authority on sheep raising and wool grading and as a successful horse-breeder. In 1844, another partner joined him in a potentially profitable wool brokerage business in Akron. The partnership was doing well enough by 1846 to open an eastern office and stock a large warehouse in Springfield, Massachusetts. He moved to Springfield to manage the eastern operation, but it soon became evident that he was a poor businessman. He set firm prices for his wool and, when buyers would not meet them, he stubbornly refused to come down. His mounting business debts and dwindling receipts did not seem to faze him. He angrily accused his customers of predatory practices, saying that they waited until he was in dire straits before offering to buy at unconscionably low prices. In 1849, he refused an offer of sixty cents a pound for a large shipment of wool and defiantly announced that he would take it to England for a higher price. But when he arrived in London, he had to sell it for an even lower price. He went on from England to visit France, Germany, and Switzerland but eventually returned to Massachusetts to face the grim reality that his wool business was heavily in debt and had to be closed down.

Once again Brown was on the move, this time to the Adirondacks of upstate New York, where Gerrit Smith had set aside 120,000 acres of land to be parceled into homesteads for free blacks. Still a committed abolitionist, Brown offered to move to the Smith property and help the blacks there build houses and establish farms. Smith sold him 244 acres in the remote village of North Elba, near Lake Placid. The price was only one dollar an acre, and the generous Smith was willing to wait indefinitely for payment. After the deed to his new property was made out, Brown sent his family to North Elba with orders to start building a farmhouse. As soon as he wound up his tattered business affairs in Massachusetts and Ohio, he joined them there.

It had been nearly forty years since Brown had seen the slave boy beaten with iron shovels on his cattle drive to Michigan, but in all that time his antislavery fervor had never cooled. In northern Ohio, there were many settlers from New England who shared his opposition to slavery and wanted to do something to end it, but they could not agree just what it should be. In church, he made a point of showing his support for black worshipers, inviting them into his pew when there were no other available seats, even trading his family's place near the front of the room for the blacks' cramped and crowded seats at the back, where they were unable to see or hear the preacher. Traveling across the country on his many business trips, he encountered parties of fugitive slaves fleeing along the Underground Railroad, hoping to make it to Canada, where they would be safe from recapture. When opportunities arose, Brown hid fugitives in barns and transported them to the next safe house. Fugitives were always welcome in his own home, where he provided them with food and shelter and built secret chambers for them to hide in when slave catchers came through. He was encouraged in 1834 when he saw the first copies of *The Liberator,* a newspaper published by the Massachusetts abolitionist William Lloyd Garrison. Garrison advocated an immediate and complete end to slavery, but he argued that it had to be done by peaceful means. Brown eventually came to disagree with Garrison, concluding that peaceful means were inadequate to the task.

In his reading of the Bible, Brown focused on passages that supported his beliefs about slavery. A verse from the Gospel of St. Matthew was one of his favorites: "Therefore all things whatsoever that men should do to you, do ye even so to them; for this is the law and the prophets."[13] Owen Brown claimed that this verse had helped convince him that slavery was wrong and had to be opposed, for what man would argue that other men should enslave him? John Brown himself was fond of saying: "I believe in the Golden Rule and the Declaration of Independence. I think they both mean the same thing."[14] Another biblical passage that meant a lot to him was Job's protestation of righteousness: "I was a father to the poor: and the cause which I knew not I searched out. And I brake the jaws of the wicked, and plucked the spoil out of his teeth."[15] Pondering this passage, he became convinced that he was an instrument "raised up by Providence to break the jaws of the wicked." And the "wicked" were the men who held other men in slavery.[16]

Brown was horrified when he learned in 1837 that Elijah Lovejoy, publisher of an abolitionist newspaper in Alton, Illinois, had been murdered by a proslavery mob, which also wrecked his newspaper office and sunk his printing press in the Mississippi River. The following Sunday, Brown rose in his church and, according to the recollections of two of his neighbors, announced to the congregation: "I pledge myself, with God's help, that I will devote my life to increasing hostility to slavery." Years later, his half-brother Edward Brown remembered John's statement on this occasion as even more dramatic and defiant: "Here before God, in the presence of these witnesses, I consecrate my life to the destruction of slavery."[17]

Another event that galvanized Brown's antislavery resolve was the Fugitive Slave Act of 1850, in which Congress authorized the appointment of special U.S. commissioners to issue certificates for the capture of runaway slaves.[18] A certificate could be issued on the affidavit of any slaveholder who sought the return of an escaped slave without first conducting a hearing or trial and without giving the alleged runaway any opportunity to present a defense. Commissioners were entitled to a fee of ten dollars when a certificate was granted but only five dollars when it was denied. Marshals and deputies who refused to enforce the certificates were subject to penalties of a thousand dollars, and citizens who interfered with a capture or who concealed or at-

tempted to rescue a fugitive were subject to stiff fines and imprisonment. By foreclosing any judicial proceedings before a
runaway was arrested, the new law made it possible for unscru-
pulous whites to claim that freed blacks were slaves and to enlist
the aid of federal marshals to take them south into captivity. The
law was drafted by U.S. Senator James M. Mason of Virginia
(whom Brown would later encounter in Harper's Ferry and
Charlestown) and supported by Senator Daniel Webster of Massachusetts as part of a national compromise to stave off Southern threats of secession when California was admitted to the
Union as a free state. Not surprisingly, the law shocked many
Northerners, who previously had little knowledge of slavery and
preferred to shrug it off as a "distant evil" for which they were
not personally responsible. Now it was thrust into their faces,
with federal marshals boldly coming into Northern cities and
searching from house to house for runaways. Throughout the
North, blacks were gripped with terror at the realization that
they could never live safely as free men and women in the
United States and that they had to flee across the border into
Canada. Brown was living in Springfield, Massachusetts, when
the Fugitive Slave Act took effect. He was friendly with the little community of free blacks in Springfield, attended church
with them, and often had them as guests in his home. He was
determined that they should not fall victims to the new corps
of federal slave catchers. He recalled the Old Testament story
of Gideon, who bravely defended besieged Israelites after God
commanded him to do so on Mount Gilead, then joined the
black pastor of his Springfield church and a young runaway
to form a defensive organization called the League of Gileadites. He drafted a charter for the organization, which included
the observation that "nothing so charms the American people
as personal bravery" and the biblical admonition: "Whoever is
fearful and afraid, let him return and depart early from Mount

Gilead."¹⁹ Brown hoped that the League of Gileadites would spread to other Northern towns and cities, but it never did.

Even among abolitionists, Brown's attitude toward blacks was unusual for its time. Many opponents of Southern slavery were unwilling to socialize with blacks on equal terms. They accepted prevailing notions that blacks were inferior beings who could survive as free men and women only if they were separated from whites—perhaps sent off to some remote location on the Great Plains or shipped to Central America or Africa. Brown rejected all of these ideas and fully embraced the concept of racial equality. He at one time proposed to operate a school for blacks and even wanted to adopt a black boy and "give him a good education, learn him what we can about the history of the world, about business, about general subjects, and above all, try to teach him the fear of God." After he took up residence on Gerrit Smith's land in North Elba, he worked closely with local blacks, helped them build houses and plant crops, and invited them into his home. One day three men from Boston who had been tramping through the nearby woods came up to the Brown house, explained that they had lost their way and had walked all night without eating. Brown's oldest daughter, Ruth, welcomed them, gave them food, and told them that her father would soon be home. In a little while Brown drove up in a buckboard wagon, two blacks riding with him. He greeted the visitors and invited them into his house for dinner. One was the Boston lawyer and celebrated author of *Two Years before the Mast,* Richard Henry Dana Jr. A few years later, Dana published a recollection of his visit to the Brown house, a "humble" log cabin one story in height with a few outbuildings. He remembered Brown as "a grave, serious man . . . with a marked countenance and a natural dignity of manner." The dinner table in his cabin was crowded with perhaps a dozen men and women, including three blacks. Dana was surprised when Brown addressed the blacks by their surnames preceded with Mr. and Mrs. "It was plain that they had not been so treated or spoken to often before," Dana wrote, "perhaps never until that day, for they had all the awkwardness of field hands on a plantation." When it came time to leave, Dana and his companions tried to persuade Ruth Brown to accept five dollars for the hospitality she had shown them. When she refused so grand an offer, they insisted that she at least take the amount that their food had cost, and they gave her a dollar bill. She reluctantly accepted but immediately went up into the garret of the house and returned with change. She would accept enough to cover the bare cost of the meals she had served, but not one penny more. Dana and his companions left Brown's house with the firm impression that the Browns "acted on a principle in the smallest matters."[20]

While Brown was helping free blacks establish homes in the Adirondacks, the focus of the slavery controversy in the United States was shifting to the west—and assuming a dramatic new dimension. On May 30, 1854, President Franklin Pierce signed the Kansas-Nebraska Act,[21] a hotly debated new law that opened federal territory west of Iowa and Missouri to settlement and repealed the Missouri Compromise of 1820, which had provided that no slavery would be permitted in any part of the Louisiana Territory north of 36° 30', the southern boundary of Missouri, except in Missouri itself, which was a slave state. In place of the repealed law, a new principle of "popular sovereignty" was introduced, under which the people of the territories would decide for themselves whether to permit or prohibit slavery. The law delighted Southerners, for it gave them a chance to establish slavery in a part of the country from which it had been excluded for more than thirty years, and they launched a vigorous effort to settle enough slaveholders in Kansas to organize the territorial government and send a proslavery delegate to Congress. Northerners were also interested in Kansas, not just because of the slavery issue, but also because it promised good lands for farming, particularly in the east. The Southerners had the geographical advantage, however, for Kansas adjoined Missouri, Arkansas was just a little distance away, and both Missouri and Arkansas were slave states. By the middle of 1855, enough Southerners had gone into Kansas to establish a territorial capital, elect a legislature, and enact a set of harsh proslavery laws. Among other things, the new laws limited jury service to men who supported slavery, disqualified antislavery candidates from holding public office, imposed stiff fines and imprisonment on anyone who denied the legality of slavery in Kansas, and prescribed the death penalty for inciting slaves to conspiracy or rebellion. Northerners complained bitterly. The laws were blatantly unjust and clearly violated the spirit of the Kansas-Nebraska Act, which was to give pro- and antislavery forces equal voices in the government of the territory. Worse, they had been enacted as a result of rampant election fraud. Determined to assert their rights, the Northerners established their own capital, elected their own legislature, and adopted a constitution that not only prohibited slavery but prohibited the migration into Kansas of any blacks, free or slave. As anger grew on both sides, violence broke out. There were gunfights, stolen cattle and horses, and farmhouses and outbuildings that were burned to the ground. Kansas—now called "Bleeding Kansas" in the newspapers—found itself in a virtual civil war, with angry factions contesting one another for control of the government and with lawlessness increasing daily.

Brown initially seemed unmoved by news of the troubles in Kansas. He was busy in North Elba helping his black neighbors with their farms and still attempting to settle the messy trail of debts he had left behind him in Massachusetts and Ohio. But several of his adult sons had decided to move to Kansas to find good land for settlement and to lend support to the antislavery forces. Brown's half-sister Florilla and her husband had also gone to Kansas, where they built a cabin near Osawatomie. Brown's sons wrote and asked him to help them in Kansas. At first, he declined their invitation, but by the middle of 1855 he had a change of mind. He decided that the slavery controversy in Kansas was too important for him not to get involved. He knew that "border ruffians," as the lawless settlers from Missouri and Arkansas were called, went about the country well armed, so he decided to take a good supply of guns and rifles with him when he left New York at the end of the summer. He arrived in Kansas in October 1855 and set about building a cabin. He met with other antislavery settlers, attended rallies, and made his views on the crisis known. He helped to organize a company of antislavery volunteers called the Liberty Guards and was quickly elevated to the rank of captain. In November, a gang of pro-slavery thugs threatened to attack the antislavery town of Lawrence. Brown led his Liberty Guards to the scene and helped to turn back the attackers.

The spring of 1856 opened with new bands of ruffians arriving in Kansas almost daily from Missouri and from as far away as Alabama and Georgia. They were hard-drinking men armed with pistols and rifles and knives, and they were eager to confront the antislavery settlers. Newspapers reported gunfights and murders. In May, Lawrence again came under attack. Brown and his sons were on their way to their second defense of the town when they were informed that it was too late: Lawrence had been burned to the ground. Outraged, Brown decided that the time had come "to strike terror into the hearts of all proslavery people."[22] With four of his sons, one son-in-law, and two other men following behind, he rode to the proslavery settlement of Pottawatomie where, on the night of May 24, 1856, he and his men took five proslavery men out of their cabins and killed them with broadswords. Brown himself did none of the killing, but he witnessed it and approved. At first, the "Pottawatomie Massacre" was almost universally condemned as a brutal display of violence. Later, however, some settlers tried to justify it as reasonable retaliation for the proslavery violence that preceded it. They argued that slave supporters had escalated the conflict with their own provocations and that Brown and his men were merely trying to defend themselves and their allies. Many, however, were unconvinced. To them, Pottawatomie seemed a mass murder scene.

Brown's opponents were not willing to forget Pottawatomie, and they continued to bear down on him. In June 1856, a large band of proslavery forces attacked Brown and his followers at a place called Black Jack, but Brown was able to fend them off. Reporters from eastern newspapers were now alerted to Brown's exploits and, with a kind of lurid fascination, began to tout his military exploits in their papers. In August, when Osawatomie was attacked by 250 proslavery men from Missouri, Brown led a band of thirty or forty in defense of the settlement. He was able to hold off the attackers for a while and eventually escaped with most of his men, but not before the settlement was burned and his son Frederick was killed. Learning of the encounter, the newspapers referred to him as "Osawatomie Brown" or, almost reverentially, "The Old Man." The incident steeled Brown with renewed determination. As he watched the smoke rising from the ashes of Osawatomie, he declared solemnly: "I have only a short time to live—only one death to die, and I will die fighting for this cause. There will be no more peace in this land until slavery is done for."[23]

There was a respite in the fighting in the fall of 1856, and Brown took advantage of it to make a trip back East. He visited Frederick Douglass, the black journalist and orator, at his home in Rochester, New York. Douglass was an escaped slave who had become one of the country's most persuasive advocates for the abolition of slavery, and he and Brown had been friends since the days when Brown lived in Massachusetts. Brown spent some time in North Elba with his wife and younger children and then visited Boston, where his reputation as a Kansas freedom fighter had preceded him. He was introduced to prominent abolitionists and invited to address a committee of the Massachusetts legislature, which was considering a proposal to lend financial support to the abolitionists in Kansas. In nearby Concord, he met the Transcendentalists Ralph Waldo Emerson and Henry David Thoreau. He gave lectures at public gatherings in Massachusetts and Connecticut, soliciting aid for the freedom fighters in Kansas. In Collinsville, Connecticut, a blacksmith and forgemaster named Charles Blair attended one of his lectures and later entered into an unusual contract with him. Blair agreed to make one thousand pikes, with double-edged knives mounted on the ends of six-foot-long wooden poles. Brown told Blair that he wanted to give the pikes to settlers in Kansas so they could defend themselves from the attacks of slaveholders.[24] After a brief visit to New York City, Brown set out again for Kansas, armed with Sharps rifles and a modest supply of cash, obtained from New England abolitionists who had decided that his cause was worthy of their financial support. He began to grow a beard to help conceal his identity. He conferred with Hugh Forbes, an Englishman he had met in the East and asked him to train volunteers for the "provisional army" he would need to carry out his plan. Forbes was a soldier of fortune who had fought with Giuseppe Garibaldi in Italy and knew something about freedom fighting.

But Brown's thoughts were already moving beyond Kansas to the real home of slavery in America, the Southern states. He called this region "Africa," because of the millions of black slaves who lived there. In Brown's mind, slavery amounted to constant warfare against its victims. Slaves were held in subjugation only because of the constant violence that was inflicted on them. If they were not whipped, beaten, and threatened with death, they could not be held against their wills. When a war is being waged, Brown reasoned, talk is not an adequate response; action is required. He had been thinking for years about the necessity of mounting a violent campaign in the South—a campaign that would bring war into the heart of the slaveholding empire. Now he believed the time was ready to mount an attack directly against the great slaveholders. "I will give them something else to do than to extend slave territory," he said. "I will carry the war into Africa."[25]

2

CARRYING THE WAR INTO AFRICA

Brown decided to launch his first Southern attack at Harper's Ferry. The little town seemed a good target for a variety of reasons. First, it was in a powerful slave state but close enough to free territory (Pennsylvania) to make entry and egress easy. It was adjacent to rugged mountains (the Blue Ridge, the Shenandoahs, and the Alleghenies) where he could "hole up" after his raid and establish camps in which the liberated slaves could gather. There were strategic heights, secluded canyons, even caves scattered throughout the mountains in which he could defend himself and his followers when Southerners launched their attacks against him—as they inevitably would. The town was a station on the Underground Railroad, through which fugitive slaves were transported north to freedom, and there were a good number of free blacks in the neighborhood who could be expected to rally to his banner and help bring the slaves out from the "quarters" in which they lived.[1] Finally, the U.S. arsenal in Harper's Ferry had one of the largest stores of military weapons in the country. If he could secure those weapons for his cause, he would be in a commanding position to work his will.

In May 1858, Brown traveled to Chatham, Canada, across the river from Detroit, where he hosted a "convention" of twelve whites and thirty-four blacks who expressed a willingness to help him in his plan. He showed them a curious document he had drafted earlier that year at Frederick Douglass's house in Rochester. Titled a *Provisional Constitution and Ordinances for*

the People of the United States, it called for a "provisional" government for the United States, modeled roughly on the existing structure, but with important differences. There was a separate office called commander in chief and specific provisions
condemning "profane swearing," "filthy conversation," "intoxi-
cation," "quarreling," and "unlawful intercourse of the sexes."
It provided that it was not to be construed "so as in any way to
encourage the overthrow of any State Government, or of the
General Government of the United States . . . but simply to
Amendment and Repeal. And our Flag shall be the same that
our Fathers fought under in the Revolution." The preamble recited Brown's own deeply held beliefs on the subject of slavery. "Throughout its entire existence in the United States," it
had been "none other than a most barbarous, unprovoked, and
unjustifiable, war of one portion of its citizens upon another
portion." Further, it violated the principles that the country
had been founded on: "the only conditions" of slavery were
"perpetual imprisonment, and hopeless servitude or absolute
extermination; in utter disregard and violation of those eternal
and self-evident truths set forth in our Declaration of Independence."[2] The *Provisional Constitution* was adopted by the dele-
gates with little debate and printed in pamphlet form. Brown
was elected commander in chief in the "provisional" government. No one could be found to accept the office of president.[3]

Brown had hoped to launch his attack on Harper's Ferry as
soon as he left Chatham, but his plans changed when he learned
that Hugh Forbes had disclosed his intentions to some senators
in Washington. The Englishman had apparently hoped to receive money from Brown's New England supporters, and when
that didn't happen he turned against Brown. Brown postponed
the execution of his Harper's Ferry plan and returned to Kansas
with a nom de guerre (Shubel Morgan) and a new determination to carry his war to the slaveholders. In December, he led

his followers on a raid across the border into Missouri, where they "liberated" eleven slaves together with some horses, wagons, and supplies. One slaveholder was shot and killed. Governor Robert M. Stewart of Missouri offered a reward of $3,000 for Brown's arrest, and President Buchanan added $250 to the amount. Brown was scornful, publicly stating that he would give "two dollars and fifty cents for the safe delivery of the body of James Buchanan in any jail of the Free states."[4] He then took the slaves he had freed to Iowa, where they got on a train for a trip through Chicago and Detroit to freedom in Windsor, Ontario, Canada.[5]

In the spring of 1859, Brown returned to the East. He was a wanted man in Kansas and Missouri, but it did not seem to trouble him. He visited his family in North Elba and went to see Gerrit Smith at his home near Syracuse. Smith had joined five well-known Bostonians in an informal group of Brown supporters that in years to come would be referred to as the Secret Six. The Bostonians were Theodore Parker, a celebrated preacher and author; Samuel Gridley Howe, a humanitarian and newspaper editor married to the well-known poet Julia Ward Howe; George Luther Stearns, a wealthy industrialist and philanthropist; Thomas Wentworth Higginson, a prominent minister and author; and Franklin Sanborn, a young schoolmaster and journalist who was secretary of the Massachusetts State Kansas Committee, which helped antislavery settlers emigrate to Kansas. All were committed abolitionists. He told them of his Southern plan. They approved in general terms, though it is questionable how much any of them knew of the details.

Brown trusted Frederick Douglass with more confidential information than he did any of the Secret Six. Both men knew how risky the Harper's Ferry plan was, so they agreed to meet in an old stone quarry near Chambersburg, Pennsylvania, to discuss it. There Brown told Douglass the details of his plan and asked for help in carrying it out. Douglass shared Brown's belief that violent action was necessary to defeat slavery, but he thought his Harper's Ferry scheme incredibly dangerous. Capturing the armory and arsenal would constitute "an attack upon the federal government, and would array the whole country against us." Brown was going into "a perfect steel-trap," Douglass warned, and "he would never get out alive." Brown tried to change Douglass's mind. "I will defend you with my life," he said. "I want you for a special purpose. When I strike, the bees will begin to swarm, and I shall want you to help me hive them." (The "bees" were the liberated slaves that Brown expected to crowd around him.) Douglass was not persuaded, but a young black man who had come with him from Rochester was. Shields Green was a twenty-three-year-old who had escaped from slavery in South Carolina and found refuge in Douglass's home. When Douglas asked Green what he planned to do, he said he had decided to go with the "old man."[6] And so he did.

One of Brown's followers from Kansas, a twenty-seven-year-old native of Connecticut named John E. Cook, went to Harper's Ferry in the summer of 1858 to study the layout of the town and the surrounding country. A crack shot with rifle or pistol, Cook found work and made the acquaintance of a young Harper's Ferry girl, whom he married in April 1859. All the while, he gathered information for Brown's use. Brown himself came down to Harper's Ferry in July 1859, to consult with Cook and establish his headquarters nearby.[7] He rented the Kennedy Farm on the Maryland side of the Potomac, telling his neighbors there that his name was Isaac Smith and that he was a cattle buyer from New York. They were suspicious of him at first, for he seemed to go about the farm with surveying instruments and a magnetic needle, and they thought he might be prospecting for minerals. Eventually, however, they accepted him as an odd but harmless neighbor.

The Kennedy Farm had two houses on it: a small farmhouse two stories high, built partly of stone and partly of logs, and an even smaller cabin that stood six hundred yards away. The men who joined Brown at the farm were an interesting and in some ways remarkable group. Sixteen were white, and five were black. Four of the blacks were free men, and one was a fugitive slave. At least twelve had fought with Brown in Kansas or known him there. Three were Brown's sons Owen, Watson, and Oliver. Besides the Brown brothers, there were two other pairs of brothers: Barclay and Edwin Coppoc, Quakers from Iowa who, despite the pacifist strictures of their religion, were willing to take up arms against slavery; and William and Dauphin Thompson, neighbors of the Browns in North Elba. At fifty-nine, Brown was the oldest, followed by Dangerfield Newby, a free black, who was forty-four. Brown's son Owen was thirty-five. All the rest were under thirty, and three, including Oliver Brown, were only twenty. The average age was twenty-five years and five months.[8] All of the men had been born in the United States except for one, a Canadian-born wagon maker and amateur astrologer named Stewart Taylor. If he did not have the same nationality as the other men, Taylor did share their convictions, for like all the others he was "heart and soul in the anti-slavery cause."[9]

A little while after Brown arrived at the Kennedy Farm, he decided that he should have some women with him to help assuage the neighbors' suspicions. He wrote his wife in North Elba, asking if she could come down to Maryland and, if she could not, to send his daughter, Annie, and his daughter-in-law, Martha, Oliver's wife. Mary Ann Brown could not leave North Elba, but Annie and Martha were able to make the trip. They arrived at the Kennedy Farm on July 19, where they assumed the duties of cooking and housekeeping for the men while helping Brown simulate the appearance of a normal household.

There were perhaps eighty people in all who knew about Brown's plan to foment a slave uprising in the South, and though all had been pledged to secrecy, it was inevitable that some word would get out. It happened in late August, when an anonymous letter was sent to John B. Floyd, secretary of war in the Buchanan cabinet, advising him of a "secret association, having for its object the liberation of the slaves at the South by a general insurrection." The letter stated that one of the leading men in the association was "in an armory in Maryland—where it is situated I have not been able to learn" and that "the leader of the movement" was "Old John Brown, late of Kansas." A former governor of Virginia, Floyd was somewhat concerned about the letter, but he found the reference to an armory in Maryland confusing. As secretary of war, he knew there was no armory in Maryland and assumed that "there was nothing of truth in the entire epistle." "Besides," he later declared, "I was satisfied in my own mind that a scheme of such wickedness and outrage could not be entered by any citizens of the United States." And so he filed the letter away but took no action on it.

Oblivious to the letter sent to Floyd, Brown made final preparations for his attack on Harper's Ferry. He received a supply of Sharps rifles and Maynard pistols sent by his Massachusetts supporter George L. Stearns, and a bulky shipment of the pikes that had been manufactured for him in Connecticut. The pikes arrived disassembled, so it was necessary for him and his men to attach the iron blades to the wooden poles to make them usable. Brown intended to distribute the pikes to the slaves he liberated, believing that they probably would not know how to use guns but could handle spears. As he waited for all of his men to arrive, he took short trips into Harper's Ferry to buy newspapers and provisions. Near the end of September, believing the time for action was fast approaching, he sent Annie and Martha back to North Elba. He familiarized his men with his *Provisional Constitution* and instructed them all in the duties they were expected to carry out. He warned them to resort to violence only in case of necessity, and to "consider that the lives of others are as dear to them as yours are to you. Do not, therefore, take the life of any one if you can possibly avoid it; but if it is necessary to take life in order to save your own, then make sure work of it."[10] He trimmed his beard to a length of about an inch and a half to help him conceal his identity. Late on Sunday, October 16, he informed his men that the time had come to mount their attack. He ordered three of them to stay at the farm, guarding the weapons there and bringing them on in the morning, when they would be distributed to blacks in the town. Brown himself and the eighteen others would immediately proceed to Harper's Ferry. In short order, the horses and wagon were made ready, and the "Provisional Army" headed by "Isaac Smith" was on the road.

By eleven o'clock, Brown and his men were inside the gate of the armory. While some of the men held the guard in the building that doubled as a guardhouse and engine house, others fanned out through the armory and the adjacent arsenal, securing possession of the grounds. Without one shot having been fired, the federal properties in Harper's Ferry were now securely in Brown's hands.

Still acting as Isaac Smith, Brown now sent five of his men to the country home of Colonel Lewis Washington, five miles west of town. Washington was a great-grandnephew of George Washington, a member of the staff of the governor of Virginia, and one of the most prominent citizens of the district. Brown's men broke in the back door of Washington's house, roused him from his sleep, and ordered him and three of his slaves to come with them to Harper's Ferry. With Washington they brought two relics that he had inherited from his illustrious ancestor: a ceremonial sword believed to have been a gift from Frederick the Great of Prussia and a large horse pistol given by the Marquis de Lafayette. Lewis Washington was shocked when Aaron Stevens, the white man in charge of the group, told Osborne Anderson to step forward and receive the sword from Washington.[11] Stevens understood that the sword was a symbol of liberty and wanted Washington to understand that the liberty was now passing to a black man. Leaving Washington's house, the men stopped at the home of John H. Allstadt, one of Washington's neighbors, and ordered him, his nineteen-year-old son, and seven slaves to join Washington and his slaves. The whole group then headed to Harper's Ferry.[12] At the armory, Brown greeted Washington and Allstadt courteously, but he made clear that they were being held as hostages for the safety of him and his men. Their slaves were henceforth to be treated as free men.

Brown now sent three of his men back across the Potomac in Lewis Washington's wagon to collect weapons from the stash he had left on the Kennedy Farm. By previous arrangement, some of those weapons had been moved from the farm to a nearby schoolhouse, where they could more readily be brought into Harper's Ferry when needed.

At a little past one o'clock in the morning, Brown was surprised when an eastbound passenger train pulled into the Baltimore and Ohio depot, a short distance from the armory gate and just short of the entrance to the Potomac bridge. Told that there were men on the bridge "carrying rifles," the conductor, A. J. Phelps, decided to walk out and investigate. With three men accompanying him, he proceeded warily into the darkness and quickly encountered two of Brown's men. They pointed their rifles in his direction and ordered him and his companions to go back, which they did. As Phelps neared the trestle that led up to the bridge entrance, he heard a gunshot, and Hayward Shepherd, the free black man who was the baggage master at the depot, came running after him with the news that he had been shot. Shepherd was taken back to the depot where, gravely wounded, he died the next morning. Thus, ironically, the first blood spilled in Harper's Ferry was that of a man who belonged to the very race Brown had come to Harper's Ferry to liberate.

As morning approached, armory employees began to report for work, not suspecting that the complex had been seized by Brown and his men. As they arrived, they were met with rifles pointed in their direction and ordered into the engine house with the other hostages. Eventually, the little building held about forty men, whites and blacks, confined under guard of Brown's Provisional Army. Brown detained the Baltimore and Ohio train until daylight before permitting Conductor Phelps and all his passengers to continue their progress toward Baltimore. It was a major mistake, for the train stopped at the first station east of Harper's Ferry, where Phelps telegraphed the railroad headquarters that the town had been captured by a large party of men who had come "to free the slaves." The president of the railroad quickly relayed the news to Governor Henry Alexander Wise in Richmond and President James Buchanan in Washington.

Meanwhile, residents of the town found a cache of arms in a building that Brown's men had neglected to secure. They took them out, stationed themselves at strategic points around the engine house, and began to fire on it. The shooting was sporadic but deadly. One of Brown's men pleaded with him to take his men and leave the town while they still had a chance to fight their way out. Brown refused. He was still in command in the engine house, with Lafayette's pistol stuffed into his belt and Frederick the Great's sword tied to his side.[13] Blacks who had come into town from the neighboring countryside were armed with pikes, which they carried about the engine house.[14] But militia units now began to come from neighboring towns— Charlestown, Martinsburg, Shepherdstown, and Winchester— and some from as far away as Frederick, Maryland, and Baltimore. By noon, the Maryland end of the Potomac bridge had been taken from the three men Brown had stationed there to guard it, Oliver Brown, William Thompson, and Dangerfield Newby. Brown and Thompson made it to the armory grounds, but Newby was shot down as he attempted to join them. An iron spike had been loaded in the musket that hit him, and it sliced through his neck, killing him instantly.[15] Some townsmen found his body and hacked off his ears and genitals before leaving the corpse for hogs to chew on.[16] And so the second man to lose his life at Harper's Ferry was also a black man. The loss of the Potomac bridge was a serious setback for Brown, for it put the weapons he had left behind at the Kennedy Farm beyond his reach. What's worse, it made it impossible for him to retreat back across the river. Militiamen were now stationed at all of the entrances to the town, but the blacks who had gathered around Brown managed to evade them, either by plunging into the rivers or by disappearing into the woods.

Brown now sent Thompson outside to bargain for truce terms. Thompson held a white flag aloft and took one of the hostages with him as he ventured forth. But the townspeople ignored the flag, seized Thompson, and hauled him off to the Wager House, where they bound him and put him under guard. Brown then ordered two more of his men (his son Watson and Aaron Stevens) to go outside with another white flag and another hostage and again seek a truce. As the three men emerged from the engine house, they encountered a hail of rifle shots, and Watson Brown and Stevens fell to the ground. Watson managed to drag himself back inside the engine house, and one of the hostages, an arsenal employee named Joseph Brua, volunteered to go outside and help Stevens. Brua lifted the wounded Stevens and carried him into the Wager House, then heroically went back to the engine house and took his place as a hostage.

Meanwhile, twenty-year-old William Leeman, another of Brown's men, attempted to escape from the back of the engine house. He made it as far as the Potomac, where he was wounded in a shower of bullets. When he sought refuge on a little island in the river, George A. Schoppert, a visitor from Richmond, waded out to him. "Don't shoot," Leeman pleaded. "I surrender." But Schoppert leveled a pistol at Leeman's head and fired point-blank, killing him instantly. For the rest of the day, townspeople, some of whom had been drinking, lined the river bank and fired round after round of rifle shots into Leeman's lifeless body.

The people of the town were infuriated when three of their own men were killed by rifle fire. Thomas Boerley, an Irishman who kept a grocery store in the town, was hit as he stood on a street corner attempting to shoot several of Brown's men he saw standing outside the engine house. George W. Turner, a farmer and slaveholder who lived west of Harper's Ferry, was struck by a bullet as he walked down High Street, on the ridge above the armory. Then Fontaine Beckham, the elderly mayor of Harper's Ferry, was shot as he peered around a water tank on the Baltimore and Ohio trestle at the edge of the armory compound. The shooter, one of Brown's men (later identified as Edwin Coppoc) had seen Beckham and interpreted his movements as menacing. One of the hostages cried, "Don't fire, man, for God's sake. They'll shoot in here and kill us all." But Coppoc ignored the warning and sent a rifle ball through Beckham's heart. Oliver Brown, who was standing at Coppoc's side, took aim at another man on the trestle, but was himself shot before he could fire. Now two of John Brown's sons lay dying on the floor of the engine house.

The death of Fontaine Beckham outraged the townspeople. His grandnephew, Henry Hunter, was drinking at the bar in the Wager House when he learned of the death and flew into a rage. He enlisted the aid of the saloonkeeper and went up-stairs, where William Thompson was being held, tied to a chair with his arms behind his back. Several people were in the room when Hunter entered and announced that he had come to kill Thompson. But a woman named Christine Fouke, sister of the hotel proprietor, interceded, insisting that she would not permit such a shooting in the hotel. Hunter seized Thompson by the throat and hauled him down to the Potomac bridge where, with a crowd looking on, he shot him through the head. Thompson fell through the trestle, and as his body approached the water it was riddled with four or five more bullets. With the crowd spurring him on, Hunter now returned to the hotel for Aaron Stevens, intending to kill him in the same way, but he was per-suaded to spare Stevens because he had already been badly wounded. For a couple of days afterward, spectators on the bridge could see Thompson's body lying on the river bottom. They used it for target practice, repeatedly riddling it with rifle shots.[17]

The townspeople now mounted another attack against the engine house. As they did, three of Brown's men—John Kagi and two blacks, Lewis Sheridan Leary and John A. Copeland—made a dash for shallow water along the Shenandoah River, but they quickly fell under rifle fire. Kagi and Leary were shot dead in the water, and Copeland was badly wounded. The townspeople dragged Copeland ashore, shouting "Lynch him! Lynch him!" but a Harper's Ferry physician, John Starry, intervened, insisting that Copeland be carried away under guard.

Back at the engine house, Brown surveyed his losses. Two of his sons lay dying on the floor. The Canadian Stewart Taylor was dead, killed by a sniper's bullet. The slaves Brown had taken from Lewis Washington and John Allstadt were at the back of the building, some sitting and others lying on the floor. Brown's remaining hostages were sullenly silent. Brown wanted to negotiate a retreat from Harper's Ferry. He asked the townspeople and militia who now surrounded him for permission to cross back over the Potomac bridge with his hostages. If he and his men were granted safe passage, he said, his hostages would be released unharmed on the other side. But Colonel Robert W. Baylor, now commanding the assembled militia units, refused. He demanded Brown's surrender and promised only that he would be dealt with by government authorities when he did. Brown refused to surrender.

As darkness fell, angry men milled about in the streets of the town. Many stopped to slake their thirsts in the crowded bars before going out into the darkness, waving rifles and firing them into the sky. In the confusion, two of Brown's men—a white named Albert Hazlett and the black man Osborne P. Anderson—managed to mingle with the crowd and then slip across the Potomac into Maryland, where they met the three men Brown had left to guard his weapons at the Kennedy Farm. They all fled north on foot.

At about eleven o'clock in the evening, a detachment of ninety marines from the U.S. Naval Yard in Washington, D.C., marched into the armory grounds under the command of Lieutenant Colonel Robert E. Lee of the U.S. Army. The detachment had been ordered to Harper's Ferry that afternoon after President Buchanan conferred at the War Department with Secretary Floyd and Colonel Lee, both of whom were prominent Virginians. It happened that the marines were the only federal troops available in Washington for this urgent assignment. It also happened that Lee was on leave from his cavalry duty in Texas and, when Buchanan called him to the War Department, he was at his home at Arlington, just across the Potomac from

Washington. Rumors (wildly exaggerated) had reached the president and secretary of war that as many as three thousand men were marching on Harper's Ferry to join the meager force then in the town, and Buchanan and Floyd conveyed the urgency of the matter to Lee. By chance, another cavalry officer from Virginia, the twenty-six-year-old Lieutenant J. E. B. Stuart, was in the War Department that day. Stuart had obtained leave from his frontier duty in Kansas to come to Washington and try to persuade the War Department to adopt two of his inventions, a "lightening horse hitcher" and a device that enabled cavalrymen to attach and remove their saber scabbards quickly and easily.[18] Stuart had heard independent reports of the turmoil at Harper's Ferry and volunteered to serve as Lee's aide-de-camp. The marines, Lee, and Stuart traveled by train to within a mile of Harper's Ferry and, in the dark of night, marched over the bridge into the town.

The scene was tense but quiet when Lee passed through a back gate into the armory compound. Anxious not to endanger innocent lives by hasty action, he decided to wait until morning.[19] Meanwhile, he drafted a written demand for Brown's surrender:

> Colonel Lee, United States army, commanding the troops sent by the President of the United States to suppress the insurrection at this place, demands the surrender of the persons in the armory buildings. If they will peaceably surrender themselves and restore the pillaged property, they shall be kept in safety to await the orders of the President. Colonel Lee represents to them, in all frankness, that it is impossible for them to escape; that the armory is surrounded on all sides by troops; and that if he is compelled to take them by force he cannot answer for their safety.
> R. E. LEE,
> Colonel Commanding United States Troops.[20]

Reasoning that the rebels in the engine house would refuse his demand, Lee offered the "honor" of assaulting them to two state volunteer units, one from Maryland and another from Virginia. Both declined to accept, reminding Lee that he was the one who was "paid for doing this kind of work." Lee then tapped Lieutenant Israel Green, commander of the marine unit, for the job. Lee ordered Stuart to approach the engine house and submit a written demand for surrender to the men inside. If, as expected, they refused, Stuart was to wave his hat, at which point Green and twelve of his best marines would storm the building, using swords and bayonets as their weapons rather than rifles, to avoid unnecessary bloodshed.

Stuart went up to the entrance to the engine house about 7 A.M. There were three heavy wooden doors. Brown opened one of them a crack to "parley" with Stuart. He refused to accept the terms of Lee's demand, still insisting that he and his men be given safe passage across the Potomac. Stuart recognized Brown from Kansas—it was "Old Osawatomie Brown" or "Old Brown," he later said.[21] (Up until that moment, nobody in town knew for sure that the leader of the rebel band was not "Isaac Smith," as he claimed.) When Stuart concluded that further talk was useless, he waved his cap, and the marines rushed forward. The door slammed shut, but the marines attacked it with sledgehammers and, when they were unable to breach it, used a heavy ladder as a battering ram. The ladder opened a ragged hole in the lower part of the door.

Lieutenant Green thrust himself inside, swinging his sword as he did, and his men followed with their bayonets. Some of Brown's men fired their rifles, and a cloud of smoke soon filled the building. Marine Private Luke Quinn was shot and killed almost instantly, and Private Matthew Rupert was wounded. Two of Brown's men, Dauphin Thompson and Jeremiah Anderson, were run through with bayonets and swords and killed. The hostages huddled at the back of the building. Brown was kneeling between the fire engines with a rifle in his hand when Lewis Washington pointed to him and told Green, "This is Osawatomie."[22] Green raised his sword over Brown and brought it down with all his force. Brown fell to the floor and rolled over on his back, still holding his rifle, and Green thrust his sword straight at Brown. It struck its target, but did not penetrate deeply. The force was strong enough, however, to bend the blade double.[23] Brown lay helpless on the floor. It was all over in three minutes.

The dead bodies in the town were collected. Ten members of Brown's Provisional Army were either dead or dying, including two of his own sons. Four townspeople and one marine were dead. Nine civilians and one marine had been wounded. Seven of Brown's men had managed to escape during the fighting, but five, including Brown himself, were taken captive. One of Lewis Washington's slaves (known only as Jim) had died in the Shenandoah River, apparently drowned while attempting to evade gunfire, and one of John Allstadt's slaves (called Phil) had been captured along with Brown, apparently because he had joined with Brown in resisting the marines' attack on the engine house. All of the rest of the slaves had either disappeared in the melee or were formally restored to their masters.

Bleeding profusely, Brown was laid on the grass in the armory yard, where militiamen and townspeople crowded around him, shouting taunts. Brown later described his wounds as "several Sabre cuts in my head; & Bayonet stabs in my body."[24] Lee and the other officers examined the wounds and determined that, though painful, they were not life-threatening. In the next few days, however, Brown's injuries would be the subject of some discussion, and they would play at least a minor role in his trial. Lieutenant Green told J. E. B. Stuart that his sword "was so dull (being a common dress sword) he could not hurt Brown with it." Stuart bragged that his own sword was "like a razor" and that had he led the attack on the engine house, "my sabre would have saved V[irgini]a the expense of B[rown]'s trial."[25]

At about noon, Colonel Lee ordered that Brown be carried to the paymaster's office in the armory, where he was laid on a bag of straw on the floor, next to his wounded comrade Aaron Stevens. Both Brown and Stevens were covered with dirt and blood; their hair was matted, and they groaned softly. Men filtered through the paymaster's office gawking at them. One of the first who stopped to talk to the captives was Alexander R. Boteler, newly elected U.S. congressman from the district, who had come from his home in nearby Shepherdstown to observe the conflict. Boteler asked Brown if he was hurt anywhere except on his head. "Yes, in my side—here," he answered, indicating the place with his hand. Boteler told him that a surgeon would soon be in to attend to his wounds. "Captain, what brought you here?" Boteler asked.

"To free the slaves," Brown answered.
"How did you expect to accomplish it with the small force you
    brought with you?"
"I expected help."
"Where, whence, and from whom, Captain, did you expect it?"
"Here and from elsewhere," he answered.
"Did you expect to get assistance from whites here as well as
    from the blacks?"
"I did."
"Then, have you been disappointed in not getting it from ei-
    ther?"
"Yes," Brown muttered. "I have—been—disappointed."[26]

A little while later, Governor Wise came into the room accompanied by Andrew Hunter, a prominent lawyer from nearby Charlestown, the county seat.[27] As soon as he heard of the violence in Harper's Ferry, Wise embarked a train in Richmond with ninety Virginia militiamen as his escort. Hunter met the governor at the train station and took him to the room where Brown and Stevens lay on the floor. Wise told Brown that he should not say anything that he did not want to say. As Hunter later recalled, the governor told Brown that his case "would not in any degree, and could not, be affected by anything he told." Brown replied that "he knew that very well, that he had never begged quarter, and he would not do so." He assured Wise that he had nothing to conceal. "I can hardly describe his manner," Hunter later recalled. "It struck me at the time as very singular that he should so freely enter into his plans immediately. He seemed very fond of talking."

The conversation soon turned to Brown's purpose in attacking Harper's Ferry. Brown asked someone to get a copy of the pamphlet in which his *Provisional Constitution* was printed and urged Wise to examine it. The governor read a few of the articles from the pamphlet aloud. He asked Brown where he intended to set up the "provisional government" that the constitution called for. Brown rose up and, as Hunter recalled, answered, "Here, in Virginia where I commenced operations."[28]

Wise continued to ask questions until it was apparent that Brown was too weak to continue, and he and Hunter left. But they returned again the following morning to ask more questions. In the afternoon of the following day, a new set of questioners appeared in the persons of James M. Mason, one of Virginia's U.S. senators; Clement L. Vallandigham, a congressman from Ohio; and Charles J. Faulkner, a former congressman from the Harper's Ferry district.[29] Mason had come to Harper's Ferry from his home in Winchester, about thirty-five miles to the south, and Vallandigham had stopped while en route from Washington to his home state. Mason, Vallandigham, and Faulkner were all supporters of slavery and appalled by

Brown's raid.[30] Faulkner had recently been defeated for reelection by Boteler, but he was soon to be elevated by President Buchanan to the prestigious post of U.S. minister to France. Mason, Vallandigham, and Faulkner were soon joined by Lewis Washington, Phelps, Lee, and Stuart. While a newspaper reporter took notes, the men put a series of probing questions to Brown and Stevens. Determined to maintain decorum, Lee announced that no one was to annoy the wounded men: if they did, he would remove all visitors from the room. But Brown seemed eager to speak—he said that he was "glad to make himself and his motives clearly understood"—so the questions continued.[31]

Brown said it was by his "own folly" that he had been captured. "I could easily have saved myself from it had I exercised my own better judgment, rather than yielded to my feelings."

"You mean if you had escaped immediately?" Mason asked.

"No," Brown answered. "I had the means to make myself secure without any escape, but I allowed myself to be surrounded by a force by being too tardy."

"Tardy in getting away?" Mason continued.

"I should have gone away, but I had thirty-odd prisoners, whose wives and daughters were in fears for their safety, and I felt for them. Besides, I wanted to allay the fears of those who believed we came here to burn and kill. For this reason I allowed the train to cross the bridge, and gave them full liberty to pass on. I did it only to spare the feelings of those passengers and their families, and to allay the apprehensions that you had got here in your vicinity a band of men who had no regard for life and property, nor any feelings of humanity."

"But you killed some people passing along the streets quietly," Mason countered.

"Well, sir," Brown answered, "if there was anything of that kind done, it was without my knowledge."

Mason wanted to know "who sent you here—who provided the means." Vallandigham in turn wanted to know if Brown had been helped by anybody in Ohio.

"No man sent me here," Brown said. "It was my own prompting and that of my Maker, or that of the devil, whichever you please to ascribe it to. I acknowledge no man in human form."

Asked again why he had come to Harper's Ferry, Brown answered: "We came to free the slaves, and only that."

Vallandigham asked Brown if he expected "a general rising of the slaves."

"No, sir," Brown answered. "Nor did I wish it. I expected to gather them up from time to time and set them free."

Brown assured his questioners that he respected "the rights of the poorest and weakest of colored people, oppressed by the slave system, just as much as I do those of the most wealthy and powerful. That is the idea that has moved me, and that alone."

When the questions were done, the reporter asked Brown if he would like to say anything more. He answered:

> I have nothing to say, only that I claim to be here in carrying out a measure I believe perfectly justifiable, and not to act the part of an incendiary or ruffian, but to aid those suffering great wrong. I wish to say, furthermore, that you had better—all you people at the South—prepare yourselves for a settlement of that question that must come up for settlement sooner than you are prepared for. The sooner you are prepared the better. You may dispose of me very easily: I am nearly disposed of now; but this question is still to be settled—this negro question, I mean—the end of that is not yet.[32]

The questions and answers, and Brown's concluding statement, took several hours. It was an ordeal for a man who had just narrowly escaped death in a battle with sword-wielding marines. But Brown welcomed the opportunity to explain himself, his motives, and his actions—and to challenge his accusers. In the days and weeks ahead, he would welcome the opportunity to do so again and again. And the Commonwealth of Virginia would, perhaps unwittingly, give him a stage from which to do just that—in words that would soon be heard around the world.

3

FRAMING THE CHARGES

Brown was a determined, even willful man. Yet as he lay on the floor of the paymaster's office in Harper's Ferry, answering questions put to him by the governor of Virginia and three members of Congress, with a detachment of marines and companies of militia patrolling the streets outside, it was apparent to all that he was firmly in the hands of his captors—and that those captors, not he, would decide his future. He had no influence to wield, no determination to exert. He acknowledged as much when he told his inquisitors: "You may dispose of me very easily: I am nearly disposed of now."[1]

Before Brown could be disposed of, however, it had to be decided when, where, and by whose authority the disposition would be made. It seems likely that the men who gathered around him all suspected that some kind of a trial was in the offing. After all, serious crimes had been committed in a state and a nation that prided themselves on observance of the rule of law. Before there can be a trial, however, charges must be filed, and before charges can be filed, jurisdiction over the crime and the accused must be established. To the uninitiated, these preliminary steps may be dismissed as mere formalities. To those whose lives hang in the balance, however, they are fundamental to the judicial process and fraught with life-and-death consequences.

*

Despite the talk of a trial, there was from the outset a real possibility that Brown would be lynched. The people in Harper's Ferry, soon joined by visitors from neighboring farms and towns, were enraged by his attack on the armory and the lives that were lost in the fighting. Their rage was intensified by excessive drinking and the realization that they had been unable to capture Brown without outside help. When Brown's men were carried outside the engine house, there were steady calls for lynching, and when Brown himself was laid on the grass in front of the building, the cries reached a crescendo. The treatment that earlier captives had received when they fell into the mob's hands demonstrated that its thirst for summary justice went beyond mere words. The mob was not satisfied when the black man Dangerfield Newby was killed by a spike shot through his neck, but went on to mutilate his body. When William Leeman, trapped on an island in the Potomac, begged for his life, he was shot to death at point-blank range, and his lifeless body was used for target practice. And when William Thompson was dragged out of the Wager House and riddled with bullets, the townsmen showed not only that they thirsted for revenge but that they were capable of exacting it with their own hands. When Governor Wise arrived in Harper's Ferry, he immediately recognized the danger of lynching and warned the people against it.[2] The fact that Brown was not lynched may be attributed to the governor's intervention and to the presence of Lee's troops. Lee was a by-the-books officer who would never have tolerated mob violence in any place subject to his military authority.

Although Brown was not lynched, he might well have been subjected to something similar: a summary court-martial, or what is sometimes called drumhead justice. Martial law may be imposed in times of emergency, when civil authorities are incapable of preserving public safety.[3] Martial law has been described as "the will of the commanding officer of an armed force, or of a geographical military department, expressed in time of war within the limits of his military jurisdiction."[4] It is justified only in cases of "necessity," that is, only when order cannot be maintained and life and property protected by the ordinary processes of law. The necessity that justifies martial law generally arises from invasion, insurrection, or civil war. When Governor Wise received the first news of an attack on Harper's Ferry, he had reason to fear that the town was the target of an invasion from the North and that a general insurrection might be in the offing. As commander in chief of the land and naval forces of Virginia, it was his duty to protect the commonwealth from the dangers posed by the invasion and insurrection.[5] Brown himself was largely responsible for the governor's apprehensions, for he exaggerated the size of his Provisional Army when he spoke to his hostages in the engine house, claiming that he was awaiting large reinforcements from the North.[6] When the hostages were released, they repeated his claims, stretching them even further, giving rise to rumors that his forces would soon number in the thousands.[7]

Governor Wise's first decision after receiving reports that Harper's Ferry had been attacked was to address a telegram to Colonel John Thomas Gibson of Charlestown, commander of the Jefferson County militia, directing him to assemble his men for the defense of the commonwealth.[8] He then ordered the Third Regiment of Virginia Cavalry to assemble in Richmond and ready itself for an immediate trip to Harper's Ferry. The only rail route from Richmond to Harper's Ferry ran northward through Washington to a junction just south of Baltimore and then westward through Maryland to Harper's Ferry, a distance of more than two hundred miles. Before Virginia troops could make this journey, however, Wise had to telegraph President Buchanan and Maryland's Governor Thomas Hicks for permission to send his regiment through their territory. By the time

the Virginia forces reached Washington, Wise had learned that
Lee and the marines had already captured Brown, so he sent
most of his troops back to Richmond.[9] When the governor himself reached Harper's Ferry, he was accompanied by a modest escort of Virginia militiamen. The governor congratulated Lee on
his capture of Brown, but he was distressed that Virginia forces
had not done the job. He believed that the militiamen who arrived in Harper's Ferry before Lee should have subdued the
raiders or, at the very least, accepted Lee's offer of the "honor"
of storming the engine house after Brown refused to surrender.
He was anguished that Brown's small force had been able to
take Harper's Ferry with so little local opposition, whereas the
U.S. marines were able to end the whole affair in a few minutes.
Three days after his first appearance in Harper's Ferry, Wise delivered a dramatic speech in Richmond in which he declared that
he would have given his "right arm to its shoulder" for Brown
to have been captured by Virginians rather than federal troops.
"I would proudly have risked my life to have gotten my guard
there in time," he said, "and to have taken the place with our
own Virginia boys."[10] If the Virginians' failure to rise to the occasion did not reflect unfavorably on their courage (Wise tact-
fully declared it did not), it did reveal a certain reluctance to defend the commonwealth from "Yankee" attack. The governor
was anguished.

Notwithstanding his disappointment over the militias' per-
formance in Harper's Ferry, Wise ordered them to march back
and forth from Harper's Ferry to Charlestown, to dissuade additional "enemies" who might be lurking in the Maryland hills
from attacking the town. He then organized a volunteer "police
guard" to protect the armory and arsenal until the federal government could provide adequate defense (he was outraged that
the United States had not provided military protection for its
Harper's Ferry properties). J. E. B. Stuart and a detachment

of marines had gone to the Kennedy Farm after Brown was captured, and Maryland militiamen had searched the school-house where some of Brown's weapons had been moved during the raid. At both places they found abundant evidence that his movement did in fact have a military posture. Brown had left behind letters disclosing his plans for a slave uprising, copies of his *Provisional Constitution* providing for a provisional army headed up by a commander in chief, and enough rifles, pistols, and pikes to arm a substantial force. If Wise had any doubts that the threat to Harper's Ferry was military, the discoveries in Maryland removed them. The governor later wrote Buchanan that had he arrived at Harper's Ferry before Brown and his men were captured, he would have "proclaimed martial law" and stormed the engine house "in the quickest possible time." He would have given the insurrectionists "no quarter" and, if any of them survived the initial attack, he would have "tried and executed them under sentence of Court Martial." "But," he lamented, "I was too late."[11]

Brown was bloodied but not bowed when Governor Wise first encountered him. "Well, Governor," he said, "I suppose you think me a depraved criminal. Well, sir, we have our opinions of each other."

"You are in the hands of the State," Wise answered sternly, "and I have questions to ask, which you can answer or not as you choose."[12]

Brown answered the governor's questions frankly, speaking courteously but defiantly. While Brown and the governor were talking, a bystander called Brown a "robber." Brown was indignant, for he considered slaveholders and their defenders as the real "robbers" and told the bystander so. Wise then said: "Mr. Brown, the silver of your hair is reddened by the blood of crime, and you should eschew these hard words and think upon eternity. . . . It is better you would turn your attention to matters concerning your eternal future, than be dealing in denunciations which can only injure you."

Brown would not back down. "Governor," he said, "I have, from all appearances, not more than fifteen or twenty years the start of you in the journey to that eternity of which you kindly warn me; and whether my tenure here shall be fifteen months, or fifteen days, or fifteen hours, I am equally prepared to go. There is an eternity behind and an eternity before; and this little speck in the center, however long, is but comparatively a minute. The difference between your tenure and mine is trifling, and I therefore tell you to be prepared. I am prepared. You all have a heavy responsibility, and it behooves you to prepare more than it does me."[13]

Wise came away from his first meeting with Brown thinking it was a mistake to dismiss Brown as a madman. "He is a bundle of the best nerves I ever saw," the governor said, "cut and thrust, and bleeding and in bonds. He is a man of clear head, of courage, fortitude and simple ingenuousness. He is cool, collected and indomitable . . . ; and he inspired me with trust in his integrity, as a man of truth."[14] But Wise's admiration for Brown was not unqualified. Brown was, after all, "a fanatic, vain and garrulous."[15] Brown and his men were "deliberate, cunning, malignant malefactors, desperately bent on mischief, with malice aforethought."[16] If there was inconsistency in the governor's words, it should have surprised no one, for despite his many talents Henry Wise was not a notably consistent man. Most Virginians considered him a talented but flawed politician in whom ambitions, ideals, resentments, and passions were mixed together in a peculiar web of contradictions.

Wise had been a force in Virginia politics from the middle 1830s on, first as a six-term member of the U.S. House of Representatives, then as U.S. minister to Brazil, later as the dominant force in the state constitutional convention of 1850 and

1851, and, since 1856, as governor of the commonwealth. Almost six feet tall, with flaxen hair worn long behind the ears and deep-set eyes that varied from hazel to gray in color, he was so thin and pale that it seemed at any moment as if a strong wind might blow him away.[17] Just short of fifty-three years old when he met Brown, he was a slaveholder but not a member of Virginia's plantation aristocracy; a lawyer by profession who spent much of his time on his modest farm on the Eastern Shore of Chesapeake Bay; a forceful, sometimes eloquent speaker; and a thoughtful public official who gave way to frequent bursts of temper (he shot and seriously wounded one of his political opponents in a duel in 1835, and he acted as the second in several other duels). Originally a Democrat, later a Whig, then a Democrat again, he was a lifelong admirer of Andrew Jackson, though he opposed many of the great Tennessean's policies. He went to college in Pennsylvania and studied law in Winchester, lived for two years in Tennessee, and sought during his three and a half years as minister to Brazil to suppress the illegal but still thriving Atlantic slave trade, so he had a somewhat cosmopolitan outlook on life. (He was both relieved and pleased when, during his tour of duty in Rio de Janeiro, he found that the slave trade was dominated by Northerners.)[18] Yet he was as dedicated to Virginia as any of his political opponents, and pricklier than most when his loyalty to the state was questioned. He gave a good deal of thought to the subject of slavery, expressed doubts about its economic future, yet declared unapologetically that it was justified "by the natural as well as divine law, the prescribed law in the book of books . . . and by all the dispensations of Jesus Christ on earth."[19] Like Jackson, he condemned John C. Calhoun's doctrine of nullification, but he defended the right of states to secede from the Union. Secession was not a prospect that he welcomed, however, and he argued frequently in favor of preserving the Union. "I know of but one thing worse than disunion," he said, "and that is dishonor."[20] It was a line that, in gatherings of Virginians, was guaranteed to win him enthusiastic applause.

Wise was an impulsive executive, very unlike the cautious man who then occupied the White House. Other than sending Lee and the marines to the scene of Brown's attack, James Buchanan did little to assert federal authority in Harper's Ferry, despite the critical presence of the armory and arsenal there. Wise, in contrast, made it his business in the days and weeks after Brown's raid to be almost constantly involved in affairs in that troubled corner of Virginia, traveling back and forth from Richmond, deciding when, where, and how Brown and his co-conspirators would be punished for their transgressions against the Old Dominion.

After the letters and other documents Brown left in Maryland were brought into Harper's Ferry, Governor Wise examined them. He stayed up late one night in a public room of the Wager House with his staff and soldiers gathered around him, and he read the documents aloud to the assembled throng, offering comments as he went along. A Pennsylvanian named Joseph Rosengarten happened to be in the room during the reading and later commented on the alacrity with which Wise seized on each letter as confirmation that Brown had planned a monstrous insurrection in Virginia. "The purpose of all this was plain enough," Rosengarten said. "It was meant to serve as proof of a knowledge and instigation of the raid by prominent persons and party-leaders in the North. The most innocent notes and letters, commonplace newspaper paragraphs and printed cuttings, were distorted and twisted by the reading and by the talking into clear instructions and positive plots."[21] Wise slept that night in the Wager House and the next morning supervised the transfer of Brown and his men from Harper's Ferry to the Jefferson County seat.

As worked out by the governor, the transfer to Charlestown was in itself a kind of military exercise. In theory, the prisoners were in the joint custody of James W. Campbell, the sheriff of Jefferson County, and Jefferson T. Martin, the U.S. marshal for the Western District of Virginia. In fact, they were under the guard of Lieutenant Israel Green and his marines and were closely watched by the governor and Senator Mason. Brown and Aaron Stevens, still suffering from their wounds, were taken from the armory to the train in a wagon, while the three other prisoners, the Iowa Quaker Edwin Coppoc and the blacks Shields Green and John Copeland, walked between files of soldiers. Townspeople, following behind, lusted for vengeance. "Lynch them! Lynch them!" they cried. Wise replied, "Oh, it would be cowardly to do so now!"[22] When the train with Brown aboard reached Charlestown, a similar procession accompanied the prisoners through the streets to the Jefferson County Jail in the center of the town.

With the prisoners safely behind bars, charges now had to be filed against them. The state court with general jurisdiction over felonies in Jefferson County was the circuit court, which had just opened its fall term in Charlestown. By mandate of the Virginia Constitution, the circuit court was required to hold sessions at least twice a year in each of the six counties constituting the Thirteenth Circuit.[23] When convened in Jefferson County, it was denominated the Circuit Court of Jefferson County.[24] The federal court was the U.S. District Court for the Western District of Virginia, which was scheduled to convene the following Monday in Wytheville, some 250 miles to the southwest. Newspapers initially reported that the United States sought to try the prisoners for the murders of the marine private Luke Quinn and Harper's Ferry Mayor Fontaine Beckham because they were either on federal property or at the edge of the armory grounds when shot.[25] The state sought to try the prisoners for the murders of George Turner, Thomas Boerley, and Hayward Shepherd, all of whom were shot outside the federal grounds.[26]

There was in the U.S. Constitution, in federal and state statutes, and in the interpretation of those statutes ample legal basis for the assertion of federal jurisdiction. At the outset, the Constitution authorized Congress to exercise "exclusive legislation in all cases whatsoever" over land purchased by the United States "for the erection of forts, magazines, arsenals, dockyards, and other needful buildings." The only condition attached to this power was that the places must be purchased "by the consent of the legislature" of the states in which they are located.[27] Called the enclave clause, this provision was the authority from which Congress derived its power over the District of Columbia (which was acquired by cession from Maryland and Virginia) and over federal forts, arsenals, naval yards, lighthouses, hospitals, and similar installations at various places throughout the country. From an early date, the phrase "exclusive legislation" in the enclave clause was interpreted to mean "exclusive jurisdiction" and to give the United States "complete sovereignty" over D.C. and the other described places.[28] Chief Justice John Marshall and Associate Justice Joseph Story of the Supreme Court both held that when a place was acquired by the United States under the enclave clause, it ceased to be a part of the state in which it was located. It became "extraterritorial." In the words of Justice Story, "It was as to the state as much a foreign territory as if it had been occupied by a foreign sovereign."[29]

Acting pursuant to the enclave clause, Congress on April 2, 1794, authorized the establishment of "three or four arsenals with magazines" at places the president of the United States deemed "most expedient" and best suited to "accommodate the different parts of the United States." Each site was to be purchased with the consent of the state legislature concerned and to have a national armory associated with it.[30] An armory and arsenal had previously been established in Springfield, Massachusetts, and President George Washington was satisfied to let it remain there. But it was incumbent on him to designate another site or sites in the southern part of the country. As a young man, Washington had often tramped through the mountains and valleys of western Virginia, where he admired the spectacular site of Harper's Ferry. He favored Harper's Ferry as the location of a second arsenal and armory, in part because the flow of the Potomac and Shenandoah Rivers could power the machinery that would be needed for the facility, in part because the site could be easily defended against attack.[31] On November 28, 1794, the General Assembly of Virginia consented to the purchase of no more than 640 acres of land "for the use of the United States, for the purpose of erecting a magazine and arsenal thereon."[32] Federal officers negotiated the purchase of land from private owners, and in 1796 and 1797 deeds were issued transferring approximately 427 acres of land in Harper's Ferry to the federal government. Construction of the armory and arsenal buildings began in 1799.[33]

No conditions or reservations were attached at the time to the transfer of land, either by the private sellers or by the Commonwealth of Virginia.[34] When the Code of Virginia was enacted in 1849, it included a general provision ratifying the purchase of sites for federal lighthouses, forts, magazines, hospitals, custom houses and public stores in Virginia, including the Harper's Ferry site. The code recited the various acts of the General Assembly under which Virginia had consented to the purchase of these sites, but it claimed that Virginia retained "concurrent jurisdiction with the United States" over all of the federal sites, "so far as it lawfully can, consistently with the acts before mentioned." The code further provided that Virginia courts, magistrates, and officers could "take such cognizance, execute such process, and discharge such other legal functions" within the

federal sites "as may not be incompatible with the true intent
and meaning of the said acts."[35] The 1849 code might have appeared on its face to be an attempt by Virginia to retroactively
assert "concurrent jurisdiction" over the federal enclaves in the
state. If this was its purpose, however, it would have been inef-
fectual, for Virginia had already consented to the United States
purchases without conditions, and it could not thereafter withdraw or qualify its consent. Further, the enclave clause explicitly provided that when the state issued its consent, the United
States legislative power (or jurisdiction) became "exclusive." It
is clear, however, that Virginia's intent in 1849 was much more
modest, for other states had previously attempted to reserve the
power to execute civil and criminal process in federal enclaves,
and the federal government had not objected. The purpose of
reserving this power was simply to ensure that persons who
committed crimes on state land could not flee into the federal
enclaves and thus make them sanctuaries for lawbreakers. If a
crime was committed on state land, the perpetrator could be
pursued into the federal enclave and arrested.[36]

In 1854, the secretary of war under President Franklin
Pierce, Jefferson Davis of Mississippi, asked the U.S. attorney
general, Caleb Cushing of Massachusetts, to render a formal
opinion clarifying the legal rights and obligations of persons employed in the Harper's Ferry armory. Virginia authorities were
then attempting to collect taxes from the federal employees, arguing that although they worked and lived in the federal enclave, they were still Virginia citizens and were subject to the
state's taxing power. Davis, of course, was an intensely pro-
Southern politician who took consistently pro-Southern positions in disputes between the North and South, and both Pierce
and Cushing, despite their Northern roots, were Democrats of
the doughface persuasion whose political views were much like
Davis's. In the dispute over taxation at Harper's Ferry, however,

Cushing could not agree with Virginia's claimed taxing power. In the formal opinion he delivered to Davis, Cushing recited the constitutional and statutory provisions under which the United States obtained title to the armory and arsenal and concluded from them that federal employees in Harper's Ferry were not citizens of Virginia and were not subject to taxation by the Commonwealth. Even if the state had not expressly ceded jurisdiction to the United States, exclusive jurisdiction vested in the United States "by virtue of the Constitution." Cushing noted that there were only two requirements for the vesting of exclusive jurisdiction under the enclave clause: purchase by the United States and the state's consent to the purchase. "By that consent," Cushing wrote, "the State voluntarily and knowingly parts with its jurisdiction." The attorney general went on to cite a decision of the Supreme Judicial Court of Massachusetts that held that the state had no jurisdiction over criminal offenses committed within the federal armory in Springfield. The situation of Harper's Ferry was analogous, he said.[37]

Cushing's opinion was not the last word on the subject, for although opinions issued by the attorney general have "great weight," they are not binding.[38] The opinion was, however, almost certainly correct, for it was in accord with court decisions rendered at about the same time;[39] it reflected the considered views of Justice Story, who was a persuasive legal scholar as well as a Supreme Court justice; and in 1885 it was cited approvingly in a U.S. Supreme Court opinion relating to federal jurisdiction at Fort Leavenworth, Kansas. In his *Commentaries on the Constitution* (1833), Story explained the importance of maintaining exclusive federal jurisdiction over the federal enclaves, writing that "the public money expended on such places, and the public property deposited in them, and the nature of the military duties which may be required there, all demand, that they should be exempted from state authority. In truth, it would be wholly improper, that places, on which the security of the entire Union may depend, should be subjected to the control of any member of it."[40] In the 1885 case, Associate Justice Stephen Field noted that the sole purpose of Virginia's reservation (or attempted reservation) of "concurrent jurisdiction" at Harper's Ferry was "to prevent the place from becoming a sanctuary for fugitives from justice, for acts done within the acknowledged jurisdiction of the state." For all other purposes, Field said, the "extraterritoriality of the armory at Harper's Ferry was complete, in so far as regards the state."[41]

From the outset, Congress asserted its constitutional authority to legislate for federal sites such as Harper's Ferry. In 1790, it passed a general statute providing penalties for crimes committed "within any fort, arsenal, dockyard, magazine, or in any other place or district under the sole and exclusive jurisdiction of the United States." The penalty for willful murder committed within such a federal enclave was death. Penalties were prescribed for other crimes and for aiding and abetting the commission of crimes. When a crime was punishable by death, the death was to be inflicted "by hanging the person convicted by the neck until dead." Rather ghoulishly, the law also authorized the convicting court, at its discretion, to order the body of the convicted person to be "delivered to a surgeon for dissection."[42]

In 1825, Congress passed a statute designed to apply state criminal law to offenses committed in federal enclaves that were not already covered by federal law.[43] Under this statute, called the Assimilative Crimes Act, if such an offense would have been punishable by state law had it occurred in the state in which the enclave was located, the offense would be punished in the same way in a prosecution in federal court. The Assimilative Crimes Act was not applicable to offenses tried in state court. Its only purpose was to permit prosecutions in federal court of offenses committed in federal enclaves that were not otherwise covered by federal law; in effect, to fill in the gaps of the federal law.[44]

At the same time that Congress prescribed penalties for crimes committed in federal enclaves, it enacted some more general criminal statutes. The first and arguably most important was the treason statute. As evidence of the seriousness with which the founding fathers regarded the subject, treason is the only crime defined in the U.S. Constitution. Justice Story acknowledged the gravity of this offense in his *Commentaries on the Constitution* when he wrote:

> Treason is generally deemed the highest crime which can be committed in civil society, since its aim is an overthrow of the government, and a public resistance by force of its powers. Its tendency is to create universal danger and alarm; and on this account it is peculiarly odious, and often visited with the deepest public resentment. Even a charge of this nature, made against an individual, is deemed so opprobrious that, whether just or unjust, it subjects him to suspicion and hatred.[45]

The founders were aware, however, that treason prosecutions could easily be abused. James Madison warned that "new fangled and artificial treasons" could be invented by "violent factions" to attack each other,[46] and Story observed that when treason was not precisely defined, it could be used to oppress citizens, as it often had been in England. Story recalled that the French philosopher Montesquieu was so concerned about abusive treason prosecutions that he declared, "If the crime of treason be indeterminate, that alone is sufficient to make any government degenerate into arbitrary power."[47] In an essay on the treason clause of the U.S. Constitution, James Wilson reflected that during the reign of King Henry VIII, the treason power was invoked so indiscriminately that "the learned as well as the unlearned, the cautious as well as the unwary, the honest as well as the vicious, were entrapped in the snares."[48] To guard against abusive treason prosecutions, the Constitution included a precise definition of treason against the United States—the only definition of a crime anywhere in the charter—and it spelled out the evidence required to prove it. Thus Article III, Section 3, provides:

> Treason against the United States shall consist only in levying war against them, or in adhering to their enemies, giving them aid and comfort. No person shall be convicted of treason unless on the testimony of two witnesses to the same overt act, or on confession in open court.

Article III, Section 3, also gave Congress power to "declare the punishment of treason." The national legislature did this in 1790 with a statute that provided that "if any person or persons, *owing allegiance to the United States of America,* shall levy war against them, or shall adhere to their enemies, giving them aid and comfort within the United States or elsewhere, and shall be thereof convicted, on confession in open court, or on the testimony of two witnesses to the same overt act of the treason whereof he or they shall stand indicted, such person or persons shall be adjudged guilty of treason against the United States, and shall suffer death."[49]

Congress's addition of the words "owing allegiance to the United States of America" to the constitutional definition reflected the understanding that treason was a crime against allegiance.[50] Chief Justice Marshall acknowledged this in 1820 when he wrote that "treason is a breach of allegiance, and can be committed by him only who owes allegiance either perpetual or temporary."[51] Allegiance is generally defined as the loyalty and obedience that citizens and residents owe to their sovereign (or government) in return for the protection they receive from that sovereign (or government).[52] In England, Sir William Blackstone called it the "tie or *ligamen* which binds every subject to be true and faithful to his sovereign *liege* lord the king."[53] Blackstone recognized two kinds of allegiance. The allegiance owed by a person born in the king's dominions was, according to Blackstone, "natural and perpetual," whereas that owed by a foreigner (or alien), based on the protection he received while he was present in the king's dominions, was "local and temporary." Both types, however, were sufficient to form the basis for treason prosecutions.[54] In America, the law recognized the same types of allegiance, although the duties were owed to the United States and to the individual states instead of to the British kings. Thus an American citizen could be charged with treason because, as a citizen, he owed the government "permanent" allegiance; but a foreigner who came into the country to visit or to reside for a period of time could also be charged with treason, because he owed the government "temporary" allegiance during the time he was in the country.[55] Court decisions on treason were rare in the United States, because treason prosecutions were so much rarer there than they had been in England, where the dignity and majesty of the king were the subjects of frequent and sometimes bitterly vindictive prosecutions.

If Brown and his fellow Harper's Ferry raiders had been brought to trial in the U.S. District Court for the Western District of Virginia, there would have been ample authority in the Constitution and in congressional statutes to maintain their prosecutions. Any objections to federal jurisdiction would have been difficult to sustain, particularly as to the death of Luke Quinn, who was clearly shot within the grounds of the U.S. armory, and possibly in the death of Fontaine Beckham, who may also have been on the armory grounds when he was shot. Further, if charges of treason had been brought in the U.S. court, the prosecution would have had a strong case, for Brown and his fellow captives were all American citizens and clearly owed allegiance to the United States. (The one Canadian who joined the Provisional Army, Stewart Taylor, was killed by a sniper's bullet during the raid.)

But the Commonwealth of Virginia also had claims to jurisdiction over the Harper's Ferry raiders, at least as to the killings of Thomas Boerley, George W. Turner, and Hayward Shepherd, who were shot outside the federal enclave. Like all other states, Virginia had statutes prescribing penalties for a host of crimes. As set forth in the Code of Virginia, "willful, deliberate and premeditated" killing was declared to be murder in the first degree and was punishable by hanging.[56] Murder of the second degree, which was defined as any murder other than first degree, was punishable by imprisonment for not less than five nor more than eighteen years if committed by a free person.[57] Different penalties applied to crimes committed by slaves.[58] The Virginia state constitution had no treason provision, but Virginia statute law defined treason against the state and, in doing so, followed the definition in the U.S. Constitution as far as it could be followed, while adding some language of its own. Thus the Code of Virginia provided:

> Treason shall consist only in levying war against the state, or adhering to its enemies, giving them aid and comfort, or establishing, without authority of the legislature, any government within its limits, separate from the existing government, or holding or executing, in such usurped government, any office, or professing allegiance or fidelity to it, or resisting the execution of the laws, under colour of its authority.[59]

The Virginia Code also followed the federal Constitution in requiring that treason be proved "by the testimony of two witnesses to the same overt act, or by confession in court." Treason against the Commonwealth of Virginia, like treason against the United States, was punished with hanging.[60]

Wise himself recognized that the federal government could properly exercise jurisdiction over Brown and his fellow raiders. In his Richmond speech, the governor revealed that the United States had already filed charges against Brown and the others, and "there was no difficulty about jurisdiction." But Virginia also had jurisdiction, and Wise insisted that Virginia's jurisdiction be exercised first. "I told the officers of the United States that they might have the bodies of the prisoners after Virginia tribunals were done with them," he declared.[61] The *Richmond Enquirer*, which was edited by the governor's son and reliably reflected his views, reported that the delivery of Brown and the other prisoners to Charlestown was a "concession" to the governor. "Gov. Wise claims them as murderers," the *Enquirer* stated, "whilst the claim of the [federal] government on them is for a minor offense."[62] (Some might have wondered why two murders committed in a federal enclave and a charge of treason against the United States were regarded as "a minor offense.") But Wise was a forceful man, and in any contest with the United States he was determined to make his views prevail. President Buchanan, on the other hand, was not a forceful man, at least not as to any issue that pitted North against South. The *New York Times* reported that Buchanan met for several hours on October 18 with his secretary of state, Lewis Cass, and his secretary of war, John B. Floyd, to discuss Harper's Ferry and that at the end of the discussion he sent Robert Ould, U.S. district attorney for the District of Columbia, to Jefferson County to "superintend legal proceedings in the premises."[63] After performing his mission, Ould returned to Washington for what the *New York Herald* described as a "protracted interview" with Buchanan, in which the president was apprised of "all of the facts connected with the affair at Harper's Ferry."[64] The *Times* commented that "the affair at Harper's Ferry" was said to be "the first case which has ever occurred in this country, involving at the same time both State and Federal jurisdiction. While the State is affected as to Slavery and locality, the General Government is interested with regard to the public property, it having exclusive control over arsenal grounds independently of the State, and also with regard to the mails."[65] Buchanan expressed no objection to Virginia's jurisdiction and issued no statement on the issue. Sometime later, he said that the question of whether Aaron Stevens, one of Brown's followers, was to be tried in state or federal court was "a matter quite indifferent to me."[66] Even if Buchanan had objected to Virginia's jurisdiction, however, it would have availed him little, for Wise was adamant. Invaders had come from the North to foment a slave insurrection in Virginia. They chose Harper's Ferry as their target because the federal government had failed to guard its facilities there. Now it was up to Virginia to defend itself, to show the rest of the country that it was capable of asserting its own rights and interests. "I would not have delivered up these prisoners to any claim of priority of jurisdiction if the President of the United States had so ordered," Wise said in Richmond. "Virginia and the other slaveholding states must rely on themselves."[67]

However much Wise's determination to hold onto Brown and his fellow conspirators was rooted in the governor's own willfulness, it had a good legal basis. As Virginia Circuit Judge Richard Parker (the man who ultimately presided over the trial of Brown and the others) expressed it, once Virginia had acquired custody of the accused men, they could not be surrendered to the demands of any other jurisdiction. No provision of the U.S. Constitution gives the federal government authority to demand the surrender of prisoners properly held by a state. The extradition clause, which provides that a person charged with a felony in one state who flees to another must be surrendered to the first state, has no application to the federal government.[68] Nor would the Constitution's supremacy clause require that Virginia surrender its prisoners. That clause provides that "this Constitution, and the laws of the United States which shall be made in pursuance thereof . . . shall be the supreme law of the land; and the judges in every state shall be bound thereby, anything in the Constitution or laws of any State to the contrary notwithstanding."[69] In the event of a direct conflict between state and federal law, the federal law is supreme and must prevail. But the fact that Virginia held prisoners for trial that the federal government might also have sought to try does not raise a direct conflict. Since Brown and the other prisoners were all charged with felonies, Virginia was entitled to hold them until trial or until the case was ended by a nolle prosequi (a prosecutor's formal notice that the prosecution is abandoned). If held until trial, the prisoners could be released to federal jurisdiction only if they were acquitted or, if convicted, only after they had suffered the punishment required by law. (If the punishment was death, of course, handing the prisoners over to federal authorities would be an idle act.) For better or for worse, Virginia had custody of Brown and the other prisoners, and Virginia was within its authority in retaining that custody until the cases against them were brought to their ultimate conclusion.[70]

Wise observed that the federal and state laws relating to the case were nearly identical. There was, in fact, only one major difference: the president had unlimited power to grant reprieves and pardons for any federal crime, but the governor could pardon or reprieve a person convicted of treason against the state only with the consent of its General Assembly.[71] Wise did not regard this difference as significant. "I will protect and guard the prisoners with the law and the mercy and the might of our own sovereignty," he declared.[72] How much of that protection would be *law* and *might* and how much *mercy* had yet to be answered, but Wise felt no urgency to provide an answer, for he was sure of his course and determined to pursue it. "As for myself," he told the crowd in Richmond, "I have manifested only my devotion to the duty of protecting the honor of the State of Virginia and the safety of the lives and property of her people."[73]

Wise might have noted one other difference between the state and federal laws. If Brown and his fellow raiders were tried in federal court, the judge could allow both the prosecution and the prisoners enough time to prepare their cases. The Virginia courts, in contrast, were subject to a severe time constraint, for the applicable Virginia statute provided that when an accused person was indicted for a felony, he had to be arraigned and tried at the same term of the court in which the indictment was found, "unless good cause be shown for a continuance."[74] The circuit court had opened its term in Jefferson County on October 20 and was obligated to move on to Winchester in neighboring Frederick County no later than November 10, so if indictments were found against Brown and his fellow raiders, they would have to be tried quickly. Assuming that "good cause" for a continuance could be shown, the trials might be postponed until the court's next term in Charlestown, but that would not be until the following April. During the intervening six months, Brown and his fellow prisoners would have to be held in the Charlestown jail; troops would have to guard them against a possible rescue attempt from the North or a local attempt at lynching, both of which Governor Wise regarded as real possibilities. And the excitement surrounding the case would continue. This was not a welcome prospect for Wise or any of the other Virginia officials. But proceeding at once to try Brown in Charlestown would open Virginia up to charges of rushing to judgment. It was not a good choice, but a choice that had to be made. The choice was, perhaps not surprisingly, to proceed to trial at once.

Virginia took the first steps to prosecute Brown and his fellow prisoners on October 20, when Justice of the Peace Roger Chew filed a formal commitment and warrant commanding the sheriff of Jefferson County to commit John Brown, Aaron Stevens, Edwin Coppoc, Shields Green, and John Copeland to the Jefferson County Jail to be held for trial on charges of murder and conspiracy to foment a slave insurrection. It is interesting to note that this formal commitment and warrant made no reference to the crime of treason, but merely recited that Brown and the other prisoners had been charged with conspiracy and murder (treason would not be added to the litany of charges until six days later).[75] The commitment and warrant commanded the sheriff to summon at least eight justices of the peace to assemble in the courthouse in Charlestown on October 25 to examine the charges against the men.[76]

The "examining court" was, as described by the *Enquirer*, "a form peculiar to Virginia."[77] Virginia statutes required that it be composed of at least eight justices of the peace drawn from the county and that it meet not less than five nor more than ten days after the warrant to hear witnesses and determine if there was probable cause to hold the accused persons for trial.[78] If not, they were entitled to be discharged. The committing justice could not be one of the examining justices.[79]

Under Virginia practice, the formal charges for trial would be set forth in an indictment handed down by the grand jury. As commanded by statute, a grand jury was summoned at the beginning of each term of the circuit court and required to listen to a charge from the presiding judge.[80] The charge to the grand jury was, at the minimum, a statement of the jurors' legal duties, though a particular magistrate might extend it to an invocation of general principles of justice and fidelity to the law.[81] As judge of the circuit court in that part of Virginia, it was the duty of Richard Parker to give the charge to the grand jury that October.

A short, stout man with a handsome face that seemed to bear a perpetually stern expression, Richard Parker was the third in a line of distinguished Virginia jurists bearing the same name.[82] Born in Richmond in 1810, he had graduated from the University of Virginia in 1827 and practiced law in Winchester and Charlestown. For ten years he served as military storekeeper and paymaster at the U.S. armory and arsenal in Harper's Ferry. Elected to Congress in 1849, he served in that position for about a year and a half before resigning to become a Virginia circuit judge. As judge, Parker lived in a large house on the southern edge of Winchester, where he owned about ten slaves, whom he rented out to other employers in the neighborhood.[83] Boyd B. Stutler, a lifelong student of John Brown, paid closer attention to Richard Parker than any other Brown scholar. Stutler described the judge as a conscientious jurist who was "modest," "plodding," and "methodical," a slaveholder who was "intensely pro-Southern in his views" but nonetheless had a strong sense of principle and judicial rectitude.[84]

Addressing the jury, Judge Parker began his charge with general remarks:

> In the state of excitement into which our whole community has been thrown by the recent occurrences in this county, I feel that the charge which I usually deliver to a grand jury would be entirely out of place. Those occurrences cannot but force themselves upon your attention. They must necessarily occupy a considerable portion of that time which you will devote to your public duties as a grand jury.

Very quickly, the judge turned to the sensational case that was on everybody's mind that day:

> However guilty the unfortunate men who are now in the hands of justice may prove to be, still they cannot be called upon to answer to the offended laws of our commonwealth for any of the multifarious crimes with which they are charged, until the grand jury after diligent inquiry, shall decide that for these offences they be put upon their trial. I will not permit myself to give expression to any of those feelings which at once spring up in every breast when reflecting upon the enormity of the guilt in which those are involved who invade by force a peaceful unsuspecting portion of our common country, raise the standard of insurrection amongst them, and shoot down without mercy Virginia citizens, defending Virginia soil against their invasion.

Parker was treading perilously close to prejudging Brown's case when he referred to the "enormity of the guilt" of Brown and his fellow prisoners. But he redeemed himself by reminding the jurors that he was "a minister of justice" and bound to enforce the laws "faithfully, and in the very spirit of justice herself." Thus, he said, every person accused of a crime was "innocent until he shall be proved guilty by an honest, an independent and an impartial jury of his countrymen," and the men about to be put on trial were entitled to "a fair and impartial trial." Parker continued:

> We owe it to the cause of justice as well as to our own characters, that such a trial should be afforded them. If guilty, they will be sure to pay the extreme penalty of their guilt, and the example of punishment, when thus inflicted by virtue of law, will be, beyond all comparison, more efficacious for our protection than any torture to which mere passion could subject them. . . . Let us all,

gentlemen, bear this in mind, and in patience await the result, confident that that result will be whatever strict and impartial justice shall determine to be necessary and proper.[85]

The judge's exhortations to justice and fairness were commendable. But sentiments and exhortations are theoretical, whereas trials are real. It remained now for Judge Parker and the Circuit Court of Jefferson County to demonstrate that Virginia justice was as good in fact as it was in theory.

4

THE INDICTMENT

Charlestown was now the center of the storm that had so suddenly and rudely settled over Virginia, and it soon became evident that it was even less prepared than Harper's Ferry to deal with it. With a population of about sixteen hundred, Charles town was about half the size of Harper's Ferry, but it had no manufacturing base and little in the way of business, and its grid of streets, laid out in neat squares, blended comfortably into the countryside. To the east, the Blue Ridge Mountains hovered low on the horizon.

Charlestown owed its economic existence to the rich farm land—sometimes called the Garden of Virginia—that surrounded it, and its political importance to the courthouse, which occupied the most prominent site in the town. The courthouse had been built in 1836, replacing a smaller structure that dated from 1803.[1] Although not large, it was a handsome building, built in the style of a Roman temple, with brick walls, four Doric columns that supported a triangular pediment and, atop it all, a cupola that could be seen for miles away. A bell in the cupola announced the beginning of court sessions and summoned witnesses and lawyers. Inside the building, a hall or passageway lined with brick walls led from the entrance to a large, open courtroom capable of seating more than five hundred people.[2] At the back wall, pierced by three high windows, an elevated platform extended the full width of the courtroom with a railing in front and a flight of six steps at either end. On the platform was a long table with chairs behind it for the judge and the magistrates. Beneath the railing was a desk for the clerk, a double row of chairs for the jurors, and tables and chairs for the lawyers and parties, all separated from the spectators by a second railing. The room was illuminated after dark by gaslights, hung from the ceiling by long tubes, and heat was provided by two iron stoves connected to chimneys by long, soot-covered pipes.[3] Above the courtroom, the building's second floor was occupied by a large hall that was used for meetings and social events.

Charlestown became the county seat when Jefferson County was carved out of neighboring Berkeley County in 1801, but the town traced its founding to 1787, when Charles Washington, George Washington's youngest brother, obtained a charter from the Commonwealth of Virginia.[4] The town was named for Charles Washington, and its streets honored members of his family, some eminent and others more humble: George, Lawrence, Samuel, and Mildred. The courthouse stood at the northeast corner of George and Washington Streets. Directly opposite it, at the southwest corner, was the Jefferson County Jail, a two-story brick building with shuttered windows and a portico-sheltered entrance in front and a narrow yard surrounded by high brick walls in back. Facing both the jail and the courthouse, at the northwest corner of the intersection, was a larger brick building in which the town markets were held.

Soon after Brown was brought into Charlestown, the streets filled with Virginia militiamen, ordered there by Governor Wise; journalists, sent by their editors to cover what promised to be a very sensational story; and crowds of curious onlookers. The town's scant supply of hotel rooms and guest houses was jammed to capacity, and the barrooms and taverns echoed with clanking glasses and excited, sometimes angry, conversations. Though Charlestown was off the major east-west railroad that sliced through Harper's Ferry, it was easily accessible by connecting lines that led to Richmond, Washington, Baltimore, Cincinnati, Philadelphia, New York, and even Boston. Newspaper and magazine editors in all of those cities had sent their most resourceful reporters to Jefferson County to gather the facts of the developing story. Graphic artists were sent too, and they were well supplied with sketch pads and pencils to capture pictures that would help to draw readers' attention. It was not yet possible to reproduce photographs on printed pages, so wood cuts or engravings had to be made from on-the-scene sketches to illustrate the magazine and newspaper stories.

The basic facts of Brown's raid on Harper's Ferry were already known to most of the country, and emotional responses to them ran high. Most Northerners, even those who opposed slavery, condemned the raid as rash and unjustified. Many, at the outset, dismissed Brown as a madman who was so fanatically committed to the abolition of slavery that he was willing to engage in the most bizarre and essentially futile violence. Some, however, justified his raid as a bold stroke for freedom that was morally defensible, however lamentable its cost in the loss of innocent life.[5] Southerners almost uniformly expressed alarm at the assault, fearing that it might be the harbinger of a bloody insurrection like that led by Nat Turner almost thirty years earlier. A slave who lived on a plantation in southeastern Virginia, Turner headed up a revolt that terrorized Virginia plantations for two months in the late summer and early autumn of 1831. More than fifty whites were brutally killed before the uprising was finally snuffed out, and seventeen blacks were hanged. In the excitement that preceded and followed the hangings, hundreds more blacks lost their lives, some under circumstances of ghoulish cruelty. Since that time, any whiff of a "servile insurrection" reminded white Virginians that their slaves could rise up at any time and go on a similar rampage. It was a prospect they dreaded and were determined to prevent.

It is hard to know whether Virginians were more alarmed by hints of domestic revolt or threats from the North. If their slaves became unruly or disobedient, they were swiftly and harshly disciplined to make sure that Nat Turner's outrage would not be repeated. But Virginians—in fact, all Southerners—were growing increasingly sensitive to criticism aimed at them from the North. Abolitionists condemned the South for its unyielding defense of slavery in a world in which the institution was increasingly deplored. Some Northerners who opposed slavery but did not identify themselves as abolitionists condemned Southern attachment to the "peculiar institution." Southerners not only defended slavery, they celebrated it; they exalted it as divinely ordained and justified it as essential to the maintenance of a truly civilized society.[6] Northerners who opposed slavery condemned it not just for its cruelty but for its affront to basic American values. The Declaration of Independence boldly proclaimed that "all men are created equal," but slavery in the American South mocked that proclamation. It was true, of course, that the immortal words of the Declaration had been written by Thomas Jefferson, a Virginian and one of America's best-known founders. But Southerners and Northerners alike knew that Jefferson was a lifelong slaveholder, and defenders of slavery argued with vehemence that the Declaration was never meant to apply to men or women of African descent.[7] It was a "white man's charter," written by white men for white men, and destined to remain such as long as the Union of the American states endured. Northerners increasingly disagreed. They chided Southerners, sometimes even threatened them. Southerners—slaveholders and non-slaveholders alike—were alternately embarrassed and enraged by Northern criticism, and they were increasingly convinced that if a Republican were ever elected president of the United States, slavery would be imperiled. The Republican Party had been formed in 1854 by an alliance of former Whigs and Democrats who were opposed to the spread of slavery into the western territories. The Republicans were not primarily abolitionists (although some abolitionists joined their ranks). They were, however, Northerners who believed that slavery was an anomaly in a nation dedicated to the principles of liberty and equality. They believed that Southerners themselves would eventually recognize that slavery could no longer be maintained and would choose to abolish it. Republicans accepted the widespread belief that the Constitution left "domestic institutions" such as slavery to be dealt with by each individual state and that it gave the federal government no power to "meddle" with those institutions. But they were convinced that if slavery could not spread, it would wither away. It would, in the words of Abraham Lincoln, be put "in the course of ultimate extinction."[8] John Brown was not a Republican. But the Republican Party seemed to Southern defenders of slavery to threaten the very foundations of the Southern slaveholding system. In Harper's Ferry, many thought, Northerners and what they liked to call "Black Republicans" had signaled their true intentions to demolish slavery. In Charlestown, the very foundations of Southern culture were being put to a critical test.

The Jefferson County Jail was nominally subject to the control of Sheriff James Campbell but was actually entrusted to his deputy, John Avis, who held the title of jailer. Built in 1806, it had a large vestibule in which visitors came and went, a hall that ran the width of the building, and commodious rooms in which the prisoners were kept.[9] Avis was a respected Charlestown resident, a veteran of the Mexican War, and one of the militiamen who had hurried to Harper's Ferry when the news of Brown's raid first reached the county seat. He lived in the jail with his wife and family. Brown and Aaron Stevens were confined together in a room furnished with two beds, chairs, and a writing table. Heat was provided by a heavy iron stove in the center of the room, with a chimney pipe that led to the roof. One window admitted light, though it was heavily barred. The *Tribune* reporter called it a "pleasant room."[10] At the outset, both men lay on their beds, nursing the painful wounds they received in the raid. Edwin Coppoc and Shields Green were held together in another room, and John Copeland was confined in a third chamber.

Brown had been in the jail only a short while when he began to receive letters, some addressed to him in Harper's Ferry and forwarded to Charlestown, others sent in care of Sheriff Campbell or John Avis.[11] Brown himself also began to write letters, initially for the urgent purpose of locating a lawyer or lawyers who might come to Charlestown and take up his defense. On the Friday after he arrived in Charlestown, he sent urgent missives to three lawyers he knew in Massachusetts and Ohio. One was Thomas Russell of Boston, a judge of the superior court, a Republican, and an ardent foe of slavery who had supported the settlement efforts of free-state men in Kansas. The second was Reuben A. Chapman, who had done some legal work for Brown when Brown lived in Springfield, Massachusetts, and shared his antislavery sentiments. The third was Daniel R. Tilden, a personal friend who was a probate judge in Cleveland, Ohio. All three were leading lawyers in their communities. Tilden had served two terms as a member of Congress from Ohio, and Chapman would in a few years become chief justice of the Supreme Judicial Court of Massachusetts. Because Brown was still suffering from his wounds, he asked Sheriff Campbell to help him draft the letters. While Brown dictated, Campbell wrote. Each of the three letters was drafted in identical words. Brown told the lawyers that he was seeking "able and faithful counsel for myself and fellow-prisoners (five in all), as we have the faith of Virginia pledged through her Governor and numerous other prominent citizens to give us a fair trial." He believed that they needed counsel from "without the slave states" to properly bring out the facts, particularly "such facts as might be considered mitigating in the view of others upon our trial." He had some assets: $250 in gold that was being held for him by the sheriff, and some property he had left behind in Harper's Ferry and at the Kennedy Farm, including pistols, rifles, and pikes; and he was willing to pledge as much of this as might be necessary to obtain a good lawyer or lawyers. "Can you or some other good man come on immediately," he asked the attorneys, "for the sake of the young men prisoners at least?" Brown said that his wounds were "doing well," but he closed with a warning: "Do not send an ultra Abolitionist."[12]

While he waited for replies to his letters, Brown was supplied with newspapers that enabled him to read stories about himself. He studied them carefully, made notes in the margins, and expressed his agreement or disagreement with particular points. He also read the leather-bound Bible he had brought with him, underlining passages that seemed to him particularly instructive or revealing. His clothes were dirty and bloodstained when he came into the jail, but he was given a change of clothes, and his old clothes were washed, so he soon struck a more presentable image, although he still groaned from his wounds.[13]

A small group of reporters received permission to interview Brown in the jail on Friday, October 21. Writing later, the *New York Herald* reporter described the jail rooms as "large and nicely kept" and said that the prisoners were "treated very well by the jailer." Brown was lying on his back when the reporters entered his room. A letter he had just written lay open on the table, and Brown asked the *Herald* reporter if he would copy it for him, as he still found it difficult to write for himself. While Stevens lay on his right side, groaning, Brown and the reporters "exchanged civilities, very courteously." Brown turned to jailer Avis and asked how many of his Harper's Ferry men were now in prison, and their names. Before he answered any questions,

Brown insisted that the reporters tell all the facts, those that were favorable to him as well as unfavorable. "Have any of you here," he inquired, "ever stated this fact, that we had no idea or thought of killing or wounding or injuring any persons who did not interfere with us? The prisoners we had will testify that they heard me continually order my men not to fire into houses, not even when we were fired upon, lest we should kill innocent persons."

"But," the *Herald* writer answered, "people wonder why Beckham was killed, who was unarmed."

"They have no business to wonder," Brown said. "Your own citizens will testify that such were my orders; that is the fact and you know it."

"I know you say it," the writer answered.

When the writer again asked why Mayor Beckham had been shot when he was unarmed and doing nothing to harm Brown or his men, Brown became defensive. "Then I know nothing about that at all," he said. "I did not know he was killed. I utterly deny any possible connection with the killing of any unarmed man. I did my utmost to protect innocent persons and my prisoners."

Brown told the reporters that he had "the promise and the faith of the State of Virginia that he should have a fair trial and no mock trial; not that it would make any difference in the result," but that he might have "justice as to the faith of their motives."[14] The *Herald* writer asked Brown if he had read his paper's reports of the raid and his capture. The *Herald* was a pro-Democratic, antiabolitionist newspaper that was hostile to Brown and generally sympathetic to the slaveholding interests in Virginia. Brown told the writer that he had read the paper "a great deal," and added: "I will give the *Herald* credit for one thing—although I do not agree with its sentiments, of course— it is very fair in its reports to all sides."[15]

While preparations were being made for Brown's trial, troops took up guard stations at all of the entrances to Charlestown. They deposited rifles and ammunition in the jail, where they could be used in case the building came under attack, and they placed cannons in front of the courthouse and the jail. Governor Wise was determined that if there was an effort to rescue Brown, it would not succeed. By Tuesday morning, October 25, the date set for commencement of the court proceedings, Charlestown gave the appearance of an armed camp.

Judge Richard Parker adjourned the circuit court on Tuesday morning to permit the examining court to move into the courtroom. Eight magistrates were on the bench as the courthouse doors opened to a throng of several hundred spectators. The examining court was a panel of prominent citizens headed up by Colonel Braxton Davenport; its other members were Dr. William Alexander, John J. Lock, John F. Smith, Thomas H. Willis, George W. Eichelberger, Charles H. Lewis, and Moses W. Burr.[16] All of these men were slave owners. Davenport, with thirty-three slaves, owned the largest number on the panel, and Alexander, with twenty-eight, had the second largest. Eichelberger owned thirteen, Lewis eleven, Willis eight, Burr seven, John Smith three, and John Lock two. In all, the magistrates who were now to examine the charges against Brown owned 105 slaves.[17]

At half past ten, the bell atop the courthouse rang out, and a military drumroll announced that Brown and his fellow raiders were to be brought out of the jail and escorted across Washington Street to the courthouse.[18] Eighty militiamen armed with rifles and bayonets stood guard as the little party approached the courthouse doors and disappeared inside the building. Brown and Stevens, still in pain, walked slowly and hesitantly, with men at their sides to help them. The reporter for the *Herald* thought the five prisoners "presented a pitiable sight. . . . Brown has three sword stabs in his body and one sabre cut over the head." Stevens had "three balls in his head and two in his breast, and one in his arm. He was also cut on the forehead with a rifle bullet, which glanced off, leaving a bad wound."[19]

Two lawyers were at the counsel table as the prisoners were brought inside the bar. Charles B. Harding was the commonwealth attorney for Jefferson County and, as such, was legally empowered to prosecute the case. But Harding was known to be a heavy drinker and to have a volatile temper, and it was generally thought that he was not up to such an important trial. Governor Wise had asked Andrew Hunter, one of the most respected members of the Charlestown bar, to take charge of Brown's prosecution. Fifty-five years old, Hunter was a native of neighboring Berkeley County and related by blood or marriage to many of the aristocratic families of Jefferson and Berkeley Counties. Educated at Washington Academy (later Washington and Lee University) and Hampden-Sidney (later Hampden-Sydney) College, he was a forceful courtroom advocate, an effective stump speaker for the Whig Party in northwestern Virginia, and a delegate to the Virginia constitutional convention of 1850–1851. For many years he had represented the interests of the Baltimore and Ohio Railroad in Virginia.[20] Hunter would nominally be Harding's assistant, but he would in fact have full authority to manage the case. Despite his eminence as a lawyer, Hunter was a curious choice for this important responsibility. His wife was the niece of Fontaine Beckham, who was shot while standing on the train trestle at the edge of the armory grounds, and his son, Henry Hunter, was the man who took the helpless William Thompson out of the Wager House and, cheered on by the townspeople, shot him to death on the Potomac bridge. In calmer times, Henry Hunter might himself have been tried for killing Thompson, but such was not to be the case in the excitement that now gripped Jefferson County. Andrew

Hunter would prosecute Brown, despite his personal connections with the events and witnesses to be examined. He would
not only represent Wise in all matters related to the trial. He
would draft the key legal documents in the case—including the
all-important indictment—and he would be provided with scriv-
eners (or amanuenses) to assist him in the task.[21] Hunter was
only too glad to take over Harding's duties, for he personally
held the commonwealth attorney in contempt (in a letter to
Wise, Hunter described Harding as a "pestiferous little prosecutor").[22] And he shared Parker's desire to get the trials over as
soon as possible. "The judge," Hunter wrote the governor, "is
for observing all the judicial decencies; so am I, but at double
quick time."[23]

Sheriff Campbell read the commitment signed by Roger
Chew aloud, after which Charles Harding suggested that the
court appoint an attorney to represent the prisoners. When Braxton Davenport asked Brown if he had counsel, Brown addressed
the magistrates:

> Virginians—I did not ask for any quarter at the time I was taken.
> I did not ask to have my life spared. The governor of the State of
> Virginia tendered me his assurance that I should have a fair trial,
> but under no circumstances whatever will I be able to have a fair
> trial. If you seek my blood, you can have it at any moment with-
> out this mockery of a trial. I have had no counsel; I have not been
> able to advise with anyone.

If any in the courtroom that morning had expected Brown to
address the magistrates in a meek or obsequious tone, they must
have reacted with some surprise to the assertive, even defiant
man who now commanded the forum. He was not speaking
to the magistrates of his examining court but to "Virginians,"
whom he apparently regarded as his real adversaries in Charlestown. He continued:

I know nothing about the feelings of my fellow prisoners, and am utterly unable to attend in any way to my own defense. My memory don't [*sic*] serve me; my health is insufficient, though improving. There are mitigating circumstances that I would urge in our favor, if a fair trial is to be allowed us; but if we are to be forced with a mere form—a trial for execution—you might spare yourselves that trouble.

Brown was neither apologetic nor compliant, but assertive, even accusatory:

I am ready for my fate. I do not ask a trial. I beg for no mockery of a trial—no insult—nothing but that which conscience gives, or cowardice would drive you to practice. I ask again to be excused from the mockery of a trial. I do not even know what the special design of the examination is. I do not know what is to be the benefit of it to the Commonwealth. I have no little further to ask, other than that I may not be foolishly insulted only as cowardly barbarians insult those who fall into their power.[24]

It was an astonishing message and must have given the spectators reason to pause. Brown had no attorneys (he had not yet heard from Russell, Chapman, or Tilden), but he was obviously not shy about speaking for himself. If the proceedings were not to be postponed (the magistrates and prosecution attorneys would have vigorously opposed any effort to do that), the best solution seemed to be to appoint a local attorney or attorneys to represent the prisoners. Accordingly, Braxton Davenport announced that he would appoint two local attorneys, Lawson Botts and Charles J. Faulkner.

Botts and Faulkner were odd choices. The thirty-six-year-old Botts was a competent and well-connected lawyer in Charlestown. His grandfather, Benjamin Botts, had represented Aaron Burr in his treason trial, and on his mother's side of the family he was related to George Washington. But he had been in the thick of events at Harper's Ferry and could well have been expected to testify in the upcoming trial. As a captain of one of the first militia units from Charlestown to reach the federal armory, he had seen much of the firing back and forth and had actually participated in the unsuccessful negotiations between Brown and the militia for a truce that would have allowed Brown to retreat across the Potomac into Maryland. He owned four slaves, who ranged in age from nine to fifty-four.[25] How a man who was a potential witness for the prosecution could also act as attorney for the defense without finding himself in an impossible conflict of interest might have been a difficult question to answer. The fact that he also owned slaves would, of course, have immediately raised a conflict of interest between him and Brown.

Charles Faulkner was an even more questionable choice. Commonly called Colonel Faulkner, he was one of the pillars of the legal establishment in northern Virginia, a friend of prominent politicians and himself a veteran officeholder. He had been a member of the Virginia legislature, a delegate to the Virginia constitutional convention of 1850 and 1851, and a member of the U.S. House of Representatives from 1851 until March 1859. He was a slaveholder (he owned thirteen when the 1860 census was taken a little more than nine months later)[26] and, while serving in the state legislature, had proposed legislation that found expression in the Fugitive Slave Act of 1850. He was fifty-three years old in 1859 and on such good terms with the pro-Southern Democrats who controlled the national government that he was about to be named by President Buchanan to the prestigious post of U.S. minister to France. Like Botts, Faulkner had been in the thick of the excitement at Harper's Ferry during Brown's raid. He had come there from his home near Martinsburg, about fifteen miles to the north, as soon as he heard that the town had been attacked and, shouldering a rifle, had helped the townspeople surround Brown in the engine house. After Brown was captured, he joined with Governor Wise in examining the papers found among Brown's possessions at the Kennedy Farm. When Senator Mason, Congressman Vallandigham, and others questioned Brown in the armory offices, Faulkner joined in the effort, asking questions himself and listening intently to Brown's answers to the other interrogators. As he later admitted, he had openly expressed his opinion that Brown was guilty and that a "just punishment" awaited his crimes. He believed that his feelings about Brown would "utterly disqualify" him from sitting as a juror in Brown's case and that he should also be disqualified from acting as Brown's attorney.[27] Notwithstanding this, Braxton Davenport appointed him and Botts to serve as Brown's counsel.

To his credit, Faulkner registered his protest. When his name was mentioned, he questioned whether the magistrates' court had authority to appoint any attorneys at all, noted that Brown did not regard the appointment of local attorneys "as a bona fide act, but rather as a mockery," and he explained that his personal involvement in the case rendered it "improper and inexpedient" for him to act as Brown's counsel.[28] But his protests were not heeded, and his appointment was confirmed.

Botts did not feel the same reluctance as Faulkner. He said he was "prepared to do his best to defend the prisoners," but he hoped the court would "assign some experienced assistant in case Mr. Faulkner persisted in his declination." Commonwealth Attorney Harding then addressed Brown directly, asking if he was willing to accept Botts and Faulkner as his attorneys. Brown replied that he had sent for his own attorneys, men who had been recommended to him by friends but whose names he did not recall. "I wish for counsel if I am to have a trial," he said. "But if I am to have nothing but the mockery of a trial, as I said, I do not care anything about counsel—it is unnecessary to trouble any gentleman with that duty."[29] It was apparent from this exchange that Brown had a knack for turning questions back on his questioners—putting the onus on them to furnish answers when he was unwilling to do so. It was a technique he would employ frequently during the trial, often to good effect.

"You are to have a fair trial," Harding shot back.

"There were certain men," Brown continued, "I think Mr. Botts was one of them—who declined acting as counsel, but I am not positive about it. I cannot remember whether he was one, because I have heard so many names. I am a stranger here. I do not know the disposition or character of the gentlemen named. I have applied for counsel of my own, and doubtless could have them, if I am not, as I said before, to be hurried to execution before they can reach me. But if that is the disposition that is to be made of me, all this trouble and expense can be saved."

"The question," Harding insisted, "is do you desire the aid of Messrs. Faulkner and Botts as your counsel: Please to answer, yes or no."

Brown was not about to back down. "I cannot regard this as an examination under any circumstances," he said. "I would prefer that they should exercise their own pleasure. I feel as if it was a matter of very little account to me. If they had designed to assist me as counsel, I should have wanted an opportunity to consult them at my leisure."

Harding then turned to Aaron Stevens and asked if he was willing to accept Faulkner and Botts as his attorneys. Stevens said that he was. Harding put the same question to Coppoc, Green, and Copeland, and got the same answer from each.

The magistrates apparently considered the matter of counsel settled, at least for the present, and they now proceeded to hear witnesses. First, however, they issued a peremptory order forbidding the press to publish detailed accounts of any of the testimony. Such reports would poison the minds of potential jurors and make it impossible to impanel an impartial jury.[30]

Lewis Washington was the first witness for the prosecution. He testified that he was asleep in his home about one o'clock on Monday morning, October 17, when he was awakened by a noise. He heard a name called, went to inquire about it, and was quickly surrounded by six men. Aaron Stevens appeared to be in command of the group. With Stevens were John Cook, Edwin Coppoc, Shields Green, John Copeland, and a man Washington later recognized as John Kagi. Washington recalled in detail the circumstances under which he and his slaves were taken prisoners, transported to the Harper's Ferry armory, and eventually confined in the engine house. After the engine house was stormed, and Brown was captured, Washington witnessed a conversation between Brown and Governor Wise. Brown was told "he need not answer questions unless he chose." Brown said that he "had nothing to conceal—he had no favors to ask." But he bragged that he "had arms enough for two thousand men, and could get enough for five thousand if they were wanted."[31]

Washington was followed in the witness stand by Archibald M. Kitzmiller, who had been in charge of the armory at the time of the raid. He was taken prisoner and, with other hostages, confined in the engine house, where he had ample opportunity to observe Brown and converse with him. Kitzmiller testified that Brown always treated his prisoners "with a great deal of respect and courtesy." Kitzmiller asked Brown what his purpose was in coming to the armory, and "he repeatedly told him his only object was to free the slaves." He was willing to fight the proslavery men to accomplish that object. At one time, Kitzmiller volunteered to go outside with Aaron Stevens under the protection of a white flag, hoping to negotiate terms for a truce. But Stevens was promptly fired on and fell. While he was lying on the ground, Stevens said to Kitzmiller, "I have been cruelly deceived." Kitzmiller said he counted twenty-two men in Brown's band, but the only ones he could recognize now were Brown and Stevens.[32]

Armistead Ball was the next to testify. He was the master machinist at the armory and was taken captive by Brown's men as he reported for work on Monday morning. After detailing the facts of his capture and confinement in the engine house, Ball recalled a conversation he had with Brown during the siege. Brown said that he had come to Harper's Ferry "for no child's play" and that he was "prepared to carry out his designs." But he did not intend "to make war against the people" and said "they would not be injured if they remained quiet." Brown said his object "was to place the United States' arms in the hands of the black men, and he proposed to free all the slaves in the vicinity." He repeatedly said his "whole object was to release the slaves." Ball asked Brown if there was some way he and the other hostages could be released. Brown said they could be released only in return for slaves. When the marines were about to storm the engine house, Brown told his hostages that he did not intend to injure them but that "they should equally occupy the post of danger with himself." If the marines did not value the hostages enough to accept his terms for a safe withdrawal into Maryland, Brown said, "they must be barbarians." Edwin Coppoc, however, was not so bold. When the marines made their assault, he told Ball and the other hostages to get behind the fire engines because he "did not want to see any of them injured." Asked if he had personally seen Brown fire from the engine house, Ball answered clearly: "I did not see Captain Brown fire once from the engine house." Ball did, however, see the black man Shields Green fire several times. Ball concluded his testimony by averring that the hostages inside the engine house "never were unreasonably exposed."[33]

John Allstadt was called next to give the particulars of his capture at his home, and of the experiences he and his slaves had when they were taken to the armory. Allstadt's testimony was interrupted when someone noticed that Aaron Stevens had lost consciousness. The magistrates ordered that a glass of water be brought to Stevens, and two doctors, Gerard F. Mason and John A. Strath, had a mattress brought into court to support the fallen man.[34] It was not clear whether Stevens had fainted or simply collapsed from the strain of his injuries and the ordeal of the legal proceedings. It was clear, however, that the wheels of justice would roll on despite the interruption, and questioning of Allstadt quickly resumed. Asked if Brown had ever fired from the engine house, Allstadt said he had—several times. He saw Brown "with a gun leveled," and he saw him fire once. He speculated that Brown shot the marine who was killed (Private Luke Quinn). He could identify all of the prisoners except John Copeland, the light-skinned black that he and other witnesses described as "the yellow man."[35]

A string of six witnesses now followed, each offering brief testimony regarding the events at Harper's Ferry. Alexander Kelly testified that he was a witness to some shooting during Brown's raid, but he could not identify any of the prisoners then in court. William Johnson testified that he saw "the yellow man" try to swim across the Shenandoah River. Copeland was armed with a spear and a rifle, and he said that Brown had put him in charge of Hall's Rifle Works. Andrew Kennedy testified that he was at the jail when Copeland was brought in. Kennedy asked him where he was from. Copeland answered that he was from the Western Reserve of Ohio and that he had been employed by

Brown at a salary of twenty dollars a month. Charles Faulkner objected to the testimony on the ground that it "implicated" the white prisoners. (He said nothing of the testimony's effects on the black prisoners.) Judge Parker ruled that the testimony could only be received as implicating Copeland himself.

Resuming his testimony, Kennedy testified that Copeland had said that their "object was to release the slaves of this country." He knew of nineteen in the party, but there were several others he did not know. Joseph A. Brua, an armory worker who was one of the hostages Brown held in the engine house, testified that he was permitted to go outside several times under a flag of truce. When guns were being fired, Brua saw Coppoc fire twice, and at the second shot Brown remarked, "That man is down." Brua then asked and received permission to go outside the engine house, where he saw that Fontaine Beckham had just been shot. Brua had no doubt that Coppoc was the one who shot Beckham.

After all the witnesses had testified, the case was submitted to the magistrates. As it was their duty under the Virginia Code to determine if there was probable cause to hold Brown and the other prisoners for trial, they did not have to decide the ultimate question of innocence or guilt. "The examination today was merely to see whether the charges are of sufficient importance to go before the Grand Jury," the *New York Herald* explained.[36] But the Charlestown magistrates were willing to go beyond mere probable cause. Parker was back in the courthouse at two o'clock when the magistrates reported their decision. As recorded in the order book of the court, it read:

> Sundry witnesses were examined and the Court being unanimously of opinion that the prisoners are guilty of the offence with which they stand charged, it is ordered and considered by

the Court that they be sent on to the Circuit Court of this county for trial according to Law; and the prisoners are remanded to jail.[37]

The grand jury, already impaneled, stood ready to receive the case without delay. The *Herald* sensed "an evident intention to hurry the trial through, and execute the prisoners as soon as possible."[38] When the magistrates' decision was brought to them, the grand jurors retired to a separate room to examine the witnesses. At five o'clock, they announced they had not yet finished their work and would resume it again the following morning.[39]

While the case was making its way from the magistrates' court to the grand jury, Judge Parker took advantage of his absence from the courtroom to walk through the streets of Charlestown and sound out public opinion on the Brown case. In short order, he found that anger against the Harper's Ferry raiders was growing. Many men were impatient with the judicial proceedings and spoke openly of storming the jail and lynching Brown and his fellow prisoners. Years later, Parker recalled that it had always been his rule to allow nobody to speak with him about a case that was to come before him for trial. This time, however, he departed from his rule, for the situation was becoming "desperate." As he explained:

> When not holding court I would stroll out and take a seat upon some good box. One after another the leading citizens of the county would come up and enter into conversation about the weather or the crops. Pretty soon the conversation would get around to John Brown and the raid, and I would encourage them to talk about it. Then I would express in the strongest language I could command my condemnation of any plot to lynch the prisoners. I would declare such a course to be nothing less

than murder and express my determination to visit direst punishment upon anybody who attempted to interfere with the majesty of the law. They would listen and often thank me for what I had stated, saying I had put the matter in a light they had not thought of. I became fully convinced from these conversations that there had been a very general sentiment in favor of lynching, and I think the talks I had with those leading citizens had a great deal to do with the abandonment of the idea.[40]

The grand jury resumed its deliberation on the morning of October 26. In the meantime, Andrew Hunter had prepared a "true bill" (or indictment) for the approval of the grand jury. Couched in the florid legal language of the time, the document represented the official accusation by the Commonwealth of Virginia against Brown, Stevens, Coppoc, Green, and Copeland. At noon, the court reconvened, and the grand jury reported that it had approved the indictment. It was long and prolix and included four counts, or allegations of distinct offenses. Three of the counts would hardly have raised any eyebrows, for they seemed to be amply supported by the evidence heard by the examining magistrates. One count charged that Brown, Stevens, Coppoc, Green, and Copeland "maliciously and feloniously" conspired with one another and with John Cook, John Kagi, Charles Tidd, and others (the latter three members of Brown's band who managed to escape Harper's Ferry during the fighting there) to "induce certain slaves . . . to make insurrection against their masters and owners, and against the government, and the constitution and laws of the Commonwealth of Virginia." Another count charged the same prisoners with the murders of Thomas Boerley, George W. Turner, Fontaine Beckham, Luke Quinn, and Hayward Shepherd. And yet another charged the prisoners with aiding and abetting John

Copeland in the murders of Boerley, Turner, and Beckham (the prosecution theory was apparently that Copeland had fired the shots that killed those three men). But the remaining count was the one that was to attract the most attention. Hunter titled it Count One, as if it was more important than all the others.

This count charged that Brown, Stevens, Coppoc, Green, and Copeland, "together with divers other evil minded, and traitorous persons to the jurors unknown, not having the fear of God before their eyes, but being moved and seduced by the false and malignant counsels of other evil and traitorous persons, and the instigations of the Devil," had committed *treason* against the Commonwealth of Virginia. To support this extraordinary charge, the indictment stated that the prisoners had done various things, among them conspiring to "feloniously and traitorously make rebellion, and levy war against the said Commonwealth of Virginia"; capturing Lewis Washington, John Allstadt, and others; setting up "a government, separate from and hostile to the existing government of said commonwealth"; professing "allegiance and fidelity to said usurped government"; and joining "in open battle and deadly warfare with the civil officers and soldiers in the law service of said Commonwealth of Virginia." All of this was done, according to the indictment, "to the evil example of all others, in like case offending, and against the peace and dignity of said Commonwealth."[41]

Note that the charge of treason appeared for the first time in the indictment. Treason had not been alleged when Brown was brought before the examining court or when he was committed to the jail in Charlestown. The charges then filed against him and his fellow prisoners had been much more conventional: murder, conspiracy, and inciting slaves to rebel.[42] Bringing treason into the picture raised the trial to a new level by forcing Brown to defend himself against the "highest crime which can be committed in civil society."[43] Why was this deadly serious and potentially inflammatory allegation added in this way, almost as if it were an afterthought?

The great Brown scholar Boyd B. Stutler argued that Andrew Hunter conceived the charge of treason for the purpose of tying the hands of Governor Wise. Hunter knew, as most Virginians did, that Wise was given to unpredictable changes of course; that he was, as Stutler described him, of "explosive, emotional, unstable character." Wise had alternately complimented Brown as "a man of clear head, of courage, fortitude and simple ingenuousness" and reviled him as "a fanatic, vain and garrulous."[44] The special Charlestown prosecutor knew, if most Virginians did not, that Governor Wise would have the power to pardon or reprieve Brown or any of the other prisoners from any crime that the Charlestown court might convict them of—except treason. Though he could find no documentary proof on the point, Stutler believed that Hunter "insisted on the treason charge even though of doubtful validity so that on conviction the power to pardon, commute or respite would be taken out of the hands of the Governor."[45] Wise had put Hunter in charge of Brown's prosecution, and Hunter clearly "took charge" of it.

There was never any serious doubt that, under the federal system erected by the U.S. Constitution, it was possible for a person or persons to be charged with the crime of treason against a state. The Constitution itself clearly recognized that possibility in the extradition clause, which provides that "a person charged in any *state* with treason, felony, or other crime, who shall flee from justice, and be found in another *state*, shall on demand of the executive authority of the *state* from which he fled, be delivered up, to be removed to the *state* having jurisdiction of the crime."[46] And there had been previous prosecutions for treason against a state (although they were notably rare and did not result in any actual punishments being inflicted).[47] It was not at all clear, however, that Brown's invasion of Harper's Ferry constituted treason against Virginia. The indictment against him and his fellow prisoners did not allege that they were citizens of Virginia or that they had a duty of allegiance to the state, and the underlying facts seemed to indicate the contrary. They were not citizens, or even residents, of Virginia (except for John Cook, who had lived in the state for something over a year). They had crossed the Potomac from Maryland not to live in Virginia and assume the duties of citizenship but to attack the federal arsenal and armory in Harper's Ferry. Yet allegiance had traditionally been recognized as an essential element of the law of treason in England and the United States, and thus of Virginia, a common-law jurisdiction that derived its law from English forms and practices.[48] The indictment did allege, however, that Brown and his fellow prisoners had professed "allegiance and fidelity" to their own provisional government and that this profession was one of the elements of their crime against Virginia. This revealed, if indirectly, that Hunter recognized allegiance as an element of the crime of treason against Virginia, despite his failure to allege that Brown or the others had any such duty to Virginia. For all that appeared from the indictment—for that matter, for all the testimony offered before the examining magistrates proved—the accused men were interlopers in the state, trespassers on its soil, men who entered it to violate its peace and quiet, but not to make their homes there or seek its security or protection. They attacked federal facilities in a federal enclave that was owned and controlled by the United States. How, then, did Andrew Hunter conclude that these men were traitors to Virginia? The answer to this question was not immediately apparent, although it would be disputed very vigorously during the trial—with Brown's lawyers arguing that he could not have committed treason against the state, and Andrew Hunter arguing that he not only could have but did.

And so the indictment was filed, and the charges were murder, conspiracy, aiding and abetting murder, and treason. The time had now arrived for the jury to be summoned. The trial itself was about to begin. And life and death—and, more important, the future of a troubled nation—hung in the balance.

5

THE JURY IS SUMMONED

After the grand jury was discharged, Judge Parker again convened the circuit court. Prosecutor Andrew Hunter opened the proceedings by noting that Charles Faulkner had left the courthouse and was no longer acting as counsel for the prisoners. Faulkner realized that his involvement in the events at Harper's Ferry and his openly expressed opinion that Brown was guilty and deserved a "just punishment" disqualified him from further participation in the case. He had discussed his situation with Judge Parker before the hearing, and Parker had agreed that he could no longer serve.[1] Lawson Botts now remained as the prisoners' only attorney, and it was clear to both Hunter and Botts that he would need help. Hunter suggested that if the court intended to appoint additional counsel, it might be proper to do so at once. Parker replied that he would assign the prisoners any member of the bar they might select. After conferring with Brown, Botts told the judge that Brown was willing to accept him. But Botts wanted Thomas C. Green, the mayor of Charlestown, to act as his assistant. Like Botts, the thirty-nine-year-old Green was a well-connected attorney. He was the son of a former judge of the Virginia Supreme Court of Appeals, a cousin of Virginia Senator James M. Mason, and a great-grandson of George Mason of Gunston Hall (1725–1792), the venerated author of the Virginia Declaration of Rights. He was also a slaveholder, owning four slaves when the 1860 census was taken, and a successful practitioner who, a few years later, would win a seat on the West Virginia Court of Appeals.[2] Parker asked Green if he was willing to accept the appointment, and he answered that he was. Given the hostile feelings toward Brown in Charlestown, it is remarkable that the attorneys who agreed to represent him were so able. As Brown's biographer, Oswald Garrison Villard, observed: "There can be no doubt that in Messrs. Green and Botts, John Brown had assigned to him far abler counsel than would have been given to the ordinary malefactor."[3] The attorneys, all prominent slaveholders, were inevitably opposed to Brown's real purpose in coming to Virginia. He wanted to free the slaves, to deprive them of what was perhaps their most valuable property. Could they be expected to warmly embrace his cause? They were willing to accept their appointments, perhaps because they believed that, by doing so, they would show Virginians that the standards of the Charlestown bar were high enough to overcome animosities. They may also have been part of an effort by the Old Dominion's ruling elite to put Virginia's best foot forward, realizing that the eyes of the nation were now focused on Charlestown and that the quality of the justice dispensed there would reflect, for good or ill, on slaveholding interests throughout the South.

Before either of his attorneys could act for him, however, Brown wanted to be heard. He arose from the chair in which he had been sitting and addressed the judge:

> I do not intend to detain the court, but barely wish to say, as I have been promised a fair trial, that I am not now in circumstances that enable me to attend a trial, owing to the state of my health. I have a severe wound in the back, or rather in one kidney, which enfeebles me very much. But I am doing well, and I only ask for a very short delay of my trial, and I think that I may be able to listen to it; and I merely ask this that, as the saying is, "the devil may have his dues," no more.

Brown was angling for a delay, a prospect that did not sit well with either Hunter or Parker. Brown continued:

> I wish to say further that my hearing is impaired and rendered indistinct in consequence of wounds I have about my head. I cannot hear distinctly at all; I could not hear what the Court has said this morning. I would be glad to hear what is said on my trial, and I am now doing better than I would expect to be under the circumstances. A very short delay would be all I would ask. I do not presume to ask more than a very short delay, so that I may in some degree recover, and be able at least to listen to my trial, and hear what questions are asked of the citizens, and what their answers are. If that could be allowed me, I should be very much obliged.[4]

Hunter thought that Brown's request was premature. He could be arraigned first, the prosecutor said, and the question of a delay taken up afterward. Parker agreed, and ordered that the indictment be read at once, so that the prisoners could plead guilty or not guilty. Then he would consider Brown's request.

It took about twenty minutes for the court clerk to read the long indictment. During all that time, Brown and his fellow prisoners were made to stand. Stevens, whose wounds were the most severe, had to be supported by two bailiffs so he would not slump to the floor.[5] The *Herald* reporter thought that Brown "looked somewhat better, and his eye was not so much swollen." David Hunter Strother, a native of nearby Berkeley County who wrote and illustrated stories for *Harper's Weekly* under the pen name of Porte Crayon, had a seat just a few feet away from Brown. "During the reading," Strother later remembered, "one might have heard a pin drop, although the Galleries & Court Hall were crowded to suffocation." While the clerk was reading, an armed soldier entered the court and caught the eye of Judge Parker, who summarily ordered him out. Parker's "judicial dignity would not tolerate an armed man in Court," Strother said. Brown "listened with respectful attention, becoming more earnest as the reading went on, & finally quivering with nervous impatience, as the charges against him were recited in the awful & high sounding language of the law."

When the reading was concluded, the clerk addressed each of the accused men by name and asked each in turn: "How say you? Are you guilty of the offenses whereof you stand indicted, or not guilty?"[6] Strother recalled that "the other prisoners seemed almost overwhelmed by the imposing solemnity of the ceremony and if left to themselves would probably have plead [*sic*] guilty & thrown themselves on the mercy of the court." But they were instructed otherwise by their attorneys. Brown met the request for a plea "by denouncing the indictments as false and exaggerated." He proceeded to argue some of the points in the document, Strother said, but was finally persuaded to agree to the simple plea of "not guilty." The other prisoners did the same. Brown was still not satisfied "with the apparent necessity of so doing," for, according to Strother, "he insisted there were some things in the indictment he didn't want to deny."[7] It was an intriguing remark. What were the things he didn't want to deny? For all the newspaper accounts reveal, the point was not pursued, and it was eventually forgotten.

Their pleas entered, the five prisoners were asked whether they wished to be tried together or separately. As was their right under Virginia law, they demanded separate trials.[8] Parker then asked Hunter to elect whom he would try first. The answer was John Brown.

It was Wednesday, October 26, the second day of the legal proceedings in Charlestown, and only one week after Brown had been brought from Harper's Ferry to the county seat. Events were moving rapidly in Jefferson County. Brown was still suffer-

ing from the wounds he sustained at the end of the raid; he had
not yet heard from any of the Northern attorneys he had written
to asking for legal assistance; he had had no opportunity to confer with the attorneys appointed to represent him in Charlestown, to discuss the facts of the case or the witnesses he needed
to summon in the trial. Andrew Hunter was ready to proceed
with his witnesses, and Judge Parker was anxious to move the
trial along so he could meet his other circuit court commit-
ments. Brown, however, was haggard and ill prepared to defend
himself in a proceeding that threatened to end in his own death.

Lawson Botts now rose to address the judge. "I am instructed by Brown," the attorney said, "to say that he is men-
tally and physically unable to proceed with his trial at this time."
It was a curious construction. Botts did not say that Brown was
unable to proceed with his trial, only that Brown had instructed
him to say that he was unable to proceed. Did this choice of
words make a difference? Brown had heard that "counsel of
his own choice will be here," Botts continued, "whom he will,
of course, prefer." Here Botts revealed that his own duties as
Brown's attorney were probably only temporary. He was acting
as counsel for the accused man only until an attorney of his own
choice could make it to Charlestown. "He only asks for a delay
of two or three days," Botts continued. "It seems to me but a
reasonable request, and I hope the Court will grant it.[9]

Andrew Hunter replied for the prosecution. He did not think
it his duty "to oppose anything that justice required, nor to object to anything that involved a simple consideration of humanity, where it could be properly allowed." But a request for a delay of two or three days should be based on "actual facts and
circumstances, not a simple request." In Hunter's opinion, even
the delay of "a single day" would be "dangerous," for it would
put additional demands on the community and would "weaken
our present position and give strength to our enemies abroad."

Brown had been given every opportunity to summon attorneys of his own choice. As for Brown's claim that he was physically unable to proceed to trial, it would be better to have Brown examined by a doctor and to hear from the jailer before accepting such a claim. Harding concurred in Hunter's objection to the requested delay, both because "Brown was the leader of the insurrection" and because any delay in his trial would in turn delay the trials of his fellow prisoners. Thomas Green told the judge that he had had no opportunity to counsel with Brown or prepare a defense. Letters had been sent off seeking Northern attorneys, but there had been insufficient time to receive any replies. Botts said that there was so much excitement surrounding Brown's trial that Northern counsel might be deterred from coming down to Charlestown. But "now that it had been promised that the prisoners should have a fair and impartial trial," Botts "presumed that they would come and take part in the case."

Judge Parker said that a reasonable delay would have to be granted if "physical inability were shown." But the expectation that other counsel would appear was not a sufficient cause for delay, as there was "no certainty about their coming." Under the circumstances, it was natural that the prisoners would seek a delay. But the brief period remaining before the close of the court's current term made it necessary "to proceed as expeditiously as practicable, and to be cautious about granting delays." He wanted to hear from Dr. Mason, who had been treating Brown in the jail, before deciding the question of his physical ability. Mason testified that he thought Brown was able "to go on understandingly with the trial" and that his wounds were not such as "to affect his mind or recollection." Brown had "always conversed freely and intelligently about this affair." Mason had heard him complain of "debility but not of hardness of hearing." David H. Cockrell, one of the guards at the jail, added his testimony that Brown "had always been ready to converse freely." But John Avis said he had heard Brown "frequently say to persons visiting him that his mind was confused and his hearing affected." Considering all of these statements, Parker ruled that the trial would proceed, but "regard would be had as to his condition, so as to avoid his being wearied."[10]

The court now took its midday recess.

At two o'clock, the jailer was ordered to bring Brown into court. When he went to his cell, however, Avis found Brown in bed complaining that he was unable to get up. Avis summoned help and had Brown lifted onto a cot, which was carried across the street and into the courthouse, where it was set down within the bar. It was an astounding scene. The prisoner in a sensational trial whose request for a three-day delay of the proceedings had just been denied now professed that he was too weak to stand or even sit in a chair and had to be laid on his back before the judge and lawyers. Most Virginians and their supporters were sure that Brown was feigning weakness to gain sympathy. The *Herald* reported that Brown was "evidently not much injured, but is determined to resist the pushing of his trial by all the means in his power."[11] Porte Crayon (Strother) thought that Brown's stratagem was "a ruse to gain time."[12] But when word was transmitted North that Brown's trial was to continue even while he was lying helpless on a cot, it aroused indignation.

News of Brown's trial reached all parts of the country. By then a telegraph office had been opened in Charlestown to transmit news of Brown's trial to the outside world. It was paid for by the major metropolitan newspapers and connected to the special telegraph line that the same newspapers had extended from Harper's Ferry to Charlestown.[13] In Massachusetts and Ohio, where Brown hoped to enlist the aid of attorneys for his defense, there was a growing apprehension that, despite frequent and public assurances that he would receive a fair trial, he was in fact being rushed to judgment. Attorneys in those states were conferring among themselves to see what they might do to help him. John A. Andrew of Boston was a leader of the Massachusetts efforts. An outstanding attorney, one of the founders of the Republican Party in his state and a determined foe of slavery, Andrew may have communicated with Reuben A. Chapman, the Springfield lawyer Brown wrote to from the Charlestown jail, and he almost certainly made contact with Brown's most prominent supporters in Massachusetts. A few months later, Andrew was called to give testimony before a U.S. Senate committee formed to examine the Harper's Ferry raid to explain why he helped Brown obtain attorneys. Andrew explained that when he learned the Jefferson County Court was proceeding to Brown's trial with "such speed and hurried action on its part as to render it probable that there was to be no sufficient opportunity to make a full and complete defense," he considered it "a judicial outrage." Andrew said he had never seen anything like it in all his years of practice. He cited a case of kidnapping that had been recently tried in Massachusetts, in which former Attorney General Caleb Cushing was the attorney for the prisoners. In that case, two or three months passed after the arraignment before Cushing was required even to enter a plea, much less proceed to trial. Various men who shared outrage over the rush to justice in Virginia came to Andrew and urged him to go to Virginia to defend Brown. Andrew demurred. "If I should go to Virginia, I, a Republican lawyer and a Massachusetts man, should be before a court and jury so little in sympathy with myself that I should be quite as much on trial as my client should be. Besides that, I am a stranger to the local jurisprudence and practice of Virginia." Andrew believed it would be better to secure an attorney who was closer to Virginia, who knew something of its practice and who could argue Brown's case with some hope of eliciting sympathy. So he took it upon himself to write to Montgomery Blair, a Washington lawyer who had good contacts with slaveholders in both Kentucky, where he was born, and in Missouri, where he had spent his early professional life. Blair was a member of the prominent Blair family of Washington and Maryland, and although he was personally opposed to slavery and had argued the *Dred Scott* case in the U.S. Supreme Court in 1856, he was widely regarded as a moderate on the issue. Blair was either unwilling or unable to take up Brown's case personally, but he did make contact with another Washington lawyer named Samuel Chilton, who agreed to go to Charlestown. Though Chilton's busy trial practice was centered in the nation's capital, he was a Virginian by birth and education, and he had good contacts in Jefferson County. But it took time for him to postpone cases he had pending and to make travel arrangements. In the meantime, Judge Richard Parker's Jefferson County Circuit Court forged ahead with Brown's trial.

Trial by jury was generally deemed to be a right, but not a requirement, in the United States. Virginia law explicitly authorized the parties to a case to waive a jury trial and thus submit to trial by the judge sitting without a jury. But this could be done only if the crime charged was not a felony.[14] In felony cases, trial by jury was mandatory. The court was required to issue a writ of venire facias commanding the sheriff to summon twenty-four freeholders (real property owners) "residing remote from the place where the offence is charged to have been committed" to attend the court in which the accused was to be tried.[15] When the twenty-four prospective jurors were assembled, they were denominated a venire, and from their number the actual jurors in the case would be selected. In Brown's case, the writ was issued to the sheriff on October 25, commanding him to summon twenty-four freeholders to appear in the courthouse in

Charlestown on October 26.[16] The requirement that the freeholders reside "remote from the place where the offence was charged to have been committed" was intended to reduce the likelihood that they might have some personal knowledge of the case and thus hold preconceived opinions as to the guilt or innocence of the accused.

Prospective jurors also had to meet age, gender, and racial requirements. By statute, Virginia limited jury service to free white males who were twenty-one to sixty years old.[17] This excluded a large part of the population: young people and old; all who were not white; and all females. The exclusion of nonwhites was to be expected in a slaveholding state. If a man was black, it made no difference if he was free or slave for purposes of determining basic political rights such as voting and jury service.

Combining the requirement that jurors be freeholders with the requirement that they reside "remote" from Harper's Ferry conspired to produce a panel of mostly farmers, many or most of whom owned slaves. The age, gender, and race requirements ensured that the persons called to sit in judgment in Brown's case would all be white men, most of them middle-aged. All would be more or less affluent, and all would be either committed to, or at least tolerant of, slavery.

A further requirement was imposed by Virginia law. Under the Virginia Code, any person whose opinions were such "as to prevent his convicting any one of an offence punishable with death" was not allowed to serve as a juror on any trial for such an offense.[18] This ensured that the jurors who would judge John Brown would all approve of the death penalty, and it probably made it more likely that they would find him guilty.

Under Virginia law and practice, prospective jurors were initially questioned as to their qualifications to sit as jurors in the case. This phase of the proceeding was called the voir dire (meaning to tell the truth.) If any juror was shown to be actually disqualified from sitting, he could be challenged for cause. Neither the accused nor the prosecution had any right to peremptory challenges, that is, to challenge a juror or jurors without stating a reason for doing so. However, when twenty-four persons were found who were not subject to challenge for cause, the accused had the right to strike up to eight names from the panel. If a full eight names were stricken in this manner, the panel would be reduced to sixteen. From that number, twelve persons would be chosen by lot to constitute the actual jury.[19]

Judge Parker began the voir dire in Brown's case by asking if any of the prospective jurors had formed or expressed "any opinion that would prevent their deciding the case impartially on the merits of the testimony." It was a benign question, almost universally asked of prospective jurors all over the United States. But how was it to be answered? If a prospective juror had formed an opinion as to John Brown's guilt, he would of course be duty bound to disclose it. But what if he believed that slavery was a divinely ordained social institution and that Northerners who criticized it were doing the "work of the devil"? It can hardly be expected that any of the prospective jurors would disclose such an opinion, although opinions like this were common in Virginia in 1859. But the very commonness of the opinions insulated them from disclosure. If a prospective juror believed that slavery was sacrosanct, and that anybody who came down from the North to help slaves win their freedom was evil, he would at least be inclined to regard John Brown as a dangerous man. But it would never have entered his head to tell the judge that he held such an opinion.

The judge continued his voir dire of the prospective jurors. His questions were brisk, and the answers given quickly. Parker was working under time constraints—he had to try not only

Brown but five other prisoners before his term in Charlestown expired—and he was determined not to dally.

"Were you at Harper's Ferry on Monday or Tuesday?"

"How long did you remain there?"

"Did you witness any of the proceedings for which this party is to be tried?"

"Did you form or express any opinion from what you saw there with regard to the guilt or innocence of these people?"

"Would that opinion disqualify you from giving these men a fair trial?

"Did you hear any of the evidence in this case before the Examining Court?"

"What was your opinion based on?"

"Was it a decided one, or was it one which would yield to evidence if the evidence was different from what you supposed?"

"Are you sure that you can try this case impartially, from the evidence alone, without reference to anything you have heard or seen of this transaction?

"Have you any conscientious scruples against convicting a party of an offense to which the law assigns the punishment of death, merely because that is the penalty assigned?"[20]

The questions asked and answered, Parker excused anyone who was present at Harper's Ferry during Brown's raid and saw him and his co-prisoners "perpetrating the acts for which they are to be tried."

The examination of the jury had lasted about three hours. During all of this time, Brown lay on his cot, with his eyes closed and, according to the newspaper reporters, "the counterpane drawn up close under his chin."[21] His attorneys exercised his right to strike off eight names from the panel.[22] From the sixteen that remained, twelve were chosen by lot to serve as jurors. None were famous men—none were celebrities in Jefferson

County or elsewhere—but by the single act of joining Brown's jury they had assured that their names would be remembered by history. They were Richard Timberlake, Joseph Myers, Thomas Watson Jr., Isaac Dust, John C. McClure, William Rightstine, Jacob J. Miller, Thomas Osbourn, George W. Boyer, John C. Wiltshire, George W. Tapp, and William A. Martin. How many of them owned slaves is uncertain; the seven who were known to be slaveholders owned a total of fifty-four slaves.[23]

Judge Parker did not administer the juror's oath to these men, preferring to defer that to the following morning. He did, however, admonish the jurors not to talk about the case or permit others to converse with them about it. At five o'clock, the jurors were dismissed and the court adjourned, to assemble the following morning at ten o'clock. Brown, still lying on his cot, was carried out of the courthouse, across the street, and into his jail room.[24]

It had been a long day for the judge, the attorneys, and Brown, but it was not yet over. When a trial is under way, the public sees only what happens in the courtroom. When the chamber is empty, it often seems as if those responsible for the administration of justice are off the job, or too lazy to attend to their duties. It is an illusion. Behind the scenes—before the court convenes in the morning, and after it adjourns late in the afternoon—the judge, the attorneys, the clerks, the bailiffs, all have important work to do: evidence must be reviewed, witnesses interviewed, clients counseled, and strategies planned. After he got back to the jail, Brown almost certainly met with Lawson Botts and Thomas Green. How communicative he may have been with the appointed attorneys, however, is a matter of speculation. He never fully trusted the local lawyers, not because they were personally suspect, but because they were part of a culture that rested on slavery and was prepared at every turn to defend it. And Brown detested the culture as much as he detested slavery itself. As the *Baltimore Sun* reported, Brown believed he could have "a fairer trial if the defense were conducted by his own counsel, than if he were defended by the counsel present here."[25] Few would have doubted his judgment on this.

But Brown did have a strategy for his defense, and he was not shy about communicating it to his appointed lawyers. It was his contention that he had not come to Harper's Ferry with malicious intent; that he did not intend to kill any of the inhabitants of the town but wanted to help the slaves there win their freedom. His desire to free the slaves was purely benevolent, and his willingness not to harm the whites equally so. He had taken hostages—or, as he called them, "prisoners"—merely to help him carry out his benevolent goals. Once he had taken them into the engine house, he treated them courteously, even kindly. He let some of them come and go, even to go home and visit their families. He never threatened them, and he repeatedly pleaded with the townspeople to stop shooting into the engine house so the hostages would not be harmed. He had acted throughout the raid with a lack of malice, and he wanted his attorneys to prove that in court. Of course, his theory was thoroughly debatable, at least from a legal viewpoint. If his motives were benevolent and kind, why had he come to Harper's Ferry armed with rifles and revolvers and pikes? Why had five men been killed and many more wounded in the course of the raid? Why had there been so much gunfire on the Potomac bridge, and later in and around the engine house? Why had unarmed men—Hayward Shepherd and Fontaine Beckham notably—been shot and killed? Brown's courtroom strategy was not by any means irrefutable, but it was of his own devising, and he made clear that he wanted Botts and

Green to follow it. For that purpose, he gave them written directions in his own handwriting:

We gave to numerous prisoners perfect liberty.
Get all their names.
We allowed numerous other prisoners to visit their families, to quiet their fears.
Get all their names.
We allowed the conductor to pass his train over the bridge with all his passengers, I myself crossing the bridge with him, and assuring all the passengers of their perfect safety.
Get that conductor's name, and the names of the passengers, so far as may be.
We treated all our prisoners with the utmost kindness and humanity.
Get all their names, so far as may be.
Our orders, from the first and throughout, were, that no unarmed person should be injured, under any circumstances whatever.
Prove that by ALL the prisoners.
We committed no destruction or waste of property.
Prove that.[26]

Mail for Brown accumulated in the jail, and, after it was first read by Andrew Hunter, it was turned over to him. He also received telegrams that were personally delivered to him or one of his lawyers. One of the telegrams he received on Wednesday was from Daniel Tilden in Cleveland. In it, the Ohio judge asked Brown if it would "be of use for counsel to leave that night." Whether Tilden meant that he was willing to come personally, or merely that he would send another attorney in his place, is unclear: the actual text of the telegram apparently was not preserved. Brown promptly sent his reply to the telegraphic office in Charlestown for transmittal to Cleveland. The telegraph was a wonder of the day, an electric innovation that provided quick and sure communication between distant locations, and, thanks to the new line from Harper's Ferry, now connected Charlestown with newspapers in the East and Northwest. But a storm had settled over Virginia that day, one so violent that it took down the telegraph line that fed into Charlestown. For a while, reporters in town were frantic because they could not post their stories of what had transpired in Brown's trial. The line was restored within a few hours, however, and communications resumed. Knowing that Brown's message to Tilden was of possibly life-and-death urgency, the local telegraph operator promised that it "would be sent off at once in advance of the dispatches sent by the reporters." Yes, Brown told Tilden, please come at once. The jury will be sworn in the morning.[27]

Another letter relating to Brown's trial arrived at Harper's Ferry the same day that Tilden's telegram was received in Charlestown. It had been sent to Alfred M. Barbour, the superintendent of the armory and arsenal, by a U.S. Army officer stationed in New York named Henry Hill:

> I would not be surprised if, from what I have heard, there will be an attempt made by the abolitionists of the North to release Brown and his associates from the Charlestown jail. I do not desire to add to the excitement already great, but to write you as a caution. If an attempt is made it will be a hidden movement by a party of armed desperadoes employed by leaders in the free States.

Hill was a Virginian and personally known to Barbour, who immediately passed his message on to Governor Wise; to Secretary of War Floyd (also a Virginian); and to John Garrett, the president of the Baltimore and Ohio Railroad. Reporting Hill's message, the *Sun* reported that Floyd had ordered forty marines to Harper's Ferry, to join the hundreds of Virginia militiamen who were already there, and that arms had been distributed from the armory to over two thousand "citizens of Virginia."[28]

John Brown was secure in the Charlestown jail. Cannons in front of the courthouse were aimed at his cell. Sentries guarded the entrances to the town, and militiamen patrolled the streets. But the commonwealth of Virginia still trembled.

ILLUSTRATIONS

The streets of Charlestown were crowded during Brown's trial. The Jefferson County Courthouse, where Brown was condemned to be hanged, is shown on the right, the market hall in the center, and a corner of the jail where Brown was confined on the extreme left. Drawing by Alfred Berghaus for *Frank Leslie's Illustrated Weekly.* West Virginia State Archives, Boyd B. Stutler Collection.

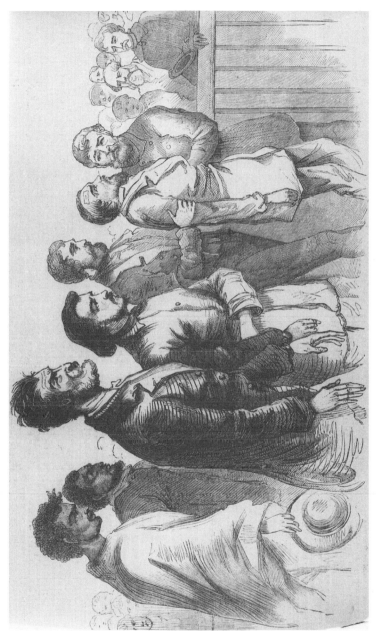

John Brown (foreground) and four of his codefendants were arraigned in the Jefferson County Courthouse on October 26, 1859. Brown was still suffering from the sword wounds he sustained in Harper's Ferry and had difficulty standing. Aaron Stevens, Brown's codefendant, was so badly injured that he had to be supported while the indictment was read. Drawn by David Hunter Strother (Porte Crayon) for *Harper's Weekly.* West Virginia State Archives, Boyd B. Stutler Collection.

John Brown in court in Charlestown on November 2, 1859. This sketch by Alexander R. Boteler, newly elected congressman from the Harper's Ferry district and an enthusiastic amateur artist, depicts Brown as he rose to receive his death sentence and deliver his famous "last speech." West Virginia State Archives, Boyd B. Stutler Collection.

Alexander R. Boteler drew this sketch of Brown on the flyleaf of a copy of the *Mason Report* (1860). It shows the short beard that Brown wore during the trial. West Virginia State Archives, Boyd B. Stutler Collection.

Henry A. Wise, the volatile governor of Virginia, who played a strong behind-the-scenes role in Brown's prosecution and, after Brown was condemned to be hanged, declined to exercise clemency. The Library of Virginia.

Andrew Hunter, the Charlestown attorney who led Brown's prosecution and drafted his last will. Library of Congress.

Judge Richard Parker, who presided over Brown's trial in Charlestown. Library of Congress.

Brown was well enough to walk from the jail to the courthouse when this sketch was made, although he often had to be carried. The cot that was used to transport him and on which he lay during much of the trial is carried before him. West Virginia State Archives, Boyd B. Stutler Collection.

Brown sits in his cell in the Jefferson County Jail as a visitor reads to him. West Virginia State Archives, Boyd B. Stutler Collection.

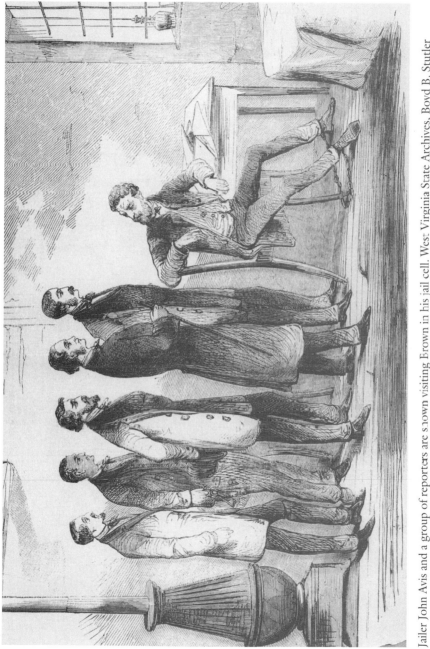

Jailer John Avis and a group of reporters are shown visiting Brown in his jail cell. West Virginia State Archives, Boyd B. Stutler Collection.

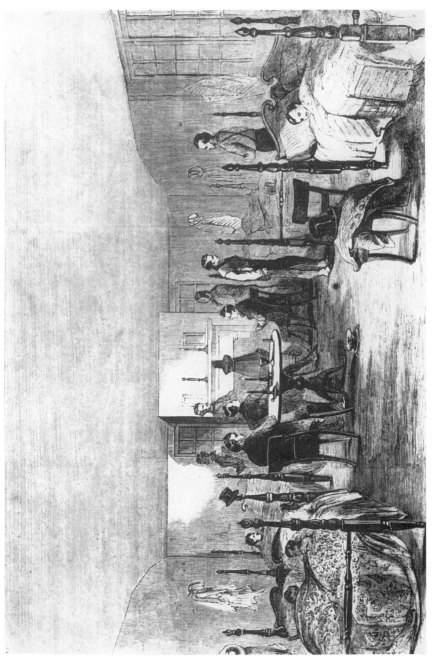

When court was not in session, the jurors were "kept together" in this sleeping room in Gibson's Hotel. West Virginia State Archives, Boyd B. Stutler Collection.

Mary Ann Brown visited her husband in the Jefferson County Jail on the day before he was hanged. This drawing shows her carriage arriving in front of the courthouse as a crowd of spectators looks on. West Virginia State Archives, Boyd B. Stutler Collection.

Execution of Brown, who is coming down the steps of the jail.

The Jefferson County Jail is shown in this drawing, with soldiers watching as Brown comes down the steps on the day of his execution. Library of Congress.

Brown walking to the wagon that carried his coffin and on which he would ride to the place of execution. West Virginia State Archives, Boyd B. Stutler Collection.

John Brown riding on his coffin to the place of execution. Library of Congress.

A sketch of Brown on his way to the scaffold, December 2, 1859. West Virginia State Archives, Boyd B. Stutler Collection.

December 2, 1859. Brown rode down George Street, surrounded on all sides by soldiers. The upper part of the Jefferson County Courthouse, with its cupola, appears in the upper right in this drawing. The back of the jail, with its walled jail yard, is in the upper center. West Virginia State Archives, Boyd B. Stutler Collection.

Brown climbing the stairs to his scaffold. Library of Congress.

Brown was hanged in an open field at the southern edge of Charlestown on December 2, 1859. The cupola atop the Jefferson County Courthouse is visible on the horizon. Drawing by David C. Hitchcock for the *New York Illustrated News*. West Virginia State Archives, Boyd B. Stutler Collection.

THE TESTIMONY BEGINS

Judge Parker convened the circuit court again on Thursday morning. Brown was well enough to walk from his jail cell to the courthouse, heavily guarded as usual. Inside the courtroom, however, he promptly lay down on his cot. The *Herald* noted that "he looked considerably better, the swelling having left his eyes."[1] Hunter and Harding were at the counsel table representing the Commonwealth, and Botts and Green were still representing Brown. Senator Mason was one of the several hundred spectators who crowded the courtroom.

Parker intended to begin the session by swearing in the jury, but his plan changed when Botts rose to read a telegram aloud to the court. Botts had received the telegram in Charlestown the previous afternoon and summoned Green soon afterward; both men then went to the jail to read it to Brown. As reported in the *Herald* and other newspapers, the telegram read:

Akron, Ohio, October 26, 1859
To C. J. FAULKNER and LAWSON BOTTS:
    John Brown, leader of the insurrection at Harper's Ferry, and several of his family, have resided in this county many years. Insanity is hereditary in that family. His mother's sister died with it, and a daughter of that sister has been two years in the insane asylum. A son and daughter of his mother's brother have also been confined in the lunatic asylum, and another son of that brother is now insane and under close restraint. These facts can be conclu-

sively proven by witnesses residing here, who will doubtless attend the trial if desired.

A. H. LEWIS[2]

William C. Allen was the telegraphic operator in Akron. After
transmitting this message to Charlestown, he added the information that A. H. Lewis was a resident of Akron and that his
statements were "entitled to implicit credit."

It can hardly have come as a surprise to anybody in Jefferson
County that John Brown's mental condition would sooner or
later become an issue in his trial. From the day he was captured
in the engine house in Harper's Ferry, he had repeatedly been
described as a "madman." Robert E. Lee had dismissed him as a
"fanatic or madman," and others had characterized his raid as an
"insane project."[3] Yet others routinely condemned him as "Mad
Brown" or "Crazy Brown."[4] The *Louisville Journal* spoke for
much of the South when it editorialized that the whole Harper's
Ferry affair "smacks strongly of the madhouse. It is worthy only
of men who are at once fiends and lunatics."[5]

Was Brown "crazy," a "lunatic," a "madman," as his critics
claimed; or was he, as his supporters insisted, a man of humanitarian purpose, a leader in a moral crusade against a great social evil? More important to the court proceedings now under
way in Charlestown, did his mental condition make any real difference to his legal responsibility for what happened? Nobody
doubted that Brown led the attack on Harper's Ferry on October 16 and 17, that he brought pistols and rifles and pikes into
the town, that his purpose was to free the slaves there, and that,
in the course of the fighting that ensued, four innocent residents
of the town were killed, one U.S. marine was shot dead and another was wounded, and dozens of civilians were captured and
held hostage. Whether Brown was sane or insane, crazy or prin-
cipled, a lunatic or a humanitarian, could not change the hard

facts of the lives lost, the property damaged, and the fear engendered in the people.

The answer to all of these troubling questions was, on one level, disarmingly simple, and on another complex and murky. Under the law of Virginia, it was clear that a man who was insane at the time of the commission of a crime or crimes was not legally responsible for those crimes. Insanity was a defense to the charges or, if not a complete defense, at least sufficient reason for suspending the proceedings.[6] It was an ancient principle rooted in the law of cultures scattered across the globe, and it had been recognized in the law of England, the American colonies, and the United States for centuries. As Isaac Ray, author of the leading nineteenth-century treatise on the subject, put it, "In all civilized communities, ancient or modern, insanity has been regarded as exempting from the punishment of crime, and under some circumstances, at least, as vitiating the civil acts of those who are affected with it." But, as Ray added, "the only difficulty . . . consists in determining who are really insane, in the meaning of the law."[7] Thus the pressing question that the Circuit Court of Jefferson County confronted on October 27, 1859, was whether Brown was insane in the eyes of the law and thereby absolved of criminal responsibility for his bloody raid.

The Code of Virginia contained an explicit statement that the words "'insane person' shall be construed to include everyone who is an idiot, lunatic, *non compos,* or deranged."[8] But the code did not define "idiot," "lunatic," "non compos," or "deranged." If criminal charges were pending against a person, and the court had "reasonable ground to doubt his sanity," the court was required to suspend the trial until a jury could decide the issue. If the jury found the person sane, the trial would proceed; if it found him insane, the jury was required to inquire whether he was insane at the time of the alleged offense. If so, the court had discretion to dismiss the prosecution and discharge the person or, "to prevent his doing mischief," send him to a "lunatic asylum." If the jury found him to be insane at the time of trial but not when the offense was committed, the court would either commit him to jail or order him to be confined in an asylum "until he is so restored that he can be put upon his trial."[9] Virginia had been a pioneer in establishing public hospitals for "persons of insane and disordered minds," passing an act for the first hospital at Williamsburg in 1769 and another at Staunton in 1825.[10]

But writing "insanity" into the law of Virginia and establishing hospitals for people of "insane and disordered minds" were easier than defining "insanity" for the purposes of the criminal law, and legislatures and courts had struggled with the problem. In eighteenth-century England, courts had ruled that an accused criminal could escape responsibility for his acts only if he was totally lacking in "understanding and memory," so that he did not know what he was doing, "no more than an infant, than a brute, or a wild beast."[11] In 1843, the law of insanity took a dramatic turn in England when a man named Daniel McNaghten was tried for murdering the secretary to Prime Minister Sir Robert Peel in an unsuccessful attempt to assassinate Peel himself. Responding to the furor caused when the jury found McNaghten "not guilty by reason of insanity," the House of Lords ruled that to establish a defense on the grounds of insanity, "it must be clearly proved that, at the time of the committing of the act, the party accused was laboring under such a defect of reason, from disease of the mind, as to not know the nature and quality of the act he was doing; or, if he did know it, that he did not know he was doing what was wrong."[12] The McNaghten rule was vigorously challenged at the time it was handed down and was criticized continually thereafter. Yet it was widely followed by courts in Great Britain and the United

States, if only because a better rule was difficult to formulate and even more difficult to apply.

Lawson Botts was doing no more than his professional responsibility required when he called Judge Parker's attention to the dispatch he had received from A. H. Lewis, and there is little reason to believe that he seriously contemplated presenting an insanity defense for Brown. If the attorney thought he could prove Brown's insanity under any test then applicable, Brown made clear that he would have nothing to do with the effort. After Brown read Lewis's telegram, he told Botts what he wanted him to tell the judge: there had never been any insanity in his father's family, although there had been repeated instances of it on his mother's side. Brown's first wife had shown some "symptoms" of insanity, which were also evident in his "first and second sons by that wife." Brown said that some parts of Lewis's telegram were "correct," but he was "ignorant" of other parts. Botts told Parker that Brown did not know whether his mother's brother had been confined in an asylum, and he was not aware that another son of that brother was then "insane and in close confinement." Brown also wanted Botts to say that he did not "put in the plea of insanity," and if he had been "at all insane" he was "totally unconscious of it." Brown observed, quite rationally, that those "who are more insane generally suppose that they have more reason and sanity than those around them." Botts said that the effort to raise the issue was made without Brown's "approbation or concurrence," and it "was unknown to him until the receipt of the above dispatch." To emphasize his determination in this matter, Brown then raised himself up on his cot and said:

> I will add, if the Court will allow me, that I look upon it as a miserable artifice and pretext of those who ought to take a different

course in regard to me, if they took any at all, and I view it with contempt more than otherwise. As I remarked to Mr. Green, insane prisoners, so far as my experience goes, have but little ability to judge of their own sanity; and if I am insane, of course I should think I know more than all of the rest of the world. But I do not think so. I am perfectly unconscious of insanity, and I reject, so far as I am capable, any attempt to interfere in my behalf on that score.[13]

Once again, Brown had spoken strongly and personally in the legal proceedings. It was clear from his statements that he did not seek to avoid responsibility for his actions in Harper's Ferry, at least not on grounds of insanity. Nor did he seek to use a claim of insanity as an excuse to delay the trial. Had he admitted the possibility that he might be insane, had he even agreed to be examined by a medical doctor to determine if he was, the trial would almost certainly have been suspended, at least long enough to inquire into the matter. The prosecutors had intimated that he was using any pretext he could think of to delay the proceedings—that he was, in legal historian Frederick Trevor Hill's phrase, "'playing possum' to waste time."[14] Now, however, he made clear that he would tolerate no such "miserable artifice."

But his statements were still insufficient to answer all of the troubling questions raised by Lewis's telegram or to satisfactorily explain his actions in Harper's Ferry, which many observers thought were bizarre if not irrational. For the time being, no effort would be made to raise the issue of Brown's possible insanity in his trial. But the question of his mental condition was not so easily put to rest, and it would be revived again after his conviction.

Though Botts made clear that he and Brown were not seeking to delay the trial on grounds of insanity, they renewed the request they made the previous day to delay the proceedings until Brown's out-of-state attorney arrived in Charlestown. Botts referred to this attorney as "foreign" counsel.[15] (Was it usual for Virginians to describe lawyers from Ohio or Massachusetts as "foreigners"?) Botts noted the telegram received the previous day from Daniel Tilden of Cleveland. He expected Tilden to arrive shortly, and he argued that Brown should be given enough time to permit Tilden to take over his case.

Andrew Hunter opposed Botts's request. He and Harding were prepared to prove that Brown "had made open, repeated, and constant acknowledgment of everything charged against him" and had even "gloried in it." "What does he mean by wishing delay for the purpose of having a fair trial?" Hunter asked. If there was to be a fair trial, it would be "a fair trial according to the laws of Virginia" and not a trial "to produce fairness in his conception, outside of what the laws recognize." As for the telegram that Botts had read, Hunter said, "We know not who this Mr. Tilden is. We know not whether he is to come here as counsel for the prisoner, or whether he wants to head a band of desperadoes."[16] There had been time enough for Tilden to arrive, and since he hadn't, "it was fairly inferable that he did not intend to come." Hunter suggested that the whole thing might be "an attempt to gain time and learn the latest day when a rescue could be attempted." Harding remarked that Brown "pretended yesterday afternoon that he was unable to walk, and was brought into court on a bed, yet he walked back to jail after the close of the trial without difficulty." Harding thought that "those were mere pretences for delay, which the Court should overrule."

Green countered that one day's delay "would be sufficient to ascertain whether the expected counsel would come or not" and that no prejudice would result to the Commonwealth from such a short delay. Green did not believe Brown had made "any acknowledgments upon which he could be convicted." As far as he knew, all of Brown's acknowledgments referred to the charge of treason, and under Virginia law they were inadequate for a conviction, because Virginia law required any confession of treason to be made "in open court."[17] As to the contention that there had been enough time for out-of-state counsel to reach Charlestown, the attorneys Brown wrote to may have been absent when the letters arrived and thus unable to reply promptly. The prosecutors may not have known who Tilden was, Green said, but he was "an ex-member of Congress and said to be a man of respectability." As to Brown's "sham sickness," that was not made a ground for the requested delay. Green did not think the trial "should be hurried through" because of fears that Brown might be "rescued," for "such fears were idle."

Idle fears or not, Parker was in no mood for delay. In this case, as in others, he could postpone the proceedings only upon a proper showing of cause. The telegram from Tilden gave no assurance that the Ohioan in fact intended to come. "The prisoner is now defended by counsel who will take care that no improper evidence is adduced against him," Parker said, "and that all proper evidence in his behalf shall be presented." If Tilden arrived before the case was closed, he could see all the testimony that had been taken, and Brown might have the benefit of his advice. As to the matter of insanity, Parker said that the issue was not presented "in a reliable form." "Instead of mere statements," the judge said, "we should have affidavits, or something of that character." For these reasons, the trial would proceed.

The jurors chosen the previous day were now brought into the courtroom. According to Virginia practice, they were to be sworn in groups of four. After the first four jurors were "elected," the clerk called their names and administered the following oath (or affirmation):

> You shall well and truly try and true deliverance make between
> the Commonwealth and John Brown, the prisoner at the bar,
> whom you shall have in charge, and a true verdict give according
> to the evidence. So help you God.[18]

The same words were repeated for the next four jurors, and the
four after that. When all twelve had been elected, the clerk addressed them again, "Gentlemen of the jury, answer to your
names." When all had answered, the clerk asked, "Gentlemen,
are you all sworn?" If they all answered "yes," the clerk then
turned to the sheriff and said, "Sheriff, make proclamation."
And the sheriff continued:

> *Oyez, oyez, oyez.* If any can inform the judge of this court, the at-
> torney for the Commonwealth, or this inquest now to be taken
> between the Commonwealth and John Brown, the prisoner at
> the bar, of any treason, murder, felony, or other misdemeanor
> committed or done by the prisoner at the bar, let them come
> forth, and they shall be heard. The prisoner stands at the bar
> upon his deliverance.[19]

Brown was again required to listen to a reading of the almost mind-numbingly tedious indictment. Parker ordered that
he need not stand for the reading, but could remain on his cot
where, the *New York Herald* reported, he lay "prostrate."

In his capacity as Commonwealth attorney, Charles Harding
now had the responsibility of presenting the prosecution's opening statement. He reviewed the facts of the case and the events
that took place in Harper's Ferry on the dates charged in the indictment. He told the jury about the men who were killed during Brown's raid, and the captures of Lewis Washington and
John Allstadt and their slaves. He said that a "government" had

been formed "within the limits of the Commonwealth" and that its citizens had been held as "prisoners of war." This constituted treason, he said, for it amounted to "levying war against the state," "giving comfort to its enemies," and "establishing a government within its limits."

Harding next proceeded to read the Virginia laws relating to "advising with a slave" and first-degree murder, both of which were punishable with death. He assured the jury that these charges would be "distinctly proven, beyond a possibility of a doubt on the minds of the jury." He would show that the "whole object" of Brown and his fellow-prisoners was to "rob our citizens of their slaves, and carry them off by violence." He was "happy to say" that this was done "against the wills of the slaves, all of them having escaped, and rushed back to their masters at the first opportunity."

The apparent reluctance of the slaves in and around Harper's Ferry to join Brown's rebellion was something that the prosecutors—in fact, all of the slaveholders in Virginia, from Governor Wise on down—mentioned often and emphatically. If, as Brown and others claimed, the slaves were badly treated by their masters, if they were really dissatisfied with their lives as human chattels, why didn't they immediately flock to Brown's side after he came into Harper's Ferry? Why were they so indifferent to his efforts to free them? It was a reassuring but fallacious argument, for there is good evidence that some slaves did in fact come into town, at least in the early hours of the raid, that they took up some of the pikes Brown had brought for them, and that they were far from reluctant to show that they supported him.[20] Those that did not join him had good reason to hold back, for they never had any assurance that his raid would succeed, and they knew that if they supported an unsuccessful effort, they would be subject to criminal prosecution or, at the very least, severe discipline from their masters. If the slaves in

Virginia and other Southern states were content with their lot, as Harding suggested, perhaps he could explain why they had been fleeing North in greater and greater numbers in the years leading up to Brown's raid; why the Underground Railroad was so active during those same years; and why, in 1850, Virginia's Senator Mason—who now occupied a prominent seat in John Brown's courtroom—had deemed it necessary to secure the passage of a new and stricter Fugitive Slave Act to stem the exodus.[21]

Harding concluded his statement by urging the jury to "cast aside all prejudices," to give the prisoner a "fair and impartial trial," and not to allow their "hatred of abolitionists to influence them against those who have raised the black flag on the soil of the Commonwealth." (An impartial observer might have asked why, if Harding wanted the jurors to disregard their "hatred" of abolitionists and ignore the "black flag" they erected on Virginia soil, he thought it important enough to remind them of these things in his opening statement.)

Harding's opening argument had made some effective points, but, like so many of his arguments, it failed to really connect with the jurors. As Cleon Moore, a deputy county clerk, remarked years later: "When Harding began to speak, if you shut your eyes and listened for the first few minutes you would think Patrick Henry had returned to earth; after that he dwindled away into ineptitudes."[22]

As Harding settled back into his chair, Thomas C. Green rose to give his opening statement for Brown. He began by telling the jurors that they were "judges of the law and the facts" in the case and that if they had "any doubt as to law, or the fact of the guilt of this prisoner," it was their duty to give him the benefit of that doubt. On this point, the law of Virginia gave jurors greater latitude than that of many other jurisdictions, where the jurors were authorized only to "find the facts," and the judge reserved the power to decide all questions of law. The Virginia jurors had broad discretion, which they might exercise either in favor of the accused or against him. How they would exercise that discretion in the case now pending in Charlestown was not hard to predict.

Green next addressed the charge of treason, arguing that "a specific act of treason" had to be proved before Brown could be found guilty. That is, it had to be proved that he "attempted to establish a separate and distinct government" within the state. If the prosecution sought to rely on his confessions to prove the treason charge, the law was clear: "No conviction can be made on confessions, unless made in open Court." There had to be sufficient evidence to prove the charge, Green argued, independent of any confessions out of court, and the law required "two distinct witnesses to prove each and every act of treason."

On the charge of "conspiring with slaves to rebel and make insurrection," Green argued the critical question of jurisdiction. He told the jurors that to find Brown guilty of a conspiracy, they had to be satisfied that the conspiracy "was done within the State of Virginia, and within the jurisdiction of this court." If there was a conspiracy in Maryland, "this court could not punish the act." Similarly, if there was a conspiracy within the limits of the armory at Harper's Ferry, "it was not done within the limits of this state, the government of the United States holding exclusive jurisdiction within the said grounds." Green recalled that U.S. Attorney General Caleb Cushing "had decided this point with regard to the armory grounds at Harper's Ferry."[23] He read Cushing's opinion on this question to the jury. It made clear that crimes committed within the limits of the armory "are punishable by the federal courts," not the courts of Virginia. "Although the Jury may doubt about the law on this subject," Green argued, "they must give the prisoners the benefit of that doubt upon the trial." He went on to argue that the Virginia court would not even have jurisdiction over the crime of murder "if committed within the limits of the armory." And if Fontaine Beckham, the popular mayor of Harper's Ferry, was "killed on the railroad bridge," Green argued that the crime was "committed within the State of Maryland, which State claims jurisdiction up to the Armory grounds." Here Green was referring to Maryland's claim to jurisdiction over the Potomac up to the low water line on the Virginia side. It was a valid claim, and Virginia accepted it, but whether the railroad bridge, or trestle, on which Beckham was killed actually stood on the Maryland side of the low water line or within the armory grounds on the Virginia side was an open question.[24]

Green went on to point out that a killing had to be "deliberate and premeditated" to make it first-degree murder, a capital offense. Any other killing was murder in the second degree, punishable with imprisonment. "If you have any doubt on these points," Green argued, "you must give that doubt to the prisoner."

Botts now made an opening statement that the newspapers called "impressive." He began by reminding the jurors that the case was "unusual" and that the crime charged was "in many respects unknown." Was Botts here alluding to the fact that no man in American history had previously been executed for treason against a state?[25] Or was he merely noting the obvious fact that Brown's raid on Harper's Ferry was unique in American history, an unprecedented attack by private citizens, launched from one state into another, never before attempted and probably never again to be repeated?

Botts reviewed the legal arguments made by Green, emphasizing each. "It is no difference how much a jury may be convinced in their own minds of the guilt of the prisoner," Botts added. "It is essential that they must have proof of positive guilt, in a case like this, involving both life and liberty." Brown believed that he was "actuated by the highest and noblest feel-

ings that ever coursed through a human breast," Botts said. He
had instructed his men "to destroy neither property nor life."
Brown's prisoners "were treated with respect" and "kept in positions of safety" throughout the Harper's Ferry raid.

It was now Andrew Hunter's opportunity to close the opening arguments. He reminded the jury that he was acting in the
capacity of "assistant" to the Commonwealth attorney, a position that had been assigned him by the governor and the judge.
He admitted that this "was probably the first case of high treason, or treason against the state," that had ever been tried in
Virginia, and he "fervently hoped that it would be the last."
But, somewhat ominously, he argued that the jury's decision in
Brown's case might well determine whether there were future
cases like it. If the jury did not decide Brown's case appropriately, perhaps there would be other Browns yet to come—other
conspirators ready to invade Virginia from the North and subject the state to more ordeals like the one they now found themselves in.

Hunter next launched into an interesting discussion of the
law of treason. He thought "his friends on the other side" were
totally mistaken in their view that the law of Virginia was like the
law of the United States on this subject. The U.S. Constitution
required proof of "overt acts" to sustain a conviction of treason,
he said, but there was no similar requirement in Virginia's constitution or laws. Virginia's definition of treason differed from
that of the U.S. Constitution because "all the powers vested in
the Federal Government were given with great jealousy." Thus
the framers had very limited authority to punish treason. Treason against the United States "consisted only in levying war
against them or adhering to their enemies and giving them aid
and comfort." And no person could be convicted of treason
against the United States "unless upon the testimony of two
witnesses of some overt act or confession in open court." The

Virginia law included within its definition of
ing, without authority of the legislature, an
its limits, separate from the existing gover
executing, in such government, any office, or pr_
giance or fidelity to it, or resisting the execution of law, unac
the colour of its authority."[26] Virginia law also declared that
treason, "if proved by the testimony of two witnesses to the
same overt act, or by confession in court," would be punished
with death.[27] "Any one of these acts constitutes treason against
this commonwealth," Hunter argued. Brown "had attempted
to break down the existing government of the Commonwealth, and establish on its ruins a new government." He had
"usurped the office of commander-in-chief of this new government." And, together with his "whole band," he had "professed
allegiance and fidelity to this new government. Brown was, in
Hunter's estimation, "doubly, trebly and quadruply guilty of
treason."[28]

Hunter then addressed the vital issue of whether Virginia
courts could punish criminal acts committed within the armory
grounds at Harper's Ferry. He allowed that Attorney General
Cushing was "an able man" but said that Cushing came from a
region of the country where opinions about the powers of the
states and the federal government were "very different." "Our
Courts are decidedly adverse to Mr. Cushing's views," Hunter
said. "In all times past," Jefferson County's jurisdiction over
crimes committed at Harper's Ferry had been "uninterrupted
and unchallenged, whether they were committed on the Government property or not." As an example, Hunter cited a case
that had occurred twenty-nine years earlier, in which an "atrocious murder" had been committed in Harper's Ferry and "the
criminal was tried here, convicted, and executed under our
laws." The reference was to the prosecution of Ebenezer Cox, a
disgruntled former employee at the armory who had entered the

ffice of the superintendent, Thomas Dunn, on January 29, 1830, and shot him at point-blank range. Cox was tried and executed in Charlestown.[29] Hunter argued that Virginia had not ceded its jurisdiction to the United States; it had merely agreed that the federal government should become a landholder within its limits. This argument was well-calculated to appeal to local sympathies, although Caleb Cushing's carefully reasoned opinion to the contrary had a better legal foundation. Did Andrew Hunter really believe that a jury of laymen in Charlestown, Virginia, was competent to overrule a formal legal opinion rendered by the attorney general of the United States? Was he arguing that the national Constitution meant different things in different parts of the country?

Hunter then proceeded to address the charges of murder and conspiracy. As to the latter, Brown's guilt was shown by "his own notorious confession." As to the former, Hunter and Harding would prove not only that Brown had actually participated in the murder of Virginia citizens, but "that he was the chief director of the whole movement." "No matter whether he was present on the spot or a mile off," Hunter asserted, "he is equally guilty." Hunter stressed his hope that the case would be considered "with fairness and impartiality, and without fear, favor or affection." He asked only that Brown might suffer the penalty prescribed by law, "which our safety requires, and which the laws of God and man approve."[30]

As the prosecutor sank back into his chair, Judge Parker declared the court's midday recess.

It had been two and a half days since the legal proceedings began in Charlestown. In that time, charges had been framed, an indictment handed down, jurors examined and sworn, and motions for delay considered and denied. Judge Parker was still intent on finishing his business in Jefferson County before he had to move on to other counties. The governor and people of Virginia were demanding the prompt administration of justice. Senator Mason was watching the proceedings from his seat in the Charlestown courthouse, determined to see the matter through to its end. There seemed little doubt that Brown would be convicted, if the normal procedures of the court were allowed to run their course. But there were still rumors of an attempt to "rescue" Brown from the Jefferson County Jail—lingering fears that Northern supporters of "Old Osawatomie" would emerge from hideouts in the nearby mountains, mass themselves at the edges of Charlestown, and "make war" on the Virginia militiamen and United States marines who were now defending the town. The suspicion was not based in fact, for the twenty-one men who joined Brown in Harper's Ferry on October 16 and 17 were in fact the only "army" that had ever been ready to defend him, and their numbers had been decimated in the fighting there: ten were killed, four were taken captive with Brown, and seven fled north. With each passing day, it became more obvious that Brown would not be rescued. But fears that he would somehow make it out of Charlestown had a life of their own, and they all but paralyzed the county.

Now, however, it was time to begin the examination of witnesses. It was half past three o'clock in the afternoon when the court reconvened and the oath was administered to the first prosecution witness. He was John D. Starry, a medical doctor in Harper's Ferry who had played a dramatic role in the events of Brown's raid. After taking his oath to tell the truth, the whole truth, and nothing but the truth, Starry began to answer questions.[31]

The doctor testified that he was at home in Harper's Ferry on Sunday night, October 16, when he heard a shot fired, then a cry, and, looking out of his window, saw two men going toward the armory gate. A "tall man" came from the gate, and two men from a train that had just pulled into the town shouted "There he goes now!" The tall man raised his rifle, after which the other men followed him to the armory gate and "exchanged shots with him." Afterward, Starry and some other men found Hayward Shepherd, the black baggage master at the railroad station, "dying in the railroad office." Shepherd said that he was on the bridge when he was ordered to stop, but he refused, and men fired upon him. Starry had seen several men "patrolling during the night" but did not know what to make of it. When he went to inquire of the armory watchman, he found a strange man "who leveled his rifle" at him. The next morning, Starry went to Archibald Kitzmiller, one of the armory clerks, and to Armistead Ball, the master machinist, and told them that an "armed body of men" had taken possession of the armory. He saw three more strange men at Hall's Rifle Works, who were notable for "a peculiar hat they wore." He did not think there were more than thirty men in all. He rode to Charlestown "to give the alarm and get assistance" and returned to Harper's Ferry about eleven o'clock in the morning with some militiamen from Charlestown. Starry "did not see or recognize Brown there at all." Cross-examined by Thomas Green, Starry said that, as he "rode past the armory, armed men were at the gate. They did not attempt to stop me. I was determined not to be stopped."[32]

The next witness was A. J. Phelps, conductor of the Baltimore and Ohio train that came into Harper's Ferry in the early morning hours of October 17. Phelps said his train arrived some time after one o'clock, heading east. When he and the engineer found no watchman on the bridge, they thought it "strange" and stopped the train. They were just about to start up again when the watchman came up "much excited" and announced that "he had been attacked on the bridge by men carrying rifles." With three men accompanying him, Phelps then set out on foot to investigate. As he and his companions entered the covered portion of the bridge, someone said, "Stand and deliver." They "immediately saw the muzzles of four rifles resting on a railing, and pointed at us." Both men turned around and headed back, but as soon as they reached the trestle that led up to the bridge they "heard the report of a gun." Shepherd then came running up to Phelps with the news that he had been shot. The ball had entered his back and come out under his left breast. The men carried the wounded man to the railroad office and "started for the doctor." But, as they did, they saw a man emerge from the covered bridge and head for the armory gate. One of the clerks from the Wager House saw him and fired, and the shot "was returned by two men at the armory gate." The clerk exchanged several shots with the men from the armory gate. The minute after Shepherd was shot, Phelps heard the men loading their rifles again. "The reports were very loud, and I wondered why the people were not aroused." He was walking back toward the railroad office when a man came out of the bridge and said, "You can come over the bridge with your train."

"I would rather not," Phelps answered, "after these proceedings. What do you want?"

"We want liberty, and we intend to have it," was the answer.

"What do you mean?" Phelps asked.

"You will find out in a day or two."

Phelps was alarmed for the safety of himself and his passengers and decided to keep his train where it was until daylight. At about three o'clock, an "old gentleman" came up and said that he had been captured by the strange men in the armory but released "on condition that I would tell you that you might cross the bridge with your train." Phelps said he would not cross until daylight, when he could see that the bridge was safe. At about four o'clock, he saw a wagon enter the armory yard, "and nearly a dozen men jumped out of it." They seemed to be putting things into the wagon, going up and down the street leading from the armory. This continued until nearly daylight, "when the wagon left the yard and passed over the bridge to the Maryland side." Sometime later, he saw a man coming down Shenandoah Street with a lantern, and "an armed man arrested him." He then saw "a short, stout negro walking with a staff with one of these men." Afterward a black boy brought a note to the clerk of the Wager House. It was a bizarre note, demanding that the Wager House provide "breakfast for forty-seven men." Phelps went out to investigate. He met a man he later recognized as Edwin Coppoc and asked what was happening. "We don't want to injure you or detain your train," Coppoc answered. "You could have gone at three o'clock. All we want is to free the negroes." Phelps was then directed to the engine house, where he met a man called "Captain Smith." Phelps now recognized him as John Brown. "Smith" said he had sent word at three o'clock that the train could pass. Phelps replied that he had declined to proceed when he was stopped by armed men. Brown was "very sorry." He said he had not intended that "any blood should be spilled"—it was "bad management on the part of the men in charge of the bridge." When Phelps asked what assurance he might have that his train could pass safely, Brown walked across the bridge with him, as the train slowly followed behind. "You doubtless wonder that a man of my age should be here with a band of armed men," Brown said to Phelps, "but if you knew my past history you would not wonder at it as much." When the train had made it all the way over the bridge, Phelps bid Brown a "good morning," jumped on his train, and headed east.

Phelps returned to Harper's Ferry on Tuesday and went in with Governor Wise and others to see Brown, who was then a prisoner, lying on the floor of the armory paymasters' office. Wise told Brown that he "was sorry to see a man of his age in that position." Brown replied that he "asked no sympathy, and had no apologies to make." The governor asked Brown if he did not think he was doing wrong in "running off with other people's property." Brown answered that he didn't. He "never had but twenty-two men of his party," but he expected "large reinforcements" from Virginia and North and South Carolina, and, Phelps thought, from New York and some of the New England states as well. He had received some arms from Massachusetts and "could arm from 1,500 to 2,000 men. He had rented the Kennedy Farm in Maryland, but all of his arms were sent to Chambersburg, Pennsylvania," addressed to "I. Smith & Sons." Brown told Wise about his *Provisional Constitution* and said it "would explain to him his whole proceedings, and what the purpose of his business was." Robert E. Lee, who was listening to the conversation, announced that he already had a copy of the constitution, and he gave it to Wise. The governor read sections of the document, which Brown seemed eager to explain. He said he was "Commander-in-Chief of the forces under the Provisional Government." There was a secretary of war, a secretary of state, a judge of the Supreme Court, and "all the officers for a general government." There was also a House of Representatives. When Phelps recalled that Brown said "an intelligent colored man" had been elected as one of the members of his House of Representatives, the courtroom erupted in what one of the newspaper reporters called a "sensation."[33] Whether the "sensation" was laughter or outrage, the newspapers did not disclose. Perhaps it was something of both, for most Virginians of the time would certainly have regarded the idea that a "colored man," even an "intelligent" one, might hold an elective office in any government as both comical and deeply troubling.

Wise asked Brown if he had taken the oath of allegiance provided for in his constitution. He had, Brown answered, as had all of the white men in his "army." They all had military titles.

Stevens, Leeman, and one of Brown's sons were captains. Edwin Coppoc was a lieutenant. Phelps thought that Brown said John Cook held a captain's commission. Brown said "he knew exactly the position he had placed himself in, and if his life was forfeited he was prepared to suffer."[34]

Green now broke into Phelps's testimony. It was late in the evening, and he had just received a telegram from Cleveland announcing that "counsel was coming, and would almost certainly be here tonight." As Phelps was a very important witness, he asked the court to adjourn until morning, "in order that counsel might have an opportunity to cross-question the witness." Green said he did not intend to remain on the case after the new attorney arrived. So far, Phelps had testified only as to "scraps" of the conversation between Brown and Governor Wise. The entire conversation had gone on for two hours, and Phelps should be questioned as to other parts of the conversation.

Not surprisingly, Hunter opposed Green's request. He said that several other witnesses to the conversation were to be called, and Brown's new attorney could question them about it. "If the cases were not pushed on," Hunter said (referring not just to Brown but to those who would be tried after him), "the whole balance of the term would not be sufficient to try these men."

Again not surprisingly, Parker decided that Phelps's testimony should go on.

Reluctantly, Green began to cross-examine Phelps. His questions brought out the fact that Brown had told Wise that "it was not his intention to harm anybody or anything." Brown said he was "sorry [that] men had been killed." It had not been "by his orders or with his approbation," and "it would not occur again, provided the people were peaceable and quiet." Phelps did not recognize Brown until he talked with him in the armory yard.

He didn't think Brown was one of the men he encountered on the bridge or in the wagon for, if he had been, "I think I would have recognized him from his peculiar beard."

Lewis Washington was called as the next witness. On direct examination by Hunter, Washington's testimony corroborated much of the testimony given by Starry and Phelps. On cross-examination by Green, however, he added important information about what happened in the engine house when it was stormed by the marines. He wasn't certain whether the marines had fired their guns after they broke into the engine house. "The noise was great," Washington explained. "We were kept in the rear of the engine house, and allowed to keep a safe position, so that there was no effort to endanger us." Washington remembered quite clearly that Brown had not been "rude or insulting" toward him or the other hostages. On cross-examination by Green, Washington revealed that he, like Phelps, had been present during the long conversation between Brown and Governor Wise in the paymaster's office. When Wise asked Brown if he had selected Harper's Ferry "as a border place between Maryland and Virginia for the establishment of his Provisional Government," Brown answered "Certainly." Brown made clear that "his object was to free the Southern slaves," Washington said. His party consisted of twenty-two men, though he had arms enough for about fifteen hundred. When Wise asked Brown if he expected that many, Brown had "no doubt he could get that number, and five thousand if he wanted them." On cross-examination by Botts, Washington testified that, when the engine house was under attack, he and the other hostages remained in the back "at the suggestion of Brown and his party." Washington heard Brown tell his men "not to fire on any unarmed man," and "he gave that order more than once." Brown's hostages were "allowed to go out, and assure their families of their safety." "Some went out several times," Washington said.

When gunfire broke out, numerous shots were fired toward the water tank where Fontaine Beckham was killed. Brown assured Washington that he would be "treated well" and that his property would not be destroyed. One of the three slaves captured with Washington was "kept in the armory yard," but another escaped and "went home." "All the Negroes were armed with spears while in the Armory yard," Washington said, although no Negro from his own neighborhood took up arms "voluntarily." He saw no wounded men dragged into the engine house, although he did overhear a conversation between Aaron Stevens and one of the white hostages "about slaveholding." Washington did not know the name of this hostage, but he recalled that Stevens asked him if he was "in favor of slavery." When the hostage answered "yes," Stevens responded, "Then you are the first man I would hang."

The questions and answers were now going rapidly. They had to, because Judge Parker and the two prosecutors were determined to try Brown and the other prisoners in time to meet their schedules. It was seven o'clock in the evening when Parker at last banged his gavel and declared the court adjourned until the following morning.

It now became the duty of Sheriff James Campbell to take charge of the jurors. In prosecutions for felony in Virginia, the jurors were always "kept together" so long as they were charged with the case.[35] This precaution reflected a concern that the minds of jurors might be influenced by public opinion. When a trial could not be completed on the day the jurors were sworn, the sheriff was obligated to furnish them with "suitable board and lodging" while they were confined.[36] In Charlestown, this was done in Gibson's Hotel, where the jurors were given meals and taken at night to a "sleeping room" set aside for their use. It was a large, dormitory-like chamber, furnished with double beds. After the court recessed, and before it reconvened in the morning, the sheriff took the jurors to Gibson's and carefully isolated them. At night, they went to bed, two by two, in the big double beds in the "sleeping room." The law reckoned that the jurors might be improperly influenced by the slightest contact with men and women outside the court. But warm and cozy contact with other jurors at night presented no similar problems.

7

THE NAME AND THE SHADOW
OF A FAIR TRIAL

As the usual crowd of spectators settled into their seats in the Jefferson County Courthouse on Friday morning, they watched Senator James M. Mason, tall and dignified, enter the chamber in the company of a slight young man whom the people of Charlestown did not know—and immediately became suspicious of. His name was George Hoyt, and he claimed to be a lawyer who had "traveled night and day from Boston to volunteer his services in the defense of Captain Brown." Already a fixture in the Charlestown courtroom, Mason was a pillar of Virginia's old aristocracy, a man of polished manners who was determined to show that the South could be generous in welcoming a New Englander into its midst, even one who came for the dubious purpose of helping John Brown. Other Virginians, however, were less inclined to welcome the newcomer. Hoyt was twenty-one years of age, but with his slight frame and boyish face he seemed at least two years younger, and his voice was overlaid with a nasal twang that marked him as a Yankee, and thus no friend of Virginia's. Could such a callow youth be a lawyer? If he was, as he claimed, a member of the Massachusetts bar, was he experienced enough to undertake the defense of a man on trial for his life? Or was he actually a spy, sent by the abolitionists to reconnoiter Charlestown and help Brown break out of the Jefferson County Jail? The people of Charlestown were wary of the newcomer, and the local newspapers had a field day ridiculing him. The *Independent Democrat,* a Charlestown weekly, called him a "young stripling of the genus homo," a "lawyer by his own avowal" whose "presence among us . . . puts our Southern courtesy to its tension." "An eye will be kept upon this *volunteer* gentleman," said the *Free Press*, another local weekly.[1]

As Brown lay impassively on his cot inside the bar, Lawson Botts announced Hoyt's arrival to Judge Parker. Hoyt said he had come to "assist" the two lawyers Parker had appointed to represent Brown. Andrew Hunter was old and wise enough to sense that something was awry. He said that Hoyt "had better be qualified as a member of the bar by producing proof from the Boston bar." Hoyt answered that he had not brought his credentials from Massachusetts. The attorneys argued about what proof was required to establish that a man unknown to Virginians was in fact an attorney in another state. After listening, Parker decided that it was not necessary to show credentials. "Any citizen's evidence would answer." Thomas Green told the judge that Botts had read letters from "fellow-students of Mr. Hoyt, alluding to him as a member of the bar." This was good enough for Parker, who ruled that Hoyt could take the oath as an attorney and enter the case on Brown's behalf.

Strangely, however, Hoyt was not yet ready to do so.

The young man from Massachusetts was in fact a lawyer in good standing in his home state, a recent law graduate who had passed the bar, but he had not come to Charlestown to defend Brown, as he suggested. He was an abolitionist and one of Brown's fervent supporters. He was living with his parents in Athol, Massachusetts, when he heard the news of Brown's capture at Harper's Ferry. He went to Boston, where he met another abolitionist and Brown supporter, a lawyer named John W. LeBarnes. LeBarnes suggested that Hoyt go to Charlestown "and act as counsel for John Brown." LeBarnes thought that "so youthful and physically fragile a person in appearance" would be more likely to gain access to Brown than another and would not be "in as much personal danger." In return for LeBarnes's promise to pay his expenses, but no fee, Hoyt agreed to go south "to watch and be able to report proceedings, to see and talk with Brown, and be able to communicate with his friends anything Brown might want to say." Further, Hoyt agreed to send LeBarnes accurate information regarding the troops at Charlestown, the location and defenses of the jail, approaches to the town, and "all other particulars that might enable friends to consult as to some plan of attempt at rescue." Hoyt and LeBarnes conferred with Samuel Gridley Howe, one of Brown's Boston supporters (and a member of the group later called the Secret Six). Howe scoffed at the idea of trying to help Brown escape, thinking it would be better for the cause of abolition if he were hanged, for then he would become a martyr. Hoyt still wanted to go. With seventy-five dollars in silver furnished by LeBarnes, he headed south on the train, arriving in Charlestown about one o'clock in the morning on Friday, October 28.[2] Botts and Green met him before court convened, and the three men discussed the case. The Charlestown lawyers made clear that they would not be associated with anybody in Brown's defense—if Hoyt wanted to take over the case, they would "wholly withdraw." But Hoyt was unwilling to take on such a responsibility. He knew nothing of the laws of Virginia, had never conducted an important criminal case, and rightly believed he would be incompetent to serve Brown's interests in the trial. As he later explained in a letter to LeBarnes, he wanted only to "remain passive and wait for developments." He walked into the courtroom with Senator Mason at eleven o'clock in the morning of his arrival in Charlestown and, within a half hour, had made clear to Judge Parker that, at present, "he did not feel disposed to take part in the case. Whenever he should feel disposed, he would do so."[3] It was, of course, an awkward situation, trying to the court and to the attorneys who were already representing Brown, and it served to heighten Virginians' suspicions of Hoyt's intentions. Parker, however, was determined to forge ahead with the trial, so he accepted Hoyt's statement and let the matter drop, at least for the time being.

If Hoyt's intrusion made Virginians uneasy, the arrival of another man in Charlestown in the early hours of the same morning gave them a feeling of triumph. John F. Cook had been one of seven of Brown's men who managed to escape after Lee and the marines stormed the engine house. Two of the escapees, Albert Hazlett and the free black Osborne P. Anderson, had made it across the Potomac during a lull in the fighting, and after surveying the town from the Maryland Heights, headed north on foot. Cook and five others—Charles Tidd, Jeremiah Anderson, Francis Meriam, Barclay Coppoc, and Brown's son Owen—had been on the Maryland side of the Potomac when Brown was captured. When they saw that their cause in Harper's Ferry was lost, they too headed north. During the day, they hid in the shelter of trees and bushes, and at night they tramped along creek beds. When they met farmers along the way, they claimed they were a band of hunters traveling through the country. Cook, however, became careless, ventured into the town of Mount Alto, Pennsylvania, in quest of food, and was promptly arrested. Governor Wise had posted rewards for all of the escapees, and Cook's captors were eager to collect the thousand dollars that was on his head. He arrived in Charlestown at one o'clock in the morning on Friday, October 28, guarded by Governor Wise's own agents. When the townspeople awoke to news of his capture, they rejoiced.[4] Cook was regarded as the most heinous of all of Brown's men, for he had lived among the people of Harper's Ferry for more than a year, pretending to be one of them while helping Brown lay plans for the raid. "If there is one among the hellish miscreants of Brown and his men," the

Independent Democrat editorialized, "who is to be distinguished among the rest for the enormity of his crime, it is this man Cook. . . . A court of justice should not be disgraced by the presence of such a black-hearted and atrocious villain."[5] Cook would, in time, stand trial in Judge Parker's court. For now, however, he was lodged in a cell in the Charlestown jail, while Brown's trial continued.

Botts opened the questioning on Friday by recalling two of the previous day's witnesses. A. J. Phelps, the B & O train conductor, was called first to answer some questions that had been prepared for him by Brown himself. Brown wanted Phelps to tell how the gunfire had started, and who fired the first shots. Phelps recalled that the first shots were fired at the baggage master, Hayward Shepherd, and that they were returned by W. W. Throckmorton, who was a clerk at the Wager House. Phelps did not know whether the firing at Shepherd was intentional, but he knew that Brown's men were not attacked until Shepherd was shot. It seemed that Brown hoped by these questions to show that his men did not initiate the gunfire, but Phelps's answers did not help him.

Botts then put more questions to Lewis Washington. Washington's answers disclosed that Brown had been negotiating for the release of his hostages "before the general firing commenced on Monday." He had frequently proposed that the hostages cross the Potomac bridge with him and his men. Once they reached the Maryland side, Brown promised, he would release his hostages unharmed and then retreat into the hills. Washington said that none of Brown's hostages "made any objection to the proposition." He recalled that Brown said at the time that he was "too old a soldier to yield the advantage he possessed in holding hostages." During the day, one of Brown's sons was wounded by a ball that entered his breast and came out on his side (this was Brown's twenty-year-old son, Oliver), but the son took up his own weapon again and "fired frequently before his sufferings compelled him to retire." Washington heard Brown complain frequently of the "bad faith" shown by the people outside the engine house, who continued to fire on his men when they went out under a white flag. During the time he was held hostage, Washington did not hear Brown "utter any vindictiveness against the people." He could not say that all of the shots fired by Brown and his men were in self-defense, but he heard Brown give "frequent orders not to fire on unarmed citizens." Brown seemed surprised that the people outside showed so little regard for the lives of the citizens inside, and he insisted that the hostages had to "take their chances" with him. When Brown was struck down by the marines, he "had a rifle in his hand" and "received a cut over the head with a sword of Lieutenant Green."[6]

When Washington's testimony was finished, Andrew Hunter rose to introduce Brown's *Provisional Constitution* into evidence. He called Sheriff Campbell to verify Brown's handwriting and thereby authenticate the text of the document. Hunter had a printed copy of the document, but it apparently included some handwriting by Brown himself, and Hunter knew this would tie Brown and the document together. Campbell had copied letters for Brown in the jail and could identify his handwriting. But Brown rose up on his cot to say that he would verify his own handwriting. He was, he said, "ready to face the music."[7] Hunter preferred to have Campbell testify as to the handwriting. After the document was entered into evidence, the prosecutor read key portions of it to the jurors: Article 7, which provided for a commander in chief with powers, among other things, to "direct all movements of the army, and advise with any allies"; Article 45, which provided that "persons within the limits of the territory holden by this organization, not connected with this organization, having arms at all, concealed or

otherwise, shall be seized at once"; and Article 48, which required all officers, citizens, and soldiers connected with the organization to take an oath "to abide by and support this *Provisional Constitution* and these Ordinances." They were strange,
even bizarre, provisions—but then the whole *Provisional Constitution* was bizarre.

Next, Hunter produced a large bundle of letters written by
Brown. They had been seized at the Kennedy Farm after the raid
collapsed. The prosecutor asked Sheriff Campbell to identify
each letter, after which he passed it on to Brown, who quickly
looked at it and announced, in a loud voice, "Yes, that is mine."[8]
Hunter then asked for permission to read some letters Brown
had received from prominent men in the North. One was from
Joshua R. Giddings, a former congressman from Ohio who was
one of the most outspoken abolitionists in the country. Another
was from Gerrit Smith, the New York philanthropist who had
warmly supported Brown's work in Kansas. Botts insisted on
the right to examine the letters before they were read to the
jury. Letters written to Brown by prominent Northerners—men
who were not witnesses in the trial—would seem to shed little light on Brown's own guilt. But it was clear to most observers that Hunter, like his mentor Governor Wise, was not content
to prove that Brown and twenty-one supporters had attacked
the U.S. armory in Harper's Ferry. He wanted to show that
there was a conspiracy of prominent Northerners to demean and
eventually destroy slavery throughout the South, and that it
was a regional conspiracy that was fast assuming national dimensions.

Hunter's next witness was Armistead Ball, the master machinist at Harper's Ferry. Ball testified that he was roused early
Monday morning with news that some men were at the armory
"carrying off government property." He reached the armory
gate, where he was met by two armed men who made him a

prisoner. He was taken to Brown, who told him his object was "to free the slaves, and not making war on the people." Brown assured Ball that his person and private property would be safe; his war, he said, was against "the accursed system of slavery." He said that "it was no child's play he had undertaken." Brown then gave Ball permission to return to his family, as he said, "to assure them of my safety and get my breakfast." When Ball got back home, he found that his breakfast was not yet ready, so he went back to Brown and was allowed to return home a second time, and to come back to the armory yet again. When the engine house came under fire, Ball and Brown's other hostages all sought protection on the floor. Brown offered to retreat across the bridge with his hostages, release them on the other side, and then "fight it out with the military at daylight." But the offer was rejected. On Tuesday morning, Ball appealed to Brown "not to persist in spilling more blood." Brown replied that he was "well aware of what he was about, and knew the consequences." There was a reward out for his capture (here Brown was apparently referring to the rewards offered for him in Kansas and Missouri). Asked about the killing of Fontaine Beckham, Ball testified that one of Brown's men (apparently he did not know the man's name) had fired "in that direction" several times. When Ball saw this man leveling his rifle at an old man outside, he urged him not to fire, "and he desisted." But a while later, he heard the same man discharge his gun and say, "Dropped him." The hostages soon learned that the dead man was Mayor Beckham. When told that "he was an old and respectable citizen, and mayor of the town," the man who shot him said he was "very sorry." Ball said the man who killed Beckham was himself killed when the marines stormed the engine house. When the final assault was made, Brown made preparations to resist the marines, but "I do not think I saw him fire."[9]

On cross-examination by Green, Ball was asked about Brown's

offer for "terms of capitulation." Ball said that the actual proposal was written out by John Daingerfield, the armory paymaster who was one of the hostages, but it was "dictated by Brown." Ball did not know that any of Brown's sons had been shot until he heard Brown say, "There lies one of my sons dead, and here is another dying." Brown frequently remarked that the townspeople were acting "indiscreetly" in continuing to fire on their own people, and he repeatedly said that "he would injure no one but in self-defense." Ball recalled that there were three or four slaves in the engine house. They were carrying spears supplied by Brown, but "all seemed badly scared." The slave called Phil was ordered by Brown to cut a porthole through the brick wall of the engine house. He worked at the task "until a brisk fire commenced outside," upon which he said, "This is getting too hot for Phil" and sat down. "Brown then took up the tools and finished the hole."[10]

The prosecution's next witness was John Allstadt, the slaveholder who lived on the farm next to Lewis Washington's. Allstadt testified that he had been roused from his sleep on Monday morning by intruders at his bedroom door who ordered him to "get up quick, or we will burn you up." When asked what they intended to do, the intruders answered: "Free the country of slavery." Allstadt and seven of his slaves were taken to Harper's Ferry, where Brown said that he would release both Washington and Allstadt if they could get two blacks to take their places. The slaves were holding spears that Brown gave them, but, according to Allstadt, they "showed no disposition to use them." Allstadt's statement that some of the slaves "were asleep nearly all the time" evoked a round of laughter from the courtroom, for white defenders of slavery were always entertained by stories that confirmed their stereotypes of blacks as dull, lazy, and cowardly. When the marines made their assault on the engine house, Brown and his men took positions behind the fire engine and "aimed at the door." Allstadt remembered that Brown was "in front, squatting." "He fired at the marines," Allstadt said, "and my opinion is, that he killed that marine." (Private Luke Quinn was the marine who was shot dead during this final assault on the engine house.) This was, of course, damning testimony. But on cross-examination by Green, Allstadt backed down. He admitted that he could not "state certainly by what shot the marine was killed. He might have been killed by shots fired before the door was broken open." Allstadt said that he was "much confused and excited at the time." He did hear "regrets expressed at Beckham's being killed."[11]

Alexander Kelly, one of the employees at the armory, was the next to testify. When he was going to work on Monday, he saw Thomas Boerley shot and killed. He said that Boerley was "armed with a gun" and that the shot that killed him "came from the direction of Shenandoah Street." Kelly was not cross-examined.

Albert Grist, a Harper's Ferry resident, next testified that on Sunday night he had been crossing the bridge over the Shenandoah River when he was "stopped by a man with a spear." The man took him to the armory, where Brown told him that his "object was to free the slaves." When Grist answered that there were not many slaves there, Brown replied: "The good book says we are all free and equal."[12] After a while, Brown told Grist that he could go home, but he was afraid some of Brown's men might try to shoot him and stayed where he was.

When Grist's testimony was finished, again without cross-examination, Alexander Kelly was recalled for a few more questions. Kelly said that he had witnessed the shootings of both Thomas Boerley and George W. Turner. Turner was on High Street and "in the act of leveling his gun" when shots came from the corner of Shenandoah and High Streets. "The men who fired had rifles," Kelly said. "One had a shawl on."[13] When Kelly's testimony was concluded, the court adjourned for its midday recess.

When the court reassembled, Andrew Hunter's son Henry was called to the stand. Young Hunter testified that he had gone to Harper's Ferry with the Charlestown Guards, a company of militiamen from his hometown, and taken a position on the Potomac bridge. After a while, he left his company and "went off fighting on my own hook." When Fontaine Beckham, Henry Hunter's granduncle, was shot, Henry "heard the whistling of the ball" and saw him fall. He tried to go to his assistance but "was withheld by a friend." He thought Beckham had a pistol in his coat pocket when he was shot, "judging from the weight and shape of the pocket." The shot that killed Beckham "came from the engine house." Hunter was cross-examined, but apparently not vigorously, for the newspaper account of the exchange reported laconically that the questions put to him "elicited nothing new."[14] Later, however, the defense would recall Henry Hunter and question him about his personal role in the grisly death of William Thompson.

The prosecution concluded its case with three witnesses who testified briefly. John Thomas Gibson, colonel commanding the Jefferson County militia, testified that he helped a portion of the militia suppress Brown's "insurrection." There was a lot of gunfire in the town when Brown and his men were there, Gibson said, some of which came from Brown's men and some from "outside citizens." He didn't think "the insurgents fired a gun at the rifle factory," he said, but they did try "to make their escape across the river."[15]

Benjamin T. Bell, who followed Gibson, testified that he had gone to Harper's Ferry from Charlestown as part of "Capt. Botts' company" of militiamen. He saw Beckham shot and "went as near to him as was safe, but perceived no breathing." "There were probably thirty shots fired from the engine house toward the [water] tank," Bell said, but there were also "twenty or thirty men firing at the engine house."[16]

Recalled to the witness stand, Dr. Starry answered a few questions about the killing of George Turner. The prosecution then rested its case.

It was now late on Friday afternoon, the third full day of the trial, only five days after Brown was first hauled into the circuit court and ten days after he was captured at Harper's Ferry. The prosecution's case had ended somewhat abruptly, and there had been little time for the defense attorneys to prepare their case. But Judge Parker was determined to push on.

The defense's first witness was Joseph A. Brua, who had been one of the hostages Brown held in the engine house. While he was a hostage, Brua heard Brown say that the hostages should "share their danger." Several times, men went outside under truce flags. When Stevens and Kitzmiller went out, Stevens was shot. It was raining, and Stevens lay "near the corner of the depot," groaning. Brown believed that anybody who went out to help Stevens would be shot, but he permitted Brua to go out and help the wounded man into the Wager House, under a pledge by Brua that he would return to the engine house and resume his place as a hostage after he was done. Brua did just that. In fact, Brown sent him out several times to ask the townspeople not to shoot, "as the lives of the prisoners were endangered." Negotiations for a truce were under way before the "general firing" began. Brown said he "had it in his power to destroy that place in half an hour. But he would not do it, unless resisted." Brua thought a shot from the water tank struck Edwin Coppoc, and then Coppoc returned the fire. Someone said, "That man's down."[17] The latter reference seemed to be to the shooting of Mayor Beckham.

Archibald Kitzmiller was then sworn as a defense witness. He testified that he made "repeated efforts to accommodate matters with Brown." Brown said that "his object there was to free the slaves from bondage, and if necessary fight the pro-slavery men for that purpose." "I was first surprised," Kitzmiller said, "then indignant, and finally disgusted with Brown." Brown told him that there was "a company of riflemen on the bridge" and that they should meet with Stevens and another man to try to work out a truce. "I saw they were our own men," Kitzmiller continued, "and waved my handkerchief." But he soon heard firing "very close." Stevens "fired in reply to a shot which struck him." He remembered that "Thompson, one of Brown's men, was a prisoner on the bridge."

At this point, Brown interrupted the testimony. He said he wanted Kitzmiller to explain "the circumstances connected with the death of Thompson."

"I was not there and did not see the last," Kitzmiller testified. "The last I saw of Thompson he was a prisoner with the Ferry people, on the bridge." He was taken prisoner at about the time that Beckham was killed. Kitzmiller did not return to the engine house because he wanted to "prevent the unnecessary shedding of blood." He originally "went out at the request of Brown to use his influence for that purpose."[18]

An argument erupted when Thomas Green offered to prove how William Thompson met his death. Thompson was one of several of Brown's men who fell into the hands of the townspeople and thereafter met terrible deaths. Thompson and Aaron Stevens had both been taken into the Wager House after they were shot. There they were bound to chairs, with their hands behind their backs. Henry Hunter and another young man named George Chambers went into the Wager House, seized Thompson, and took him outside to the trestle of the Potomac bridge, where, in the presence of a cheering crowd, they deliberately shot him through the head. To add insult to injury, his body was then either dropped or thrown into the river and, while it was falling, was riddled with bullets.

Not surprisingly, Andrew Hunter did not want evidence of this killing to be heard by the jury. Betraying some anger, he said that there had been a good deal of testimony "about Brown's forbearance and not shooting citizens," but that testimony about Thompson's death "had no more to do with this case than the dead languages." It was "intended by Brown only for outdoor effect," and was wholly objectionable unless "it were shown that Brown was informed of the killing, and still continued to exercise forbearance towards his prisoners and the citizens." Green argued that there had been communications between Brown and the citizens all during the day and that it was proper to infer that he had been made aware of Thompson's killing. Judge Parker noted that "the whole transactions of that day constituted a part of the *res gestae* [the events at issue in the case]."[19] As such, it was proper to inquire into everything that happened. He overruled Hunter's objection and permitted Green to proceed.

Henry Hunter was then called and questioned by Green.

"Did you witness the death of this man Thompson?" Green asked.

"I witnessed the death of one whose name I have been informed was Thompson," Hunter answered.

"The one who was a prisoner?"

"Yes, sir."

"Well, sir, what were the circumstances attending it?"

"Do you wish my own connection with it, or simply a description of the circumstances—shall I mention the names?"

Andrew Hunter broke in. "Every bit of it, Henry," he said to his son. "State all you saw."

"There was a prisoner confined in the parlor of the hotel," Henry Hunter said, "and after Mr. Beckham's death he was shot down by a number of us there belonging to this sharp-shooting band."

Andrew Hunter again interrupted: "Will you allow him to state, before proceeding further, how he was connected with Mr. Beckham?"

"Certainly, sir."

Henry Hunter continued:

He was my grand uncle and my special friend—a man I loved above all others. After he was killed, Mr. Chambers and myself moved forward to the hotel for the purpose of taking this prisoner out and hanging him. We were joined by a number of other persons, who cheered us on in that work. We went up into his room, where he was bound with the undoubted and undisguised purpose of taking his life. At the door we were stopped by persons guarding the door, who remonstrated with us, and the excitement was so great that persons who remonstrated with us one moment would cheer us on the next. We burst into the room where he was, and found several round him, but they offered only a feeble resistance. We brought our guns down to his head repeatedly—myself and another person—for the purpose of shooting him, in the room. There was a young lady there, the sister of Mr. Fouke, the hotel keeper, who sat in this man's lap, covered his face with her arms, and shielded him with her person whenever we brought our guns to bear. She said to us "For God's sake wait and let the law take its course." My associate shouted to kill him. "Let us shed his blood," were his words. All around were shouting "Mr. Beckham's life was worth ten thousand of these vile abolitionists." I was cool about it, and deliberate. My gun was pushed up by someone who seized the barrel, and I then moved to the back part of the room, still with purpose unchanged, but with a view to divert attention from me, in order to get an opportunity, at some moment when the crowd should be less dense, to shoot him. After a moment's thought, it occurred to me that that was not the proper place to kill him. We then proposed to take him out and hang him. Some person of our band then opened a way to him, and first pushing Miss Fouke aside, we slung him out of doors. I gave him a push, and many others did the same. We then shoved him along the platform and down to the trestle work of the bridge, he begging for his life all the time, very piteously at first. By the bye, before we took him out of the room I asked the question what he came here for. He said their only purpose was to free the slaves—that he came here to free the slaves or die. Then he begged, "Don't take my life—a prisoner." But I put the gun to him, and he said, "You may kill me, but it will be revenged; there are eighty thousand persons sworn to carry this work." That was his last expression. We bore him out on the bridge with the purpose then of hanging him. We had no rope, and none could be found. It was a moment of wild excitement. Two of us raised our guns—which one was first I do not know—and pulled the trigger. Before he had reached the ground I suppose some five or six shots had been fired into his body. He fell on the railroad track, his back down to the earth, and his face up. We then went back for the purpose of getting another one—Stevens. But he was sick or wounded and there were persons around him, and I persuaded them myself to let him alone. I said, "Don't let us operate on him, but go around and get some more." We did this act with a purpose, thinking it right and justifiable under the circumstances, and

fired and excited by the cowardly, savage manner in which Mr.
Beckham's life had been taken.

It was quiet in the courtroom when Andrew Hunter asked:
"Is that all, gentlemen?"
"Yes, sir," Lawson Botts replied.
Andrew Hunter then spoke directly to his son:
"Stand aside."[20]

The next defense witness was William Williams, the night watchman whom Brown and his men encountered on the bridge
when they first entered Harper's Ferry. Williams had been taken
back to the engine house and kept there with Brown's other
hostages. Brown told the hostages that he would not hurt any of
them, but he threatened to "burn the town" when the townspeople began to fire on the engine house. Williams heard two
shots on the bridge about the time the train arrived, but he did
not see the black baggage master Hayward Shepherd killed. At
this point, Brown rose up on his cot to interrupt the testimony:
"State what was said by myself," he commanded.
    "I think you said that if he had taken care of himself, he
would not have suffered," Williams answered.[21]
    The next witness was a man named Rezin Cross, another hos-
tage Brown held in the engine house. Cross was called to testify
to efforts Brown made to work out a truce with the townspeople. "I prepared a proposition that Brown should retain the possession of the armory," Cross said, "that he should release us,
and that the firing should stop." Brown then interposed a question: "Were there two written propositions drawn up while you
were prisoner?" he asked. "Yes," Cross answered, "there was another paper prepared by Kitzmiller and some others." Cross said
that at one point he and William Thompson went out "to stop
the firing," but Thompson was taken prisoner. Asked how he

had been treated during the time he was held in the engine house, Cross answered that Brown's treatment of him "was kind and respectful," but he heard Brown "talk roughly to some men who were going in to where the blacks were confined."[22]

All of the witnesses who had answered Brown's summonses had now been heard. But Brown had asked for additional witnesses, and when their names were called they did not answer. Brown's right to compel witnesses to attend the trial in his behalf was one of his most valuable. It was enshrined in the venerated Virginia Bill of Rights which provides, among other things, that "in all capital or criminal prosecutions, a man hath a right . . . to call for evidence in his favor."[23] To enforce this right, the Virginia Code gave accused criminals the right to demand that witnesses be summoned in their behalf.[24] After consulting with Botts and Green, Brown had done just this, making out a list of the witnesses he needed to prove his case. But now when the witnesses were needed, some of them were not in court. Had the clerk issued the summonses as requested? Had the sheriff served them?

It went without saying, of course, that all of the witnesses would be white. The Code of Virginia explicitly provided that neither blacks nor Indians were competent to testify in any case, civil or criminal, in which a white person was a party.[25] If Brown knew of a black person, whether a slave or free man, who had special knowledge of the circumstances of his case and could provide exculpatory or mitigating evidence that might save him from the gallows, it would avail him not at all.

Brown again got up from his cot. He was "evidently excited," the newspapers reported, and took to his feet to address Judge Parker.

> May it please the Court: I discover that, notwithstanding all the assurances I have received of a fair trial, nothing like a fair trial is

to be given me, as it would seem. I gave the names, as soon as I could get at them, of the persons I wished to have called as witnesses, and was assured that they would be subpoenaed. I wrote down a memorandum to that effect, saying where those parties were; but it appears that they have not been subpoenaed, as far as I can learn; and now I ask, if I am to have anything at all deserving the name and shadow of a fair trial, that this proceeding be deferred until tomorrow morning.[26]

It was late in the day, and Brown realized that his last chance to save his life was rapidly drawing to a close. But Judge Parker and the prosecuting attorneys were, as usual, pushing to conclude the trial as quickly as possible. The attorneys he had written to in Massachusetts and Ohio had not yet appeared in Charlestown—not surprisingly, perhaps, for it had been only a week since he sent out his letters asking for their help. Botts and Green had conducted themselves well enough in the interim, but they did not really believe in him or his case. They could not be expected to embrace the cause of a Northern abolitionist with the fervor and devotion they would show for one of their own—a Virginia aristocrat, perhaps, or a Jefferson County slaveholder. And Brown frankly did not trust the Charlestown lawyers. He wanted his own counsel, an attorney—or attorneys—who believed in his case, as he did, and who would fight to win it. The failure of the witnesses to answer his call now gave Brown an opportunity to ask for more time—but just a little. He explained:

> I have no counsel, as I have before stated, in whom I feel that I can rely. But I am in hopes counsel may arrive who will attend to seeing that I get the witnesses who are necessary for my defense. I am myself unable to attend to it. I have given all the attention I possibly could to it, but am unable to see or know about them,

and cannot even find out their names. And I have nobody to do any errands, for my money was all taken when I was sacked and stabbed, and I have not a dime. I had two hundred and fifty or sixty dollars in gold and silver taken from my pocket, and now I have no possible means of getting anybody to go my errands for me, and I have not had all the witnesses subpoenaed. They are not within reach, and are not here. I ask at least until tomorrow morning to have something done, if anything is designed. If not, I am ready for anything that may come up.

Brown then lay down again, drew his blanket over him, closed his eyes, and appeared to fall asleep.[27]

It was not an unreasonable request, under all of the extraordinary circumstances of the occasion. Brown, after all, was the only man in the crowded Charlestown courtroom that Friday afternoon whose life hung in the balance. He was the only man whose neck would snap if the vaunted ideal of a fair trial was not realized. George Hoyt, who had been sitting silently beside Lawson Botts all day, took this occasion to stand up and address the court. Once again, the newspaper reporters noted that the courtroom reaction was a "great sensation." At last, the "boy lawyer from Boston" was to be heard:

May it please the Court—I would add my voice to the appeal of Mr. Brown, although I have had no consultation with him, that the further hearing of the case may be postponed until morning. I would state the reason of this request. It was that I was informed, and had reason to believe, that Judge Tilden of Ohio was on his way to Charlestown, and would undoubtedly arrive at Harper's Ferry at seven o'clock tonight. I have taken measures to insure that gentleman's arrival in this place tonight, if he reaches the Ferry.

Hoyt sensed the doubts that Brown felt about his Charlestown lawyers, but he did not want to impugn them. He continued:

> The gentlemen who have defended Brown acted in an honorable
> and dignified manner in all respects, so far as I know, but I can-
> not assume the responsibility of defending him myself for many
> reasons. First, it would be ridiculous in me to do it, because I
> have not read the indictment through—have not, except so far as
> I have listened to the case and heard counsel this morning, got
> any idea of the line of the defense proposed, and have no knowl-
> edge of the criminal code of Virginia, and no time to read it. I
> had no time to examine the questions arising in this defense,
> some of which are of considerable importance, especially that
> relative to the jurisdiction over the armory grounds. For all
> these reasons, I ask the continuation of the case till to-morrow
> morning.[28]

Botts felt the need to speak:

> In justice to myself, I must state that, on being first assigned as
> counsel to Mr. Brown I conferred with him, and at his instance
> took down a list of the witnesses he desired subpoenaed in his be-
> half. Though it was late at night, I called upon the sheriff, and in-
> formed him that I wished subpoenas to be issued early in the
> morning. This was done, and there are here Messrs. Phelps, Wil-
> liams and Grist, and they have been examined.

Sheriff Campbell, who was seated nearby, stated that the sub-
poenas were delivered to an officer with the request that he
serve them at once. "He must have served them," Campbell
said, "as some of the witnesses are here."

Botts thought that he and Green had shown that they
"wished Mr. Brown to have a fair trial." Hunter assured the

court he did not wish to "interpose the slightest impediment to a fair trial." "Whether it was promised to Brown or not," Hunter said, "it is guaranteed by our laws to every prisoner." But the prosecutor reminded the court that a postponement for the purpose of hearing additional witnesses requires a showing that the testimony of those witnesses would be "material." The defense witnesses thus far had testified that Brown treated his hostages "with leniency, respect and courtesy" and that "his flags of truce—if you choose to regard them so—were not respected by the citizens, and that some of his men were shot." "If the defense choose to take that course," Hunter said, "we are perfectly willing to admit these facts in any form they desire." But unless additional testimony was "really material to the defense," there should be no delay.

Green then announced that he and Botts were withdrawing from the case. "We can no longer act in behalf of the prisoner," he said, "he having declared here that he has no confidence in the counsel who have been assigned him. Feeling confident that I have done my whole duty, so far as I have been able, after this statement of his, I should feel myself an intruder upon this case, were I to act for him from this time forward." Green explained that he had not wanted to take up the case in the first place, and he did not think the court could "insist that I should remain in such an unwelcome position."[29]

Harding, who had thus far taken little part in the proceedings, now decided to speak. "We have been delayed from time to time by similar applications," he said, "in the expectation of the arrival of counsel, until we have now reached the point of time when we are ready to submit the case to the jury upon the evidence and the law, when another application arises for a continuance." Harding disclosed that one of the witnesses Brown had subpoenaed was John Daingerfield, the paymaster at the armory. Harding said that Daingerfield had been under a prosecution subpoena but was not called to testify because he and Harding thought they had enough testimony without him.

Judge Parker now spoke. He rejected the idea of waiting for out-of-state counsel "to study our code through." Whether a delay should be granted to call additional witnesses was a different matter. "I do not know whether the process has been executed or not," the judge said, "as no return has been made."[30]

"I have endeavored to do my duty in this matter," Botts responded, "but I cannot see how, consistently with my own feelings, I can remain any longer in this case, when the accused whom I have been laboring to defend, declares in open court that he has no confidence in his counsel." Botts suggested that George Hoyt take over the case, and that Parker "allow him this night for preparation." "My notes, my office, and my services shall be at his command," Botts said. "I will sit up with him all night to put him in possession of all the law and facts in relation to this case. I cannot do more; and in the mean time, the sheriff can be directed to have the other witnesses here tomorrow."

Parker relented. It was six o'clock in the evening. Under all of the circumstances, Botts's proposal was reasonable, and his offer to help Hoyt through the night was generous. The judge declared the proceedings adjourned until the following morning.[31]

Perhaps the trial would be fair, after all—in name and not just in shadow.

8

THE QUIET WAS DECEPTIVE

By Saturday morning, the fourth day of the trial, the courtroom in Charlestown had become a stage on which a great national drama was being played out. The actors were mostly Virginians or friends of Virginians: the judge, the jurors, the clerks, the witnesses, the lawyers for the prosecution, even the two court-appointed attorneys for John Brown. George Hoyt, the boy lawyer from Boston, was an interloper in the crowd, a Northerner who had been shown to his seat by Senator Mason but scorned by nearly everyone else. Reporters from all over the country were in the courtroom, but those with Northern sympathies knew enough to keep them to themselves. Feelings ran high in the town, and the feelings were almost unanimously on the side of the Commonwealth in its struggle with "Old Brown of Osawatomie."

Outside, militiamen still paraded up and down the streets. The cannons in front of the courthouse and the jail were checked regularly to make sure they were in firing condition, ready to defend the jail against any attempt to rescue Brown. Strangers were stopped in the streets and asked to explain their business. Hotel registers were examined for unfamiliar names; if one was encountered, the unknown guest was tracked down and, as a writer for the *New York Tribune* reported, subjected to close questioning "concerning his nativity, his avocation, his political sentiments, his plans in life, and so forth."[1] Directions for the protection of the town came from Governor Wise, but he did not have to coax the residents to comply. Jefferson County had been caught unprepared when Brown and his Provisional Army invaded Harper's Ferry. It would not be subjected to such a humiliation again.

Inside, the courtroom had taken on the atmosphere of an arena, with spectators assembled to witness an athletic contest or watch horses cross the finish line of a very important race. (Charlestown was a noted horse racing center, and the people were great followers of the sport.)[2] Judge Parker sat behind his table on the elevated platform at the back of the chamber, presiding over the proceedings, but in a disarmingly casual manner. His table was strewn with papers and law books, pens and inkstands, a water pitcher and drinking glass. From time to time, he leaned back in his chair and put his feet up on the table—the better to reflect on the rulings he had to make or the objections he was called on to sustain or overrule. In front of the judge, the jurors watched and listened. Near the center of the room, the lawyers gathered around the counsel table, some with their legs draped over the arms of their chairs or their feet on the edge of the table, in the style of the judge.[3] Charles Harding, perhaps feeling the effects of too much hard drinking the night before, sometimes dozed off in his chair.[4] But no one seemed to care much about Harding, for Andrew Hunter, tall and handsome, was on duty for the Commonwealth. And John Brown lay impassively on his cot, seemingly oblivious to the arguments that were being waged about him, but ready to take to his feet when he had something he wanted to say. His critics thought it curious that he lay on the cot while the witnesses and lawyers were speaking but that, when provoked, he could instantly rise and command the audience. Was he genuinely disabled by his wounds, they wondered, or merely playing for sympathy?

While the spectators sat and listened, they also cracked peanuts and chestnuts and avidly chewed on them, tossing the broken shells on the floor. No court rules forbade this indulgence, and the people were so persistent in it that the floor was covered to within a few feet of the judge's chair with broken shells, in some places several inches deep. The noise of people moving about the room was, as a writer for the *New York Herald* observed, "like that which would be made by trampling on glass." But court officials continually attempted to stop men from smoking. "Give over that smoking in court, there," an official would say. The offender frequently would remove the cigar from his mouth for only a moment and then put it back.[5]

Out of the courtroom—in the offices of Hunter and Harding, those of Botts and Green, and in the jail cell Brown shared with Aaron Stevens—the drama also continued. When Hoyt first arrived in Charlestown, he was denied access to Brown. He was not, after all, the accused man's lawyer. He had never before met him, and, with the concern for security that gripped the town, neither the sheriff nor the jailer was prepared to accommodate a boy from Massachusetts who walked up to their door and casually announced that he wanted to talk with the most famous prisoner in the whole commonwealth. By the end of the day on Friday, however, Hoyt had become Brown's attorney of record and secured Botts's promise to stay up all night to help him prepare for the next day's battle. Now Brown's cell was opened for Hoyt, and the two men met. Hoyt had not forgotten that he was sent to Charlestown to spy on the town and assess the chances of rescuing Brown. That was certainly one of the first topics he discussed with his new client. But it was not the only one or even the most important. Hoyt quickly concluded that any effort to help Brown escape would be futile. Even assuming that Brown could be gotten out of the jail, it would be virtually impossible for him to elude the sentries and militiamen in the streets. More important, Brown told Hoyt that he did not want to escape. Perhaps he still entertained a ray of hope that things would go well in the trial; that the jury would be persuaded by some of the evidence, by the arguments his attorneys were prepared to present, or by his own statements. If not, there was a possibility that Governor Wise would step in to grant some kind of clemency. If there was no conviction on the treason charge, his hands would not be tied. If none of these eventualities came to pass, however, Brown was willing to accept the result. Precisely when Brown became resigned to his fate is difficult to determine. That he did at some point accept it, however, and that he finally realized that he could achieve far more in Charlestown by dying than by eluding death is clear.

Hoyt believed it was fortunate that he was in Charlestown when Botts and Green withdrew from the case. Yes, he was young and green in the ways of courtrooms, but he was no stranger to law books, and Botts was willing to tutor him. What's more, Hoyt believed in Brown and was willing to fight for him. As he talked with the accused man, the young lawyer's respect for him grew. As he wrote his abolitionist friends back in Boston: "I confess I did not know which most to admire, the thorough honor & admirable qualities of the brave old border soldier, or the uncontaminated simplicity of the man. John Brown is an astonishing character. The people here generally admit & applaud his conscientiousness, honor & bravery."[6]

Hoyt had kind words for Brown's court-appointed lawyers. "In justice to them," he wrote his Massachusetts friends, "I must say their management of the case was as good for Brown as the circumstances of their position permitted."[7] But "the circumstances of their position" did not permit much, and Hoyt was delighted when the Saturday morning train to Charlestown brought two new lawyers to join Brown's defense team: Samuel Chilton from Washington and Hiram Griswold from Cleveland.

Chilton came at a heavy price: a fee of one thousand dollars that was raised among Brown's most devoted Boston supporters, led by John Andrew.[8] But Chilton's reputation as a lawyer was so good and his connections with Virginia so extensive that Brown's friends felt the money was well spent. The arrangements between Andrew and Chilton were handled by Montgomery Blair of Maryland and Washington, who had declined to take Brown's case himself but contacted Chilton about it. Although he now practiced in the nation's capital, the fifty-five-year-old Chilton was born in Warrenton, Virginia, only fifty miles south of Charlestown, where he was admitted to the bar in 1826 and elected to Congress in the 1840s. He moved his practice to Washington in 1853 but still maintained his Virginia contacts. In a letter back to Massachusetts, Hoyt praised Chilton as "a very eminent lawyer, practising in the courts of Virginia, also a relative of the Judge, and the family friend of most of the wealthy & respectable people hereabouts."[9]

Griswold had come from Cleveland at the behest of Daniel Tilden, who had been expected to come to Charlestown but was unable to leave his Cleveland probate court. Tilden had apparently consulted with several attorneys in and around Cleveland before finally settling on Griswold. One was a former U.S. congressman named David K. Cartter, and another a former state representative (and future U.S. congressman) named Albert Gallatin Riddle. Both Cartter and Riddle were skilled attorneys and Republicans. Riddle had been out of town when Brown's letter to Tilden first arrived, but when he got back to Cleveland he declined the invitation to join Brown's defense team. In later years, Riddle expressed "lasting regret" that he did not go to Charlestown with Griswold.[10] The fifty-two-year-old Griswold was one of the leading attorneys of Cleveland, a Republican who had served five years as official reporter of cases for the Supreme Court of Ohio and, in 1851, narrowly lost an election to represent Ohio in the U.S. Senate. He apparently agreed to go to Charlestown without any advance arrangements about his fee, but after arriving there he obtained Brown's consent to seek payment out of the gold coin and other property that was held for him by the sheriff. In the end, Griswold received $250. Griswold had to juggle his court schedule in Cleveland before he could leave for Virginia, obtaining postponements when possible.[11] He made a good impression in Charlestown, where Cleon Moore, one of the deputy clerks, wrote that he had "established quite a reputation here, as a profound lawyer—he's from Ohio."[12]

Judge Parker called his circuit court to order at ten o'clock on Saturday morning and immediately announced that he had received a note from Brown's new attorneys requesting a "short delay" to enable them to talk with their client. Parker agreed to the request. An hour later, Brown was brought into court and laid down on his cot. The *Baltimore Sun* reported that "he looked quite feeble and haggard, and the effort of the excitement of last evening was quite visible in his countenance."[13] Chilton and Griswold were introduced to the judge, after which Chilton took the floor to make "an explanatory statement." He said that he had been asked to come to Charlestown only the day before. "I took some time to consider the proposition," he added, "and finally agreed to come in under the expectation of finding Messrs. Botts and Green still in the case. On arriving here, however, I learned for the first time the course the case had taken last evening." He spoke with Brown and consulted with Hoyt and Griswold. He did not know what evidence had been given up to that time; he had not even had an opportunity to read the indictment; if he accepted the case, he would not be able to discharge the "full duty of counsel." Griswold, he said, found himself in the same circumstances. The attorneys were not now making a formal motion to delay the proceedings—merely suggesting, as one reporter put it, that "a short delay of a few hours, if the court thought proper to grant it, would enable them to make some preparation."[14]

It was already Saturday. The following day was the Sabbath, and court proceedings on that holy day would be suspended in any case. What damage would the prosecution suffer if the judge granted a delay of a few hours so the new lawyers could prepare—read the indictment, at least, review notes of the evidence already given, perhaps even leaf through a few Virginia law books? After all, two highly regarded lawyers had arrived in Charlestown to replace two lawyers who had taken themselves off a case that was drawing national attention. A man was on trial for his life in a proceeding that Virginians had repeatedly promised would be a fair trial. The indictment was long and complex and raised difficult legal questions.

Some might have thought that a short delay was called for. Judge Parker did not. He pointed out that the court had assigned counsel to Brown. They were, the judge said, "of his own selection." (This was not strictly true, however, for Brown had not sought out Botts or Green. He had, at the most, declined to object to their appointment, all the while making clear to the judge that he was waiting for his own attorneys to arrive from the North.) The court-appointed attorneys had "labored zealously" in Brown's behalf, Parker continued, and they had withdrawn only because Brown "declared in open court that he had no confidence in them." No obstacle had been "thrown in the way" of Brown's having an "ample defense." (This assertion was highly debatable, for Brown had repeatedly asked for short delays so he could obtain his own legal counsel, and Parker had repeatedly denied his requests.) Parker then went on to state the real reason for his refusal to permit any delay. "If this was the only case of this kind before the court," he said, he would "at once grant the request." But several cases were lined up behind Brown's. The judge's term in Charlestown would end soon, and it was his duty to get through all of the cases if he could do so "in justice to the prisoners, and in justice to the state." The trial, therefore, had to proceed.[15]

The defense attorneys were in a difficult position. None of them knew much about Brown's case, but since Griswold and Chilton knew even less about it than Hoyt, responsibility for moving the defense forward fell by default to the young lawyer from Massachusetts. It was not clear just what should be done, so Hoyt did what a lawyer must do in such circumstances— he improvised. He referred to the writings that Hunter had introduced the day before, the ones that had been taken from the Kennedy Farm after Brown was captured in Harper's Ferry. Hoyt said he had "hastily examined" them, but he didn't know what purpose they were offered for. He intended to object to some and thought his colleagues might object to others.

"No need of argument about the matter," Hunter interrupted. "Designate those you wish to object to."

"I desire to know the object of the counsel in introducing those papers," Hoyt said.

"The papers will speak for themselves," Hunter shot back. "If you will designate which of them you object to, we will go on at once."[16]

One of the papers Hoyt objected to was a short narrative that Brown had written in Kansas in 1858. Hoyt called it an "autobiography." In fact, it was the beginning of a manuscript about Brown's early life that Brown had hoped to publish for the benefit of his family and "the cause of Freedom," but it was never finished.[17] Hoyt said it had "no bearing on this case."

"I withdraw it," Hunter responded.

"I object to the letter of Gerrit Smith," Hoyt continued. He was referring here to a letter the New Yorker had written to Brown. There had, of course, been many letters between Smith and Brown over the years, for the two men shared a long association and a mutual contempt for slavery. It was far from clear, however, what light a letter written to Brown from New York might shed on his guilt, or innocence, of the Harper's Ferry charges. Even if it was relevant, such a letter was objectionable as hearsay—a statement made out of court and offered to prove the truth of the matter asserted.[18] Was it possible that Hunter was fishing for evidence of Smith's participation in the "conspiracy" that led up to Harper's Ferry? Very probably. If so, that evidence belonged in a trial of Gerrit Smith, not John Brown.

"I withdraw that, too," Hunter responded.

"I handed to the clerk, last night, a list of names we wished summoned as witnesses," Hoyt continued, reading off the names of Samuel Strider, Henry Ault, Benjamin Mills, John E. P. Daingerfield, and a certain "Captain Simms." "I got a dispatch just now, informing me that Captain Simms had gone to Frederick, and would return in the first train this morning, and come on to Charlestown this afternoon. I should like to inquire whether the process has reached Captain Simms at Harper's Ferry?"

Sheriff Campbell, who was seated nearby, reported that Simms had returned to Frederick; Simms was a member of the militia from Frederick that had come to Harper's Ferry to help put down Brown's raid. "He was here yesterday," Hunter said. "I hope we will proceed with some other witnesses."[19] The prosecutor, it seemed, was growing weary of all of this talk of witnesses. It is doubtful, however, that Hoyt, Chilton, Griswold, or Brown shared his weariness.

If Simms was not available, John Daingerfield was, and he was the first witness Hoyt called that Saturday morning.

Dangerfield testified that he was an officer at the armory and one of the hostages Brown held in the engine house. Brown had opened discussions with the townspeople for the release of all of his hostages before the townspeople began to fire on the engine house. "About a dozen black men were there," Daingerfield said, "armed with pikes which they carried most awkwardly, and unwillingly." During all of the time he was in the engine house, Daingerfield had no "personal fear" of Brown or his men. After the townspeople began to fire on the engine house, he saw one of Brown's men take a shot, exclaim, "It's all up with me," and die a few moments later. He saw another man come in from the outside, wounded, and begin to vomit blood. He later learned these two men were Brown's sons. Daingerfield heard Brown complain frequently that his men had been shot down while carrying truce flags.

Hunter did not like the implications of Dangerfield's testimony. He broke into the interrogation, complaining that the defense attorneys were repeating facts that had already been brought out in the evidence. The prosecution "freely admitted" all of this, Hunter said. Hoyt responded that this was "the only feasible line of defense to prove these facts," and that it was "the duty of counsel to show, if possible, that Captain Brown was not guilty of treason, murder, or insurrection, according to the terms of this indictment. We hope to prove the absence of malicious intention." Hunter thought the whole line of questioning was "calculated to waste time." Hoyt said his questions were asked out of a "conviction of duty" and in accordance with Brown's "express commands." Parker answered that it was the responsibility of counsel "to conduct the case according to the rules of practice," not according to the client's commands. Hoyt thought Hunter's reference to delay was calculated to "impugn his honor." "Nothing of the kind was intended," Hunter retorted. "It is presumed the gentlemen will conduct the case in accordance with their duty as counsel, and their responsibility to the court."[20]

Undaunted, Hoyt continued to question Daingerfield. The paymaster had heard Brown say that he had it "in his power to lay the town in ashes" and to "carry off the women and children," but he never heard him say he would carry out these threats. "The only threat I heard from him was at the commencement of the storming of the engine house," Daingerfield continued. "He then said that we must all take equal shares with him, that we could no longer monopolize the places of safety." But Brown "made no attempt to deprive us of the places we had taken. Brown promised safety to all descriptions of property, except slave property." When the marines began their assault on the engine house, one of Brown's men asked him if he was "committing treason" by resisting the marines. Brown said that he was. The man then said, "I'll fight no longer"—he thought he was merely "fighting to liberate the slaves." During the marine attack, two of Brown's men "cried for quarter, and laid down their arms," but "after the marines burst open the door, they picked them up again and renewed the fight." After the first attack, "Brown cried out to surrender, but he was not heard." Daingerfield saw Brown "wounded on the hip by a thrust from a sabre, and with several sabre cuts on his head." When his head was cut, he "appeared to be shielding himself, with his head down, but making no resistance."[21]

When Daingerfield's testimony ended, Hunter offered no cross-examination.

Hoyt now called a succession of witnesses who had been hostages in the engine house and had observed Brown's conduct and demeanor there. Benjamin Mills, the master armorer, repeated Daingerfield's assertion that negotiations for a truce were under way before the townspeople began to fire on Brown and his men and that one of Brown's sons had gone out under a white flag and come back with a gunshot wound. Brown frequently complained that the townspeople were acting "in a barbarous manner." Brown's ears pricked up during Mills's testimony, and he rose up on his cot to ask whether he had seen any firing by Brown that was not "purely defensive." "It might be considered in that light, perhaps," Mills answered. "The balls came into the engine house pretty thick."

Mills revealed that his wife and daughter had visited him in the engine house and that "free verbal communication was allowed with those outside." "We were treated kindly," Mills said, "but were compelled to stay where we didn't want to be. Brown appeared anxious to effect a compromise."[22]

Samuel Strider agreed that Brown had tried to "protect his hostages." Brown continually said that he wished to make terms "more for their safety than his own," Strider testified.[23]

At half past one in the afternoon, the court took its midday recess, but the judge and jury and the attorneys were back in the courtroom thirty minutes later. Captain Simms had arrived from Frederick, and Hiram Griswold had decided to question him. Simms testified that he had come to Harper's Ferry on Monday with his militia company, in response to reports that "750 blacks and abolitionists combined" had seized the armory. Simms was pleased when he discovered that the reports were grossly exaggerated. Approaching the engine house where Brown was holed up, he found the door ajar and heard someone inside calling to him. He went inside, where he met Brown, Daingerfield, and the others. Brown said that he "had a proposition to make." He wanted to be allowed to go over the Potomac bridge "unmolested," after which the militiamen could try to "take him." Brown said he had "fought Uncle Sam before" and "was willing to do it again." When he complained that his men had been "shot down like dogs while bearing a flag of truce," Simms replied that they should expect to be "shot down like dogs" if they took up arms in that way. Brown said that he "had full possession of the town and could have massacred all the inhabitants had he thought proper to do so, but as he had not, he considered himself entitled to some terms." When Brown said he had shot no one who had not carried arms, Simms reminded him that Mayor Beckham had been killed "and that I knew he was altogether unarmed." Brown said that he was sorry to hear of Beckham's death and added, "I fight only those who fight me." Simms left the engine house and went over to the hotel, where he found Aaron Stevens badly wounded and lying on a bed. Some of the young men of the town were about to shoot him. Simms was appalled. He told them that if Stevens "could stand on his feet, with a pistol in his hand, they would all jump out of the window."[24]

Simms had come to the trial in response to a summons. He had "no sympathy" for Brown's conduct—he "would be one of the first to bring him to punishment" for what he had done. But he regarded Brown "as a brave man." "As a Southern man," Simms declared, "I came to state the facts about the case, so that Northern men would have no opportunity of saying that Southern men were unwilling to appear as witnesses in behalf of one whose principles they abhor."[25]

Here the defense attorneys closed their case. Hunter was satisfied with the way the testimony had gone, confident that the evidence against Brown was too strong to admit of any possibility that he might escape punishment; and he saw no need to cross-examine any of the defense witnesses. It was now time for the attorneys to make their legal arguments.

Samuel Chilton and Hiram Griswold had arrived so late in the trial that they had had almost no opportunity to question the witnesses, and if they were to have any effect at all on the ultimate decision, it would have to be in the arguments they made, both to the judge and the jury. What happened at Harper's Ferry may have been clear enough, but the legal issues raised by it, and by the long and complex indictment that Hunter had prepared, were not. Chilton had had virtually no time to reflect on the legal issues before he was called upon to address them; but he was an attorney who was used to thinking on his feet—and he now proceeded to do just that.

Chilton began by offering a motion that the prosecution "be compelled to elect one count of the indictment and abandon the others." It was a rather technical motion and supported by a rather disjointed combination of reasons. Chilton argued, first, that the language used in the second count of the indictment, which charged that Brown "conspired together, with other persons, to induce certain slaves . . . to make rebellion and insurrection," did not precisely agree with the applicable language of the Virginia Code, which imposed the death penalty for any free person who shall "advise or conspire with a slave to rebel or make an insurrection." "There is a broad distinction between advising and conspiring with slaves to rebel," Chilton said, "and conspiring with others to induce slaves to rebel." "Broad distinction" or not, Chilton's argument did seem a bit like hairsplitting, and he did not dwell on it. Chilton was on somewhat surer ground when he alluded to the "hardship" that arises when the accused in a criminal prosecution is forced "to meet various and distinct charges in the same trial." He said that the criminal law recognized "different descriptions of treason." Treason against the United States was, he said, "high treason," whereas treason against the Commonwealth of Virginia was "treason against her sovereignty." "We have no other description of treason," Chilton said, "because treason can only be committed against sovereignty, whether that of the United States, or of a sovereign State."[26]

Chilton was beginning here to get at a vital point, which was whether Brown could properly be convicted of treason against Virginia when the facts showed that he was not a citizen of Virginia and that his attack had been directed against a federal facility. The newspaper reports of Chilton's argument may not have adequately summarized the points he was making, and so it is necessary to engage in some speculation to imagine precisely what they were. By arguing that "treason can only be committed against sovereignty," Chilton seemed to be addressing the issue of allegiance. Did Brown owe a duty of allegiance to Virginia? And, if he did not, how could he be convicted of treason against Virginia?

Harding rose to make the first reply to Chilton. He admitted that one count of the indictment charged Brown with treason, but another charged him with murder. "Murder arose out of this treason," Harding said, "and was the natural result of this bloody conspiracy." Yet, "after all the evidence has been given on all these points, the objection is made that we must confine ourselves to a single one of them." Harding hoped that the court would not grant Chilton's motion.[27]

Hunter followed by arguing that when an indictment includes several counts, the prosecution should be forced to elect one count and abandon the others only when "great embarrassment would otherwise result to the prisoner." That was certainly not the case here. Hunter seemed to take offense at Chilton's suggestion that the indictment was not properly phrased. "It is my work," he said, "and I propose to defend it as right and proper." Hunter was almost dismissive of Chilton's argument about the different kinds of treason. The points made by Chilton were, he said, "too refined and subtle" for his own "poor intellect."[28]

Parker pointed out that the jury had been sworn to try the case "on the indictment as drawn." If the indictment was defective, Chilton might raise the point on a motion to arrest the judgment. But such a motion could be made only after the jury had considered the case. "There is no legal objection against charging various crimes in the same indictment," the judge said. It had been the practice in Virginia courts "to put a party upon election where the prisoner would be embarrassed in his defense." But "in this case, these offenses charged are all part of the same transaction, and no case is made out for the court to interfere and put the parties upon an election."

Having lost his effort to force an election, Chilton said he would reserve his points for a motion in arrest of judgment.[29]

Griswold now rose to address the court. Since all of the evidence had been presented, nothing remained except for the lawyers to give their closing arguments. But Brown's attorneys still hadn't had an opportunity to review the testimony of the witnesses. Griswold knew from the previous history of the case that Judge Parker was not favorably disposed to delays, but the circumstances forced him to ask for one now. The Ohioan spoke tentatively, hoping that he would not offend the judge.

Hunter acknowledged that the defense attorneys found themselves in "a somewhat embarrassing position." That was not their fault, he said, nor was it the fault of the prosecutors or the judge. It was entirely Brown's fault, for he had dismissed his own "faithful, skillful, able and zealous counsel" just the day before. Delays had consequences not only for the officers of the court, but also for the jurors. The men who were serving on Brown's jury were kept away from their homes as long as the trial continued. And, Hunter charged, the very continuation of the trial exposed the women of the community to fear. "There could not be a female in this county," he said, "who, whether with good cause or not, is not trembling with anxiety and apprehension."[30]

It is interesting to speculate what Hunter meant by this last statement. Was he suggesting that women were afraid because their husbands were kept on duty at the courthouse longer than they had expected—and were thus deprived of their domestic protection? Was he suggesting that, until Brown was safely convicted, the slaves might yet rise up and rape all the white women of the county? Or was he insinuating that Brown and his men themselves posed a special threat to the females of Jefferson County? Southern gentlemen were, it is known, chivalrously protective of the fair sex. Whatever its intent, it was a strange—and possibly inflammatory—allusion.

Although Brown was entitled to be treated with "courtesy" and "humanity," Hunter continued, the court had to remember that "the Commonwealth has its rights, the community has its rights, [and] the jury have their rights." For his part, Hunter thought that the case should continue right through to midnight if necessary to complete it. In that time, the attorneys could give their arguments, the judge could instruct the jury, the jury could deliberate and announce its verdict, and Brown would receive the sentence prescribed by law. Hunter was, of course, confident of the outcome.

The defense attorneys were appalled. Griswold and Chilton had arrived in Charlestown just that morning and were exhausted—and probably a little bewildered—by their first day in Parker's court. And George Hoyt had been traveling for most of the previous week, sitting in on Brown's trial for two days, conferring with him in the jail, consulting with Botts and Green into the early hours of the morning. Chilton said that it was impossible for him to give his closing argument now—he could not, as a press report recounted his statement, "allow himself to make an attempt at argument on a case about which he knew so little. If he were to get up at all it would only be for the unworthy purpose of wasting time."[31]

Judge Parker decided to consult the jurors. Did they want the trial to be delayed until Monday, or would they prefer to wrap the whole thing up that night? Not surprisingly, the jurors told the judge that they were "very anxious to get home." Parker assured them that he was "very desirous of trying this case precisely as he would try any other, without any reference at all to outside feeling."[32] This was a platitude, of course. John Brown's trial was not like "any other," however much Parker might have wished it were.

Hoyt told the judge that he had worked hard the previous night researching important legal points, working "until he fell unconscious from his chair from exhaustion and fatigue." He had slept only ten hours over the previous five days and nights. It seemed to him that justice to Brown demanded "the allowance of a little time in a case so extraordinary in all its respects as this." Even if he had been fully prepared, Hoyt said, he was "physically incapable of speaking tonight."[33]

Harding suggested that the attorneys all waive their arguments and "submit the case to the jury without a single word, believing that they would do the prisoner justice."[34] It was obvious that Harding, like Hunter, was confident of the outcome. But Chilton protested. If he and Griswold could not argue the case, why had they come all this distance to Charlestown? Parker asked how much time their arguments would take. Not more than two and a half hours, Chilton said. Hunter protested "earnestly" against any delay. "Then you can go on yourselves," the judge said, nodding to Hunter and Harding.

Harding led off. He reviewed the testimony of the witnesses, and discussed the law that he believed was applicable to the case. He argued with some vehemence that it was "absurd" for Brown, having led a bloody attack on Harper's Ferry, to expect that he be treated "according to the rules of honorable warfare." He seemed to have "lost sight of the fact that he was in command of a band of murderers and thieves, and had forfeited all title to protection of any kind." And he suggested that "anxious faces were hanging around the courthouse" demanding a verdict of guilty.[35] After forty minutes, Harding sat down. He was tired. Hunter may have been tired, too, for he offered no argument of his own. He had very probably decided that he would deliver the closing argument for the prosecution when the court reconvened on Monday.

It was now dark in Charlestown. As the judge banged his gavel, the courtroom emptied. Harding, Hunter, Hoyt, Griswold, and Chilton all walked out into the brisk night air. The sheriff conducted the jurors back to their quarters in Gibson's Hotel, making sure to keep them together. And Brown, still under heavy guard, went back to his room in the jail.

It was quiet in the town, for the Sabbath was fast approaching. But the quiet was deceptive, for militiamen still manned their posts outside the courthouse and jail, and sentries still guarded the entrances to the town. And John Brown had yet to rise from his cot in the courtroom and speak the words that history would remember.

9

THE VERDICT

Sunday was a day of rest in Charlestown, as it was throughout the United States in 1859. Church bells rang out in the morning, summoning worshipers from the town and the surrounding farmland. Brown was one of the most fervently religious men in Jefferson County that Sunday morning, though he was confined to his jail cell and could not go to any church. But this may not have mattered much to him. In his cell, he read his Bible assiduously, and he prayed fervently. He did not, however, put great faith in ministers or denominations. He had his own core set of beliefs, and they were firm. He believed that it was his duty as a true Christian to fight against slavery, and that in trying to help the slaves achieve freedom he was doing no more than God wanted him to do. He was convinced that Christians who temporized with slavery, who excused its cruelties, were not true followers of Christ. While he was in the Charlestown jail, local ministers came to meet him. They did so, no doubt, with the honorable intention of giving him spiritual comfort, perhaps of persuading him of the "errors of his ways." He was wary of all these "emissaries" of a religious faith he had no respect for. One of the ministers who called on Brown in Charlestown was the Reverend Norval Wilson, a Methodist. When admitted to Brown's cell, Wilson proposed a prayer. Brown promptly challenged him:

"Mr. Wilson, do you believe in slavery?"

"I do," Wilson answered, "under the present circumstances."

"Then I do not want your prayers," Brown said. "I don't want the prayers of any man that believes in slavery."

In one of his free moments in the jail, Brown penned a letter to a Reverend McFarland in Wooster, Ohio:

> You may wonder, are there no ministers of the gospel here? I answer, No. There are no ministers of *Christ* here. These ministers who profess to be Christian, and hold slaves or advocate slavery, I cannot abide them. My knees will not bend in prayer with them while their hands are stained with the blood of souls.[1]

The first letter that Brown sent to his wife from Charlestown described his legal predicament and addressed his religious beliefs.

> My Dear Wife, & Children every one
> I suppose you have learned before this by the newspapers that Two weeks ago we were fighting for our lives at Harper's ferry: that during the fight Watson was mortally wounded; Oliver killed, Wm Thompson Killed, & Dauphin slightly wounded. That on the following day I was taken prisoner immediately after which I received several Sabre cuts in my head; & Bayonet stabs in my body.

It was dreadful news for Mary Ann Brown, but she had learned years before to expect dreadful news from her husband and to accept it with the resignation of a Christian wife. John Brown now went on to expound on his religious views:

> Under all of these terible [*sic*] calamities; I feel quite cheerful in the assurance that God reigns; & will overrule all for his glory; & the best possible good. I feel no conciouness [*sic*] of guilt in the matter; nor even mortifycation [*sic*] on account of my imprisonment; & irons; & I feel perfectly assured that very soon no mem-

ber of my family will feel any possible disposition to "blush on my account."

And he affirmed his faith that God would protect his family:

"He will never leave you nor forsake you" unless you forsake him. Finally my dearly beloved be of good comfort. Be sure to remember *& to follow my advice* & my example *too:* . . . it has been consitent [*sic*] with the holy religion of Jesus Christ in which I remain a most firm, & humble believer.[2]

While Charlestown and the nation rested that Sunday morning, Brown still had work to do. Until that morning, Hoyt, Griswold, and Chilton had never had an opportunity to confer with him about his case. Now they came to the jail and "were closeted" with him for three or four hours. They would have to speak for him in court the following morning and still had much to learn about his case. What did he admit—and what did he deny? What did he want them to say in his behalf—and what did he want them not to say? They had to review notes of the testimony given by the witnesses they had not heard and plan their legal theories. Only Chilton knew anything substantial about Virginia law, so the other two relied heavily on his wisdom and experience.[3]

Afternoon and evening came. It was exactly two weeks to the day since Brown and his little Provisional Army had crossed over the Potomac bridge into Harper's Ferry. The wheels of justice in Jefferson County had moved swiftly, and Brown's case would go to the jury tomorrow. Brown was a thoughtful man and must have reflected on the jumbled events of that two weeks as he lay his head back on his pillow and drifted off to sleep.

The court met promptly on Monday morning at nine o'clock. Brown was carried into the courtroom and once again laid on his cot. The newspapers reported that he looked "better than heretofore" and that his health seemed to be improving. A sense of anticipation was palpable in the crowded courtroom as Hiram Griswold rose. "May it please your Honor and Gentlemen of the Jury," he began.[4]

The Ohioan knew that he had to establish some rapport with the Virginians who were about to judge Brown's case. He told them that he had taken advantage of the delay granted on Saturday evening to "pay such attention to the case as I reasonably could," and such as would "enable me to condense my remarks within the shortest possible space." He attempted to allay the fear, common throughout the South, that Brown's attack on Harper's Ferry was promoted, or at least approved and encouraged, by people in the North. There was "no sentiment in the North," he said, "that approved of the kind of offenses charged in the indictment." He had heard that "the universal sentiment throughout the county" was that Brown should have a "fair trial." "I was rejoiced to see that sentiment echoed throughout the whole State," he said, "through your Governor, that he should have a fair trial." All of this was commendable, of course, but it begged the real question, which Griswold stated very simply: "What is meant by a fair trial?" It was not that the "mere forms of the law should be invoked," he said, because "it is well known that these forms are but the pathway to the scaffold." It was that the accused should have "not only the forms of a fair trial, but that every principle of law and justice shall be made available, and every particle of evidence introduced by himself or by the state shall get its fair weight and consideration in his behalf."[5]

Griswold reviewed the evidence and the law applicable to it. He began with the allegation that the offenses charged against Brown had all been committed "within the jurisdiction of this Court, and within the county of Jefferson, in this State." He said there had been no evidence on this point. Not one witness had stated in open court that Brown was in Jefferson County when he conducted his raid. "There has been proof that the offences said to have been committed took place at Harper's Ferry," the attorney observed, "or in the neighborhood of Harper's Ferry. But where is Harper's Ferry? . . . [T]his must be proved. . . . We demand, on behalf of the prisoner, that the jurisdiction be proven. We maintain that it is as necessary to do so, as to prove the firing of a gun, the seizing of a slave, or the commission of any of the acts laid in the indictment."

Griswold next addressed the charge that Brown was guilty of treason. He argued that no man could be guilty of treason unless he was "a citizen of the State or government against which the treason so alleged has been committed." If Brown was not a citizen of Virginia, he could not commit treason against Virginia. "Rebellion means the throwing off allegiance to some constituted authority," Griswold said. "But we maintain that this prisoner was not bound by any allegiance to this State, and could not, therefore, be guilty of rebellion against it.[6] Griswold's argument here was forceful, but it was not definitive, for it overlooked the possibility that Brown might have a duty of allegiance to Virginia simply because he was a citizen of the United States. The federal system had created a unified whole out of separate states, tying them together with duties and protections, rights and obligations, that all Americans shared. Griswold's argument ignored the protection that Brown was entitled to receive from the state of Virginia because he was a citizen of the United States, and the possibility that in return for that protection he might owe Virginia some duties.

Treason was sometimes said to be "levying war against the state," Griswold said. "But, gentlemen, there is a great difference between levying war and resisting authority." Men often gather together to commit crimes. In this case, Brown and his men had assembled "for the purpose of running away with slaves." It was admittedly a crime to do that. "But that is not levying war against the Commonwealth of Virginia," Griswold said. "It is simply resisting the authority of the law.[7]

Griswold's argument was a good one, but it was not perfect. When Brown came into Harper's Ferry, he had not merely resisted the authority of the state. He had tried to undermine the system of slavery that was one of the bulwarks of Virginia's legal order. He had challenged the state's most basic assumptions about its social and economic institutions. How could the jurors who now listened to Griswold speak—twelve men chosen from "remote" regions of a county in one of the great slaveholding states of the American South—soberly reflect on Brown's effort to free the slaves and conclude that it was anything other than "levying war" against Virginia?

The Ohioan next considered the pamphlet in which Brown had printed his *Provisional Constitution*. None of its provisions contemplated "overthrowing the Commonwealth of Virginia." There were countless societies, associations, clubs, and other organizations in which issues were debated, bulletins drafted, and reports issued, yet no one seriously believed that they were "miniature governments," much less crimes against the state. Brown could not be convicted of treason unless it was proved that he had "associated with others for the purpose and with the object of overthrowing and of organizing a government." If the *Provisional Constitution* proved anything at all about treason, Griswold argued that it showed an attempt to "establish a government in opposition to the Government of the United States, and not to subvert the Commonwealth of Virginia." He continued:

> All the terms used, all the officers to be appointed, have reference to a government like the United States. The pamphlet does not say what territory this association, or government, is to exercise

jurisdiction over. Its proposed empire is not defined. It has fixed
no territorial limits, and, therefore, if it means anything at all, it
alludes to the government of the whole United States in general,
and not to this state or any other in particular.[8]

Griswold next took up the charge that Brown "conspired
with slaves to rebel and make insurrection" and drew the distinction between helping slaves run away and inciting them to
rebel "against the authority of their masters." Was there any evidence that Brown had done anything more than try to help
slaves run away? Lewis Washington had testified that the slaves
showed little interest in following Brown. "Let us suppose that a
body of slaves are seeking to escape," Griswold said. "They are
aided in that attempt by a body of white men; their escape may
be effected by white men—they are pursued by the authority of
the state, their capture is attempted—they resist, and defend
themselves even to the loss of life, yet that does not constitute
rebellion—they are amenable to punishment, but not to the
penalty of rebellion."[9]

Griswold now proceeded to the charge that Brown was guilty
of murder. He pointed out that murder in the first degree might
be proved by two different kinds of evidence. First, if the evidence showed that the murder was "premeditated," it would be
murder in the first degree and punishable with death. But the
same result would apply if the evidence showed that a death was
caused "without it being the original intention of the party to
commit murder." This could happen if the accused was "at the
time in the commission of some other offense—such as rape, ar-
son, robbery or burglary." This was the so-called "felony murder" rule, deriving from the common law of crimes, and applied
even in the absence of malicious intent.[10] "If a party is engaged
in the commission of any of these crimes," Griswold said, "and
death, though not designed, ensues, then the offender is liable

to the penalty of death." But when citizens at Harper's Ferry were shot, Brown and his men "were not engaged in the commission of any of these offences." And the first death, that of the free black man, Hayward Shepherd, took place under obscure, even implausible circumstances. "The night was dark," Griswold pointed out, "and his death might have been accidental. . . . I can only say as my client says to me on this subject: 'Why should we shoot a Negro?—that was not our object.'"[11]

If Griswold's argument up to this point seemed somewhat technical—the kind of hair-splitting logic that elevated form over substance and failed to connect with jurors on an emotional level—he was now determined to show that he could appeal to the jurors' hearts as well as their brains:

> Here stands a man of whom you know something. He is a man of indomitable will, of sleepless energy of purpose, possessed of a spirit of perseverance that turns back from no difficulty, and endowed with a constitution that will endure and overcome everything. He, with all these qualities fitting him for such an enterprise, was engaged for months and months prosecuting it, and how did he succeed? Despite of all his efforts, despite these energies of mind and body which he threw into the work, and that unbending will of his which never faltered nor slept, he was able throughout the length and breadth of the United States to gather round his standard some twenty-one men both black and white. Can it be supposed, gentlemen, for a moment, that there is fear to be apprehended from such a man, who, in the zenith of his power, when he had a name in history, and when something might be hoped for the cause in which he was engaged, could only, throughout the whole country, raise twenty-one men?[12]

John Brown may not have cared much for this argument. Was Griswold saying that he was a paper tiger—a man with bold plans, great ambitions, and noble purposes, who was unable to effect his goals? Perhaps—but the argument had an emotional appeal, for it humanized Brown. He was not an all-powerful ogre who, if not stopped in his tracks here at Charlestown, would run roughshod all through the South, leaving death and destruction in his path. He was a very human man, strong by some measures, pitifully weak by others.

Griswold was now ready to close:

> I feel, gentlemen, that I have not done justice to the case; but I have said what I desired to say, situated as I am, closing simply with these remarks, which I make on behalf of my client, and at his request, that he has not a particle of exception to take to the testimony of the witnesses examined during the trial. He deems it only a wonder amid the excitement of these scenes, that the truth, as he declares it to be, should be so fully developed. He believed that the desire of one and all of the witnesses was to do him ample justice; that whenever they could speak in commendation of his humanity, in the means he had taken to spare the effusion of blood, and to preserve from harm his prisoners, they came cheerfully forward to do it. He desires, also, as the least he can do, to express his grateful thanks to Captain Simms, who voluntarily came forward from another state, because, as he said, he wished to see justice done to a brave old man. Gentlemen, with these remarks I submit the case, as far as I am concerned, into your hands.[13]

As Griswold sank into his chair, Judge Parker called on Samuel Chilton.

Chilton began by assuring the jurors that he was "one of them." "My birth and residence till within the last few years were within the State of Virginia," he said, "in the midst of those institutions of slavery by which we are surrounded. . . . I have been a resident of the District of Columbia for several years past, but I still maintain my connection with this State and practice in its courts, and I trust the day will come, before I am gathered to my fathers, that I will return to spend the remnant of my days where my youth was spent, and to mingle my dust with the soil of this State." He had "no sympathy with the prisoner at the bar," he said—he looked on him "simply as a prisoner under your law." It was his duty to prove that Brown's conviction was not warranted by law—nothing more. "Conscious that this is my duty," Chilton said, "I am determined to perform it."[14]

Chilton said that he wanted Brown to have a fair trial, but more for Virginia's sake than Brown's. "I feel that there is a settled determination not to permit a stain to rest upon the fair name of the State," he said. "That it shall not be said that any man, no matter what his crime may have been, who has been taken into the courts of law of this State, and protected under that law—that it shall not be said he was denied a full, fair and impartial trial, or convicted contrary to law."[15]

Chilton addressed the treason charges against Brown: "Now, the word treason is derived from a French word signifying betrayal. It means the betrayal of a trust. Treason means betrayal of trust or confidence, the violation of fidelity or allegiance to the Commonwealth." But how could Brown be convicted of treason against Virginia when he was not a citizen of the commonwealth? Brown owed no allegiance to Virginia because he was not a Virginian. Chilton's argument, like Griswold's, ignored the possibility that Brown might owe Virginia a duty of allegiance because he was an American citizen, and because Virginia was one of the United States, a member of the federal union protected by the Constitution.

Chilton next argued that there was no proof that Brown was guilty of murder. The indictment alleged that Brown and the other prisoners had murdered four men at Harper's Ferry, but it did not specify which of them murdered which men. And the testimony elicited by the prosecution failed to answer this critical question. Whom did the prosecution claim that Brown had murdered? Whom had Stevens murdered? Whom had Edwin Coppoc and Shields Green and John Copeland murdered, if anyone at all? They had come into Harper's Ferry merely to free the slaves. "I grant, for the sake of argument," Chilton said, "that these men had assembled with a criminal purpose; that they were seeking to accomplish a criminal purpose with reference to those slaves. But it was not necessarily a part of their purpose that they should commit murder in effecting that object. There was no proof whatever that they entertained a desire to commit murder." When Brown's men took Lewis Washington and John Allstadt and their slaves into custody, they had no intention of murdering anyone. To the contrary, Brown's efforts to protect Washington and Allstadt during the siege of the engine house showed that he intended to free the slaves "without bloodshed."

There had been no proof that Brown and his men "resisted any process issued against them as violators of authority of the Commonwealth." If Brown and his associates had resisted any governmental authority, Chilton said, it was the authority of Robert E. Lee and the marines who stormed the engine house at Harper's Ferry. They were federal officers. If Brown's resistance was any crime at all, it was not treason against Virginia, but "treason against the United States, in seizing the property, and in resisting the constituted authorities of those States."[16] Chilton's contention was valid—up to a point. Although Brown had ultimately been subjected by U.S. marines, Virginia state militiamen had attempted to subject him before that. He had not merely resisted federal authority in Harper's Ferry—he had openly fought against state officials who had attempted to bring peace to the town.

Chilton had carefully examined the pamphlet containing Brown's *Provisional Constitution* and regarded it as a "ridiculous, nonsensical production." "Why, gentlemen," he exclaimed, "it could only have emanated from the brain of a man of unsound mind." "The government and constitution spoken of define no territory over which it is to have sovereignty, no property which it will protect. It specifies no place as the seat of power, but it merely says, in the words of the pamphlet, that slavery is a great evil."[17] This did not show an intention to commit treason, Chilton argued, but merely that a group of men had "associated together as other companies do for specific purposes, such as we see railroad and other companies associate together." "They came here to free the slaves," Chilton said. "That was their only object." He referred specifically to the section of the *Provisional Constitution* stating that "it was no part of their object to interfere with existing governments." "Now this is in the very document given in evidence," Chilton said, "and upon which I understand the prosecution relied to establish this setting up of a government within the limits of the State."[18] The prosecution's own evidence contradicted its claim that Brown intended to establish a government in opposition to the government of Virginia.

Chilton next addressed the specifics of the murder charge against Brown. Hayward Shepherd, the baggage master, had been killed under such ambiguous circumstances that it was impossible to determine who had shot him or for what purpose. Perhaps his death was nothing more than an accident. While Brown and his men were in the engine house with their hostages, they "begged and earnestly remonstrated with the citizens not to fire lest they should injure their own friends," but the townspeople continued to fire at them. "Here in the midst of this wild, unbridled excitement a conflict ensued—a conflict which the prisoner at the bar endeavored to avoid, for the purpose of saving human life; and shots were fired at random and were returned at random. . . . Who could perfectly tell, in the maelstrom of lawless frenzy and tumult, while the tempest was raging around, when lives were not only imperiled, but sacrificed, and homicides were the result of indiscriminate firing, by whom the shots were fired that caused death? . . . I cannot think that the law requires a man under such circumstances not to return the deadly fire of his assailants in self-defense. The people of Harper's Ferry ought not to have fired upon Brown and his men under these circumstances. It must have been manifest to everyone that if a little time had been allowed—if this attack had not been made, the prisoner and his associates would now be in the custody of the law without bloodshed and without the sacrifice of life."[19]

Chilton concluded with a plea that the jurors base their decision solely on the laws of the Commonwealth of Virginia and not on passions or fears. If the laws governing the guilt or innocence of an accused criminal could not be "upheld in integrity and truth and independence," Chilton argued, dire consequences would ensue:

> Then, farewell to all the blessings of a free government, and soon will follow that which is so much dreaded—the dissolution of the Union; soon will follow a revolution of all the practices, all the precedents, of all the securities, of all the conservatism which binds us together. And property and liberty, and reputation and every interest which governments are established to preserve and protect will vanish. And soon, I say, when justice is overridden and the law laid in the dust, soon will follow all the evils I have so feebly endeavored to paint.[20]

As Chilton resumed his seat, Andrew Hunter rose to present the prosecution's closing argument. Hunter was still confident that the jury would see the case as he saw it, despite the obvious strength of Griswold's and Chilton's arguments, and he pro-

ceeded to address their points in a methodical way. He denied
any effort to excite the passions of the citizens, though he recognized that the case had stirred up emotions. Virginia found itself
in an unusual situation, and despite "all the temptations to the
contrary" it had decided to observe the requirements of the law.
Governor Wise might have declared "martial law," Hunter said,
and administered "drum-head justice," but he had elected instead to take the "high conservative ground." Virginians were
"justly proud" of the chief executive's decision not to "force this
thing beyond what prudence requires of us."[21]

Hunter next responded to the tricky jurisdictional arguments
that the defense attorneys had made. He denied that it was necessary for the prosecution to show that Brown's crimes were
committed within the territorial limits of Jefferson County, because the Code of Virginia explicitly provided that Virginia had
power to execute criminal process up to the Maryland bank
of the Potomac River. If the jurors had any doubt on this question, Hunter said that they "could read the Code for themselves." It was no answer to the indictment to argue that the
crimes were committed within the federal jurisdiction in Harper's Ferry. Hunter here made the curious assertion that "not
one murder out of the four lives taken was committed on the armory grounds."[22] But the indictment clearly alleged that five
men were killed in Harper's Ferry—Hayward Shepherd, George
Turner, Thomas Boerley, Fontaine Beckham, and Luke Quinn
—not four, as Hunter argued. And of these five men, Marine
Private Quinn was clearly shot in the federal enclave. Beckham
may also have been on federal territory when he was shot down
—the evidence on this point was murky—and Hayward Shepherd was shot on the Potomac bridge, which was beyond the
low water mark on the Virginia side and thus within Maryland's
jurisdiction. Hunter was bending the evidence almost to the

breaking point to show that all of this clearly happened within the jurisdiction of Virginia.

Hunter next addressed the charge of treason and the defense assertion that Brown couldn't be prosecuted for treason against Virginia because he wasn't a citizen of the state. He began by insisting that Brown was in fact a citizen of Virginia, despite Griswold's and Chilton's claims to the contrary, because, when he came to Harper's Ferry, he intended to "reside and hold the place permanently."[23] A "resident" is generally deemed to be any person who permanently resides in, or makes his or her domicile in, a particular place, and under the Code of Virginia, "all free white persons" who were born in Virginia or thereafter became residents were deemed citizens of the state.[24] It required no legal formality to become a citizen of Virginia. Merely moving to the state would be sufficient (providing, of course, that the person was free and white). But what evidence was there that this is what Brown intended to do when he crossed the Potomac River to Harper's Ferry on the night of October 16, 1859? It is true that when Governor Wise first questioned Brown in the paymaster's office in Harper's Ferry he asked him where he intended to set up his "provisional government," and Brown answered, "Here, in Virginia where I commenced operations."[25] Other evidence, however, indicated that Brown had intended to confiscate the federal arms in Harper's Ferry, gather slaves around him, and then withdraw into the mountains— whether in Virginia or in neighboring Maryland was unclear. Did this show an intention to hold Harper's Ferry permanently? To become a resident and thereby to become a citizen of the state?

Hunter's next argument was stronger. He asserted that Brown was subject to prosecution for treason against Virginia because he was a citizen of the United States and, as a citizen of the United States, he owed a duty to Virginia. Hunter said:

The Constitution of the United States provides that citizens of
each state shall be entitled to all the immunities of citizens of the
several states. Brown came here with the immunities given by
the Constitution. He did not come divested of the responsibilities belonging to those immunities. Let the word treason mean
breach of trust, and did he not betray that trust with which, as a
citizen, he is invested when within our borders? By the federal
Constitution, he was a citizen when he was here.[26]

Hunter was referring here to the privileges and immunities
clause of the U.S. Constitution, which provides that "the citizens of each state shall be entitled to all privileges and immunities of citizens in the several states."[27] This is one of the most
important, though little understood, provisions of the Constitution. Its immediate effect is to prohibit individual states from
discriminating against citizens of other states. It guarantees that
a citizen of one state who goes to another will be entitled in the
other state to the same privileges and immunities (or fundamental rights) that the other state accords its own citizens.[28] In this
way, it guarantees a uniform level of citizenship in the different
states—what Justice Story called a "general citizenship."[29] Alexander Hamilton recognized the pervasive importance of the
privileges and immunities clause when he wrote that it could be
"esteemed the basis of the Union."[30] It may not be too much to
ask those who enjoy the benefits of the general citizenship guaranteed by the clause to refrain from "levying war" (or committing any other treasonous acts) against the states that confer
those benefits.[31] The duty of an American citizen not to commit
treason against the individual states may well be regarded as the
equivalent of a duty of allegiance to them. Brown, after all, was
as much a citizen of the United States in Virginia as he had been
in Maryland or Connecticut or Ohio or New York, or in any of
the other states he passed through in his eventful life. As a citi-

zen of the United States, he was entitled in Virginia to all of the privileges and immunities that Virginia accords its own citizens. The argument that Andrew Hunter based on the privileges and immunities clause was not elaborated at any length,[32] and much of it was left to conjecture and speculation. But its import was clear enough.[33] Brown enjoyed the privileges and immunities of citizenship when he was in Virginia, and those privileges and immunities carried with them a duty of loyalty to Virginia and obedience to its laws.[34] Echoing Hamilton's characterization of the privileges and immunities clause as the basis of the Union, Hunter declared that the "bond of Union" formed by the Constitution had allowed Brown "to come into the bosom of the Commonwealth." But Brown had come there "with the deadly purpose of applying the torch to our buildings and shedding the blood of our citizens." And, Hunter added, "that bond of Union . . . may ultimately prove a bad bond to us in the South."[35]

Hunter's last reference was a clear allusion to the possible dissolution of the United States itself—to the secession of the Southern states from the Union and their establishment of a separate and independent government. It was a threat the jurors would have no difficulty in understanding, for Southerners had made it over and over in years past, and they would continue to make it with greater frequency in the months ahead. Raised in John Brown's trial, the threat carried an obvious and ominous implication: if Brown was not convicted here in Charlestown, in the courtroom of Judge Richard Parker of the Circuit Court of Jefferson County, the Union itself was imperiled. The country might shatter. The sections could go their own ways, and civil war might well be the result.

Hunter continued his argument by answering Griswold's and Chilton's claim that Brown's *Provisional Constitution* did not set up a "government" in opposition to that of Virginia; that it really did no more than specify the rules for a private association or club. Brown's Provisional Government was the "real thing," Hunter said, "and no debating society, as his counsel would have us believe. . . . The whole document must be taken together. The property of slaveholders was to be confiscated all over the South, and any man found in arms was to be shot down. Their conduct at Harper's Ferry looked like insanity, but there was too much method in Brown's madness. His purposes were too well matured, and he and his party declared there were thousands in the North ready to join them."

Hunter scoffed at the suggestion that Hayward Shepherd may have been shot by mistake or that Brown could not have killed him because he was a black man and Brown had no "object" to kill blacks. He similarly discounted the claim that Brown's gunfire was defensive and was directed only against armed men. "Beckham was killed when unarmed," he reminded the jurors. He emphasized the felony murder rule, arguing that it was an adequate basis for finding Brown guilty of murder. "If the party perpetrating a felony undesignedly takes life," Hunter argued, "it is a conclusive proof of malice." "If Brown was only intending to steal Negroes, and in doing so took life, it was murder with malice."[36]

Hunter concluded his argument at 1:30 in the afternoon. It had been four and a half hours since the attorneys' arguments began. During that whole time, Brown continued to lie on his back, as the newspapers reported, "with his eyes closed."

It was time now for the jurors to begin their real work. Chilton asked Judge Parker to instruct them that, if they believed that Brown "was not a citizen of Virginia, but of another State," they could not convict him of treason. Parker refused. He did not agree with Chilton's reading of the law, and he thought Andrew Hunter had it right. "The Constitution did not give rights and immunities alone," Parker said, "but also imposed responsibilities." Chilton then asked the judge to instruct the jury that they "must be satisfied that the place where the offense was committed was within the boundaries of Jefferson County." Parker agreed and gave that instruction.[37]

The jurors now retired to the jury room to deliberate. The trial had been short, but there had been a good deal of testimony, and the legal issues were complex. Did Virginia have jurisdiction over the crimes alleged in the indictment? Was Brown properly subject to prosecution for treason against the Commonwealth, despite the fact that he was not a citizen of Virginia and despite the fact that his raid took place almost entirely on federal land in Harper's Ferry? Did Brown show any malice against the people of Harper's Ferry when he and his men fired their guns? Were they merely shooting in self-defense? Was there any credible evidence that Brown shot anybody at all? There were many questions, and the answers to the questions were heavy with implications—first for Brown, second for the future of slavery in Virginia and the rest of the slaveholding states of the American South, and finally for the future of the American Union.

But the twelve freeholders from Jefferson County, more than half of whom were prosperous slave owners, did not seem to regard the case as difficult. They deliberated only three-quarters of an hour before returning to the courtroom and informing Judge Parker that they had reached a verdict. The newspapers reported:

> At this moment the crowd filled all the space from the couch inside the bar, around the prisoner, beyond the railing in the body of the court, out through the wide hall and beyond the doors. There stood the anxious but perfectly silent and attentive populace, stretching head and neck to witness the closing scene of Old Brown's trial. It was terrible to look upon such a crowd of human

faces, moved and agitated with but one dreadful expectancy—to let the eyes rest for a moment upon the only calm and unruffled countenance there, and to think that he alone of all present was the doomed one, above whose head hung the sword of fate.[38]

If the reporter's prose was emotional, he may be excused. It was an emotional moment—one like none other, perhaps, in the young history of the American Republic.

The jurors took their seats. The court clerk reviewed the offenses alleged in the indictment and then said:

"Gentlemen of the Jury, what say you, is the prisoner at the bar, John Brown, guilty or not guilty?"

The jury foreman, John C. Wiltshire, answered:

"Guilty."

"Guilty of treason, and conspiring and advising with slaves and others to rebel and murder in the first degree?"

Wiltshire answered:

"Yes."

The courtroom was jammed with hundreds of spectators, but they were all silent. "Old Brown himself, said not even a word," the newspaper reported, "but, as on any previous day, turned to adjust his pallet, and then composedly stretched himself upon it."[39]

10

THE SENTENCE

Dramatic though it was, the announcement of the verdict did not mark the end of the trial. If they were to save Brown from the gallows, Griswold and Chilton and Hoyt still had work to do. And even if they were not, they owed it to their reputations as zealous advocates to assert every right, insist on every privilege, and demand every concession that the laws of Virginia afforded him.

As soon as the jury was discharged, Chilton rose to present a motion for arrest of judgment. This was the customary vehicle by which defense attorneys challenged errors in the trial. If the indictment had not been properly drafted or presented, if the jury had not been properly chosen or sworn, if the judge had made erroneous rulings on the admissibility of evidence, or if any of a hundred other serious errors affecting the justice of the proceedings and the legal validity of the verdict had been committed, they could be brought to the court's attention by motion for arrest of the judgment. The motion was made before sentence was passed to give the judge the opportunity to correct the errors if they were correctable and, if not, to order the sheriff to summon a new venire of jurors and to commence a new trial.

Chilton was ready to proceed with his motion, but the judge and the other attorneys were not ready to hear it. They were exhausted by the work of the morning and the hectic pace they had been following for the previous week. In addition, Parker, Harding, Hunter, Griswold, and Hoyt had other important business looming. A new jury was being convened to try John Brown's lieutenant, Edwin Coppoc, and Griswold and Hoyt had agreed to act as his defense counsel. So Parker announced that Chilton's motion would be taken up the next day, while he tended to the business of Coppoc's trial. John Brown was again taken back to jail.

The court convened at ten o'clock on Tuesday, November 1. Griswold was on hand now to argue the motion for arrest of judgment that Chilton had presented the previous day. He began with the somewhat surprising assertion that it had not been proved "beyond a doubt that Brown was even a citizen of the United States," much less a citizen of Virginia. It had certainly been assumed all during the trial that Brown was a U.S. citizen (in fact, of course, he was), but was it possible that no evidence had actually been offered on that point? And if there had been none, was Brown's conviction therefore invalid? Griswold next argued that "treason could not be committed against a state, but only against the general [federal] government." For this point, the newspapers reported, Griswold cited one of the writings of Justice Story. This was probably Story's influential *Commentaries on the Constitution*, first published in 1833, which asserted that a state could not "take cognizance [of], or punish the offense" of treason against the United States. But Griswold may have misunderstood Story, for Story explicitly left open the possibility that a state could punish treason "exclusively against itself." Story did express some doubt whether there could ever be a treason against a state which was not "at the same time treason against the United States," but he did not rule out such a possibility.[1] In fact, there had been prosecutions for treason against individual states in Story's own lifetime, though they were very rare. Griswold next argued that the indictment had improperly joined several distinct offenses and that the verdict was defective because it was not on each count separately. It was a general verdict, not revealing which of the four counts the jury had considered and really found Brown to be guilty of.[2] Finally, Griswold argued that the jury had not found Brown guilty of offenses charged in the indictment but of other offenses entirely. They had found him guilty of murder in the first degree even though the indictment did not charge him with that offense.[3]

Hunter answered Griswold with a figurative wave of his hand. He said blandly that "technicalities should not arrest the administration of justice"; that Virginia had shown that it had jurisdiction over treason when it "passed a law assuming that jurisdiction, and defining what constitutes that crime"; and that all the rest of the points raised by the motion for arrest of judgment were without merit.[4] Hunter did not belabor his argument— he did not have to. He was addressing a sympathetic judge. The jury had taken only forty-five minutes to dispose of all of Chilton's and Griswold's arguments, and Parker should not take much more time to dispose of Griswold's plea to arrest the judgment.

But the judge had other important business to attend to before he could rule. The jury had been chosen in Coppoc's case, and he now had to preside over Coppoc's trial. So he announced that he would reserve his decision on the defense motion until the following day, while he proceeded with Coppoc. With that, Brown was again taken back to the jail.

Coppoc's trial resumed on Wednesday morning. It was not difficult for Harding or Hunter to present the evidence against the young Quaker. It was much the same as that presented in Brown's trial. The same witnesses were called up, and they repeated the same testimony. The legal arguments made by the defense and the responses of the prosecution were all familiar to Judge Parker. Quietly but firmly, he disposed of them all. The defense attorneys called no witnesses of their own, apparently content to rely on their cross-examination of the prosecution's witnesses. Griswold asked for several instructions to the jury, which Parker granted. The attorneys presented their arguments, which everybody agreed were learned and logical. Parker then gave his instructions, and the jury retired to the jury room to deliberate.

While Coppoc's jury was out, John Cook was brought over from the jail. Once Brown's right-hand man, Cook had been chastened by his capture in Pennsylvania and his forcible return to Jefferson County, and since his arrival in Charlestown he had been busy writing out a long and detailed "confession" of his role in the Harper's Ferry business. He had been Brown's "advance man" in Harper's Ferry, moving there more than a year before Brown himself arrived in nearby Maryland, gathering information about the town and the federal facilities there, even taking a local girl for a bride. Now he was regarded with special hatred by the people of Jefferson County—and understandably so, for they had accepted him as one of their own, and he had betrayed them. For his part, Governor Wise regarded him as "the worst of all these villains."[5] Brown, too, developed a contempt for Cook when he learned that he planned to confess. It happened that Cook had some high and very respectable connections in Indiana. His sister, Matilda, was married to Ashbel P. Willard, the governor of that state. A Democrat who was friendly toward slavery and slaveholding interests, Willard was aghast when he learned that his wife's younger brother had joined the abolitionist forces of "Osawatomie Brown." Mrs. Willard, too, was distressed, for she had lost contact with her brother for several years and, until she saw his name in the newspapers, supposed that he was dead. Governor Willard boarded a train for Charlestown to counsel his brother-in-law. He brought with him his state's attorney general, Joseph E. McDonald, and the U.S. district attorney for Indiana, a brilliant young lawyer from Terre Haute named Daniel W. Voorhees. Only thirty-two years old, Voorhees had already acquired a reputation as one of Indiana's finest courtroom advocates, although he had strongly racist views that led him to regard blacks with contempt and abolitionists with a kind of fury. When he, McDonald, and Governor Willard went to the Charlestown jail to meet Cook, they brought Senator Mason along. Mason offered to leave the room so the lawyers could confer with their client in private, but they insisted that he remain. They had nothing to hide from the champion of Virginia's old slaveholding aristocracy. They told Cook he should confess, "to exonerate those who were innocent, and to punish those who were implicated," and he agreed to do so.[6] While Coppoc's jury was deliberating, Cook appeared before the magistrates in the courthouse and waived his preliminary examination. It took only a few minutes for him to surrender this valuable procedural right and speed his case along to trial.[7] Voorhees agreed to act as his attorney. Willard, McDonald, and Voorhees all hoped, as the *New York Herald* reported, that if Cook made "a clean breast of it," he might, through Willard's influence with Governor Wise, "have some hope for his life."[8]

It was evening when the jail guards brought Brown into the courtroom. It had been two weeks since he was wounded in Harper's Ferry, and he had healed well enough to make the short trip from the jail to the courthouse on his own feet. But a reporter for the *New York Tribune* noted that he "walked with considerable difficulty," and that "every movement appeared to be attended with pain." The courtroom had been half empty earlier in the day, but now it filled with a throng of spectators eager to catch another glimpse of the accused man. Voices in the crowd murmured reproofs and denunciations: "Damned black-hearted villain! Heart as black as a stove pipe!" Brown paid no attention as he took a seat near his attorneys, rested his head on his right hand, and sat for a moment motionless. The gaslights that hung from the ceiling were burning, and they "gave an almost deathly pallor to his face."[9]

The scheduled business was the defense motion for arrest of the judgment. The judge had considered all of the arguments Griswold had presented on the motion and found them insufficient. The objection that a man could not be convicted of treason against a state was invalid, he ruled, for treason may be committed "wherever allegiance is due." Parker noted that most of the states had passed laws against treason. Certainly they would not have done this if the states could not prosecute treason. Griswold's objection to the form of the verdict was also insufficient.[10]

Years later, Judge Parker explained that he had intended to rule on the defense motion as soon as he opened court that morning. He had prepared an opinion the previous night in which he set forth his reasons for rejecting Griswold's arguments, and he had intended to read it. But since Coppoc's jury had not yet reached a decision, and since anything he might say in response to the motion might affect Coppoc's verdict, he decided to withhold his opinion. As he explained, "By the Virginia practice, a jury in a criminal case were held to be judges of the law as well as triers of facts, and I would do nothing to prejudice this their right." With the case safely in the jury's hands, Parker felt free to make his ruling and read his opinion. The motion for arrest of judgment was denied.[11]

While the judge read his decision, Brown sat "very firm," the *Tribune* writer said, "with lips tightly compressed." He seemed "like a block of stone." When the judge finished, the clerk ordered Brown to stand and "say why sentence should not be pronounced upon him." He rose, leaned lightly forward, and rested his hands on the table in front of him.[12]

It is not clear how much preparation he had given to the

statement he was now about to make. In a letter he later wrote to Andrew Hunter, he claimed that he was not ready for the clerk's order when it came. "I was taken wholly by surprise," he wrote, "as I did not expect my sentence before the others." He thought that he and his fellow prisoners would all be sentenced at the same time, after the last of their trials was concluded. It was a reasonable expectation, although not required by Virginia law or practice. Some of the spectators in the courtroom thought he seemed nervous and distraught when he stood up. The *Tribune* writer thought that he spoke "timidly—hesitatingly, indeed—and in a voice singularly gentle and mild."[13] Two days later, Cleon Moore, a young deputy county clerk, wrote David Strother, the writer and artist for *Harper's Weekly,* that Brown appeared "composed." The *Baltimore Sun* reported that he spoke "in a clear, distinct voice."[14] And Judge Thomas Russell of Boston, who had arrived in Charlestown just in time to witness the courtroom scene, said that Brown spoke "with perfect calmness of voice and mildness of manner." "His self-possession was wonderful," Russell added, "because his sentence, at this time, was unexpected, and his remarks were entirely unprepared."[15]

Brown's words were carefully transcribed by the newspaper reporters as he spoke:

I have, may it please the Court, a few words to say.

In the first place I deny everything but what I have all along admitted, of a design on my part to free slaves. I intended certainly to have made a clean thing of that matter, as I did last winter when I went into Missouri, and there took slaves without the snapping of a gun on either side, moving them through the country, and finally leaving them in Canada. I designed to have done the same thing again on a larger scale. That was all I intended. I never did intend murder or treason, or the destruction of property, or to excite or incite the slaves to rebellion, or to make insurrection.

I have another objection, and that is that it is unjust that I should suffer such a penalty. Had I interfered in the manner in which I admit, and which I admit has been fairly proved—for I admire the truthfulness and candor of the greater portion of the witnesses who have testified in this case—had I so interfered in behalf of the rich, the powerful, the intelligent, the so-called great, or in behalf of any of their friends, either father, mother, brother, sister, wife or children, or any of that class, and suffered and sacrificed what I have in this interference, it would have been all right; every man in this court would have deemed it an act worthy of reward rather than punishment.

This Court acknowledges, too, as I suppose, the validity of the law of God. I see a book kissed, which I suppose to be the Bible, or at least the New Testament, which teaches me that all things whatsoever I would that men should do to me I should do even so to them. It teaches me, further, to remember them that are in bonds as bound with them. I endeavored to act up to that instruction. I say I am yet too young to understand that God is any respecter of persons. I believe that to have interfered as I have done, as I have always freely admitted I have done, in behalf of His despised poor, is no wrong, but right. Now, if it is deemed necessary that I should forfeit my life for the furtherance of the ends of justice, and mingle my blood further with the blood of my children and with the blood of millions in this slave country, whose rights are disregarded by wicked, cruel and unjust enactments, I say let it be done.

Let me say one word further. I feel entirely satisfied with the treatment I have received on my trial. Considering all the circumstances, it has been more generous than I expected; but I feel

It was quickly pointed out that Brown's speech was not strictly factual, and, just as quickly, he was accused of "lying."[17] He said he had taken slaves out of Missouri "without the snapping of a gun on either side," and that was not true, for one slaveholder had been killed when Brown rescued the Missouri slaves in 1858. But in the excitement of the moment in the Charlestown courthouse, he may have forgotten exactly how he had managed the Missouri foray; perhaps he regarded it as relatively unimportant, at least as compared to what later happened in Virginia. He also said that when he came into Harper's Ferry, he "never did intend murder, or treason, or the destruction of property, or to excite or incite slaves to rebellion, or to make insurrection." This denial was only partly true. He may have thought that he could make off with slaves from Harper's Ferry and its environs, help them organize themselves, rendezvous with them in the nearby mountains, and provide refuge for the other slaves who could be expected to join them in freedom, without any killing or destruction of property. But this was a naïve dream. He should have known that slaveholders who were taken out of their homes at gunpoint and armory workers who were held as hostages in an engine house would resist his impositions. They would have summoned help and welcomed it when it came; they would have fought to establish their rights as free men and property holders. To expect them to peaceably acquiesce in his demands, to stand quietly by while he made off with their slaves, was wildly unrealistic. Andrew Hunter later charged that Brown's claim that he came to Virginia "simply to stampede slaves, not to shed blood," was inconsistent with statements he made to Governor Wise when he first spoke to him in Harper's Ferry.[18] When Hunter called the point to his attention, Brown seemed embarrassed. In a letter he wrote Hunter after the trial, he attempted to explain the "confliction" by saying that, in the "hurry of the moment" in the courtroom, he had forgotten much that he intended to say and "did not consider the full bearing of what I then said."[19]

It is undeniable that Brown made misstatements in his courtroom speech. Given the circumstances under which he spoke, it was almost inevitable that he would. But he was not *lying*, for a *lie* is an intentionally false statement made for the purpose of deception and fraud. Brown's Charlestown speech was neither deceptive nor fraudulent, merely imperfect. That he got so much right and so little wrong is in itself remarkable. He was not trying to deceive his listeners. He was not deliberately misstating his record or his purposes. On the contrary, he was admitting enough to confirm his guilt under the laws of Virginia, acknowledging that his "design" was to free the slaves, his purpose "to remember them that are in bonds." He had admitted this all along.

If he admitted his guilt under the Commonwealth's laws, he denied it under "the law of God." His reference to the holy book he saw kissed during the trial (no doubt when oaths were taken by witnesses and jurors) introduced a "higher law" into the Charlestown courtroom. He recited the Golden Rule, which had been his moral compass for most of his life, and declared that, in interfering with the institution of slavery in Virginia, he was confident that he "did no wrong, but right." And as his penalty for doing that "right," he was now willing to "mingle" his blood with the blood of his own sons (Frederick Brown, killed in "Bleeding Kansas," and Watson Brown and Oliver Brown, killed in Harper's Ferry) "and with the blood of millions in this slave country whose rights are disregarded."

Brown showed a magnanimous spirit in the speech. Here was a man who was beaten, totally and abjectly, in his courtroom struggle, yet was willing to congratulate those who beat him. He said that he was "entirely satisfied" with the treatment he had received in his trial and that it was "more generous" than he expected. He expressed admiration for "the truthfulness and candor of the greater portion of the witnesses who have testified in this case." Brown's attorneys, who still hoped to appeal his sentence, did not share his satisfaction with the trial. He was speaking for himself, not them, offering an uncontrived reflection on the proceedings, not a self-serving declaration designed to evade responsibility and prolong the legal struggle.

The most powerful message of the speech was one that was suggested but not explicitly stated. It was implicit in Brown's words but not literally declared by them: that, on the scales of moral justice, Virginia's guilt—and the guilt of all the other slaveholding states of the American South—was the real offense against the laws of God. Slavery was the real accused in the Charlestown trial, not Brown. If he was going to pay for his transgressions with his life, the institution of slavery would in time pay for its own transgressions. It, too, would die, not as a result of the Charlestown verdict, but in spite of it; not because Brown violated Virginia's "wicked, cruel, and unjust enactments," but because Virginia violated the considered judgment of Americans and, ultimately, of mankind.

The time had now arrived for Judge Parker to pronounce sentence. There was never any doubt that Brown would be hanged, for the crimes he was convicted of were all capital offenses, but the judge had some discretion to decide when, where, and how the hanging would take place. In the courts of Virginia, it was considered the "better practice" for the judge to announce the sentence immediately after the trial. This was "calculated to have a better and more lasting effect upon the audience, in whose minds the crime and its punishment are thus immediately connected." Passing sentence immediately after the trial was "always observed in the case of treason and murder."[20] The Virginia statutes provided that a sentence of death "shall not be executed sooner than thirty days after the sentence is pronounced."[21] But this was subject to a caveat that loomed large in Brown's case: "except for insurrection or rebellion." Since Brown stood convicted of "conspiring and advising with slaves and others to rebel," Parker could have ordered that the execution be carried out immediately. But this would not have permitted Brown's lawyers to seek appellate review of his conviction. Judgments of the circuit court could be appealed to the Supreme Court of Appeals in Richmond, but only after prescribed procedural formalities were complied with. First, a bill of exceptions had to be prepared, specifying the errors it was claimed the judge had committed. The bill then had to be certified by the clerk as correct, signed by the judge, and taken to Richmond. Finally, a petition for writ of error had to be prepared, incorporating all the legal arguments and authorities that defense counsel relied on to seek a reversal of the trial judgment. Virginia officials, from the governor on down to the prosecuting attorneys in Charlestown, had repeatedly assured Brown that he would receive a "fair trial." Denying him the opportunity to seek appellate review of his conviction would mock the promise of fairness. So Parker decided that he would order Brown's hanging to be delayed for thirty days. One of the leading men of Jefferson County got advance word of the judge's intention and pronounced it a terrible mistake. He predicted that there would be a "grave tumult" in the courtroom and that the people "would tear Brown to pieces before he could be taken from the building." Parker heard this and warned the jailer to be on guard for any effort to interfere with the orderly process of the court. But the judge made clear that soldiers were not to be admitted to the courtroom, for he had a "righteous repugnance" against armed men in a court of justice.[22]

The courtroom was quiet when the last words of Brown's speech were pronounced. Parker waited for a moment and then addressed Brown with the following words:

> John Brown, you have been charged with three several and dis-
> tinct offenses of the deepest originality—with the attempt to
> subvert by force the institution of slavery as established in this
> State; with advising slaves in rebellion against the authority of
> their owners; and with the willful, deliberate and premeditated
> murder of several of our citizens who, as was their duty, opposed
> the execution of these unlawful purposes, and for so doing were
> shot down by the party under your command. For each of these
> offenses the law provides the penalty of death, and now it only
> remains for me, as the minister of the law, to pronounce judg-
> ment upon you. Not a reasonable doubt can exist as to your guilt
> of each and every one of these offenses. Your own repeated ad-
> missions, and all the other evidence in the case, fully sustain the
> verdict that has been rendered. I deem it unnecessary to recapit-
> ulate any portion of this evidence, for every part of it, that ad-
> duced by yourself, as well as that introduced by the prosecution,
> contributes to prove that you had come with your followers into
> this county determined to carry into execution by force the un-
> lawful purpose of liberating the Southern slaves.
>
> You have been defended by counsel of marked ability, the jury
> gave their patient consideration to every argument addressed to
> them in your behalf.
>
> You have had the protection and benefit of every principle of
> law and of every privilege secured to persons accused of crime
> and of every indulgence in making your defense that could rea-
> sonably be extended to you, and yet you have been found by an
> impartial jury of your countrymen to be guilty of the offenses
> charged against you.
>
> In mercy to our own people—to protect them against similar

invasions upon their rights—in mercy and by way of warning to the infatuated men of other States who, like you, may attempt to free our negroes by forcing weapons into their hands, the judgment of the law must be enforced against you.

The execution of that judgment will be delayed a sufficient time to enable you to apply to the Supreme Appellate tribunal of this State for its decision upon the errors which are alleged by you and your counsel in the proceedings against you. This is a right secured to you by our law, and it is my duty to see you are not deprived of it.

The sentence of the law is that you, John Brown, be hanged by the neck until you are dead, and that execution of this judgment be made and done upon you by the Sheriff of this County, on Friday, the second day of December next, between the hours of nine in the forenoon and four in the afternoon of the same day. And the court being of opinion that for the sake of the example set the execution (and all our dealings with the accused be done in open day and before all men) of this sentence should be in public, it is therefore ordered that this judgment be enforced and executed not in the jail yard, but at such public place as is used for this purpose or at such other public place convenient thereto, as the said Sheriff may select.

And may God have mercy on your soul.[23]

When the sentence was pronounced, one man in the crowd "clapped his hands jubilantly."[24] His demonstration was greeted by frowns throughout the chamber. Judge Russell of Boston, who was in the audience, later wrote that the offender was an "excited man" whom Parker instantly ordered into custody. "It illustrates the character of the people," Russell said, "that several officials and members of the bar hastened to inform us that this man was not a citizen of the county."[25] Decorum was important in Virginia, and if it was breached the people did not want it to be by one of their own. Mindful of the threats against Brown, Parker ordered all of the spectators to remain seated until the accused man left the courtroom. Accompanied by his guards, Brown was led across the street into the jail. This time he made the trip "without even hearing a taunt."[26]

The jurors in Coppoc's case had been out less than an hour when they returned to the courtroom with their verdict. Like the twelve men who found Brown guilty, Coppoc's jurors were all freeholders from "remote" parts of Jefferson County, all slave owners or men who sympathized with slave owners, all men who were disinclined to give any quarter to insurrectionists from the North. Nobody was surprised when they found Coppoc guilty on all charges. His attorneys announced that they would move the court for an arrest of judgment, as they had in Brown's case, and Coppoc was led back to the jail. There were now six prisoners from Harper's Ferry in confinement. Two had been found guilty, and four remained to be tried.

11

THE EXECUTION

Parker, Hunter, and Harding pushed relentlessly on with the trials of Brown's co-defendants. Immediately after Coppoc's verdict was announced, jurors were summoned for the trial of Shields Green. By this time, another young attorney had arrived from Boston, and Hoyt had gone back. George Sennott was originally from Vermont, but he had moved to Massachusetts and become a member of the Boston bar before volunteering his services on Brown's behalf. He was an outspoken foe of slavery, but unlike most New England abolitionists he was a Democrat, and Brown's Bostonian supporters thought that fact might earn him a warmer welcome in Charlestown than Hoyt had received. On his arrival in Jefferson County, Sennott immediately volunteered to represent Green.

Born in South Carolina, Green had escaped from slavery after his wife died, but he had to leave a little son behind. He eventually made his way to Rochester, where Frederick Douglass took him into his home. He met Brown for the first time in Rochester and again near Chambersburg, Pennsylvania, when he and Douglass met Brown and discussed his Harper's Ferry plans. Douglass had decided there not to have anything to do with the raid, but Green was impressed by Brown and decided to go with him.[1] Some of the witnesses who saw Green in Harper's Ferry thought he was pompous and cowardly, but others extolled his courage.[2] The evidence offered in his trial was much the same as that offered against Brown and Coppoc. There was, however, an

important difference. Because he was black, Green was subject
to a host of legal incapacities under the laws of Virginia. Sennott
was a zealous advocate and immediately proceeded to make
"many ingenious arguments" in Green's behalf. One was that
under the recent decision of the U.S. Supreme Court in *Scott v.
Sandford,* Green could not be tried for treason. Dred Scott was a
poor black man in St. Louis who sought a judicial ruling that he
had become a free man when his owner took him to live in Illinois and later in the Wisconsin Territory, both of which prohibited slavery. After losing his case in the Missouri state courts,
Scott sought to assert his rights in the federal courts. But the
pro-Southern, proslavery justices of the Supreme Court denied
his claim. The decision in *Scott v. Sandford* was handed down in
March 1857 and immediately became the subject of bitter debate. A variety of reasons were assigned for the decision, but the
most famous (or infamous) was that offered by Chief Justice
Roger Taney of Maryland. Taney said that black men were ineli-
gible to citizenship because, when the Declaration of Independence and the U.S. Constitution were adopted, persons of African descent were deemed "so far inferior that they had no rights
which the white man was bound to respect." Since Dred Scott
was not a citizen of Missouri, Taney ruled, he could not bring
suit in federal court, and thus he could not establish that he was
a free man.[3] Citing *Dred Scott,* Sennott argued that if a black
man could not be a citizen, he could not commit treason against
the Commonwealth of Virginia. The argument followed somewhat logically from Taney's *Dred Scott* pronouncement, though
it was not strictly required by it. It was strong enough, however,
to persuade Judge Parker. Since Green was not a citizen, Parker
ruled, he could not be convicted of treason, and he so instructed
the jury.

Parker's ruling on this point seemed to be inconsistent with
his earlier ruling that Brown could be tried for treason against

Virginia even though he wasn't a citizen of Virginia. If citizenship wasn't required in Brown's case, why was it required in Green's? Perhaps the answer lay in Andrew Hunter's argument that Brown was a citizen of the United States and, as such, entitled to the benefits of the privileges and immunities clause of the U.S. Constitution; and, because of those benefits, he owed allegiance to Virginia.[4] Since Green was a black man, he wasn't entitled to the benefits of the clause and thus owed no allegiance to Virginia. It is hard to determine the grounds for Parker's rulings, since they were not elaborated at any length. After the judge made his ruling, however, the jury returned with a verdict convicting Green of murder in the first degree and of advising and conspiring with slaves and others to rebel, but acquitting him of treason.[5]

John Copeland's trial followed immediately upon Green's. Unlike Green, who was described in the newspapers as a Negro (and, demeaningly, in one of the Charlestown newspapers as "a regular out-and-out tar-colored darkey"), Copeland was commonly described as a mulatto, implying that he was of mixed parentage and had a lighter complexion than Green.[6] But this made no difference for purposes of *Dred Scott*, for Taney's condemnation of Africans was broad enough to include those of "mixed" heritage. Like Green, Copeland had "no rights which the white man was bound to respect." Like Green, he was not a citizen of Virginia and could not be convicted of treason against it. Sennott repeated his *Dred Scott* argument. This time, Andrew Hunter agreed to abandon the treason charge against Copeland.[7] Copeland's verdict, like Green's, convicted him of murder and advising and conspiring with slaves to rebel, but it acquitted him of treason.[8]

John Cook's trial presented problems different from those of Green's or Copeland's. Cook was, first of all, well-connected, with a brother-in-law who was the governor of Indiana and two high-powered attorneys from that state. Cook was also a white man, but he was still hated by the people of Jefferson County because he had lived among them while he plotted with Brown. There were rumors at first that Cook would be tried in federal court rather than in Charlestown. This would have put his trial off to the following spring and given his attorneys ample time to prepare his defense. Governor Wise would have had to consent to any transfer of Cook to the federal court. He entertained the idea of doing that, despite his particular resentment of Cook's role in the Harper's Ferry raid, because he wanted Brown's Northern supporters to be subpoenaed to testify in Virginia. Since the subpoena power of the Charlestown court ended at the state's boundaries, Northern abolitionists such as Joshua Giddings of Ohio, Gerrit Smith and Frederick Douglass of New York, and Samuel Gridley Howe and Franklin Sanborn of Massachusetts were beyond its reach. But the process of the U.S. District Court for the Western District of Virginia extended all over the country. Wise was transfixed with the idea that prominent Northern opponents of slavery, including the Boston abolitionists who were now praising Brown in the newspapers, were behind the Harper's Ferry raid. He went so far as to ask Andrew Hunter to get Virginia indictments against Douglass, Howe, and Sanborn for "conspiring to cause & actually causing murder &c. in Virginia," although he knew it would be hard to get them extradited (or "requisitioned") from their home states.[9] Wise vacillated wildly on the issue of whether Cook should be tried in Charlestown or in the federal court. He told Hunter that the Harper's Ferry raid should yield at least one trial in the federal court.[10] He let it be known that he was willing to turn Cook over to the federal authorities, then reversed ground and telegraphed Andrew Hunter in Charlestown that Aaron Stevens should be turned over to the federal authorities and Cook kept for trial in Jefferson County.[11] By that time, however, Judge

Parker had already begun to try Stevens in Charlestown. George Sennott had agreed to act as his attorney, and a jury had been partially chosen. To the annoyance of Wise and Hunter, Charles Harding, who was legally empowered to make prosecution decisions for the county, insisted that Stevens's trial continue in Charlestown. Harding and Hunter engaged in a heated exchange in open court, after which Stevens consented to stand aside and wait for a federal trial while Cook's trial proceeded.[12] Hunter made clear that his purpose (and that of Governor Wise) in seeking to turn Stevens over to the federal court was to "strike at higher and wickeder game." Harding was equally clear that he wanted to keep Stevens in Charlestown to vindicate his own authority as Commonwealth prosecutor.[13]

A new indictment had to be handed down against Cook. In it, Hunter took care to allege, as he had failed to do in Brown's indictment, that Cook was a citizen of the United States and a resident of Virginia, and thus eligible to be prosecuted for treason against the Commonwealth.[14] Hunter began the trial by reading the "confession" that Cook had written in his jail cell. It was a sober recital of Cook's association with Brown from their days together in Kansas down to the Harper's Ferry raid, though it slighted Cook's role in preparing for Harper's Ferry (he claimed he knew nothing of Brown's "plan of operations" until the morning of the day the raid began) and included a vague suggestion that Gerrit Smith, Samuel Gridley Howe, Franklin Sanborn, and Thaddeus Hyatt of Kansas may have been Brown's "aiders or abettors."

Thomas Green and Lawson Botts now joined Cook's defense team, apparently unconcerned that the theory of Cook's defense was antagonistic to Brown's and that zealous representation of Cook might require them to breach their ethical obligations to Brown. Thomas Green rose in open court and admitted that Cook had joined a conspiracy to induce slaves to rebel—an allegation that Brown had denied in his memorable allocution.[15] After that, Daniel Voorhees delivered a long and impassioned argument to the jury. He praised the "proud Commonwealth of Virginia" and the "calmness," "dignity," and "impartiality" of the Charlestown court. He argued that Cook was a "misguided young man" who had fallen victim to "the despotism of an iron will" (Brown's, of course). He called Brown a "pirate and robber" and described his attack on Virginia as the "mad offspring of a loathsome fanaticism." Voorhees said that Cook was wrong to be taken in by Brown, but he had repented. Voorhees begged for sympathy for his client and argued that, because of Virginia's swift and stern response to Brown's attack, "the institution of domestic slavery today stands before the world more fully justified than ever before in the history of this or, indeed, perhaps of any other country."[16] It was the kind of peroration that, in a few years, would win Voorhees the nickname of "The Tall Sycamore of the Wabash" and a twenty-year tenure as U.S. senator from Indiana. In Charlestown, it was met with a few tears among the courtroom spectators and a prompt verdict of guilty from the jurors. But the verdict convicted Cook only of murder and advising and conspiring with slaves and others to rebel and make insurrection. It found him not guilty of treason against Virginia. Ironically, Brown had been convicted of treason, though he had been on Virginia soil only a few minutes before the raid began, whereas Cook was acquitted of the charge despite the fact that he had lived and worked in the state for more than a year, even married there.[17] It was a small victory for Cook, but potentially important, for by not convicting him of treason the jury had at least opened up the possibility that Wise would grant him clemency. It was a possibility that Governor Willard considered worth pursuing. He went to Richmond and put his case before Wise. He argued on humanitarian, legal, and political grounds. Wise was then campaigning for the Democratic nomination for president in 1860. He thought that party's presidential nominee should represent the interests and viewpoints of the South but still appeal to moderate Democrats in the North and West, and he argued that he filled those requirements better than any other candidate on the political horizon. Wise listened to Willard but held his counsel on the issue of clemency.

On November 10, Judge Parker convened the circuit court at ten o'clock in the morning and sentenced Edwin Coppoc, Shields Green, John Copeland, and John Cook to death. He ordered that all four men be executed on the same date, December 16, but specified that the two blacks be hanged in the morning and the two whites in the afternoon.[18] (Even on the scaffold, Virginia law was careful to provide separately for whites and blacks.) After sentencing the four men, Parker adjourned his circuit court and left Charlestown for his next assignment in Winchester.

While Governor Willard was pleading John Cook's cause with Wise, hundreds—eventually thousands—were pleading Brown's cause with Wise. Letters poured into Richmond begging for mercy.[19] Many argued that Brown's life should be spared on purely humanitarian grounds. Others urged political considerations. They said that execution would only make Brown a martyr in the North and thus add volatile fuel to the abolitionist cause. Yet others argued that clemency would demonstrate the civility and benevolence of Southerners. One who took the latter view was Fernando Wood, the mayor of New York, a Democrat and one of the most fervently pro-Southern politicians in the North. Wood praised the way Wise had handled Brown's case but argued that clemency would win Virginia more friends than enemies. "The South will gain by showing that it can be magnanimous to a fanatic in its power," Wood told the governor.[20] But Wise also received ugly threats from letter writers who supported Brown—or claimed to. Some were frankly outrageous. The governor was not a docile man, and the more distasteful the threats became, the more inclined he was to stand firm and permit Brown to be executed. When Brown heard that threatening letters had been sent to Wise, he was chagrined. He said he could not believe that they came from his own friends.[21]

Of course, Wise could not pardon Brown without the consent of the General Assembly.[22] He could, however, grant a reprieve (or respite) and then ask the General Assembly to approve a pardon.[23] If he did this, Brown's ultimate fate might be decided by Wise's successor, who had already been chosen and would take office in less than two months. Wise's term of office was to expire on December 31, and John Letcher's was to begin on January 1, 1860.[24] But Wise did not like to defer important decisions to others. He held the power to decide what would happen to Brown, and he was determined to exercise that power.

While the letters were pouring into Richmond, Brown's attorneys explored the possibility that Wise might grant clemency if they could prove that Brown was insane. The issue of his sanity had been dramatically raised but not finally disposed of in his trial, and, for legal purposes at least, it was still an open question.[25] On November 7, Hiram Griswold wrote the governor, enclosing a petition for clemency for Brown and an affidavit that claimed that Brown was insane. "Whether any further effort will be made to obtain Brown's pardon, or a commutation of his sentence on the ground of insanity," Griswold wrote, "I do not know. I am in communication with no person on this subject. But I avail myself of this occasion to say that my conviction is that, on questions connected with slavery and the liberation of the slave, he is insane."[26] George Hoyt visited Montgomery Blair, the Washington attorney who had arranged for Chilton to join Brown's defense team, and asked his thoughts on the sanity issue. Blair thought that "a demonstration of Brown's insanity might please Wise" and persuade him to commit him to an asylum. If Brown could be presented to the nation as a "lunatic" rather than a martyr, Blair thought the sectional storm now gathering over the nation might be quelled.[27] Hoyt traveled to Ohio and collected affidavits from nineteen persons who knew Brown. They stated that some of Brown's relatives had either been insane or were "thought at times to be insane," and that Brown himself was a "monomaniac," "deranged," or "completely insane" on the subject of slavery.[28] At first blush, the affidavits seemed to present a grim picture of a family plagued by mental disorders. On closer examination, however, they implicated families related to Brown by marriage more than his own. Much of the information stated in them was hearsay, the kind of second- or even thirdhand whispers that are often dismissed as mere gossip. And it was clear that all of the affidavits were motivated by the desire to save Brown's life. After he had gathered the affidavits, Hoyt sent them to Samuel Chilton in Washington, and Chilton forwarded them to Wise. On November 10, Wise wrote a letter to Dr. Francis T. Stribling, superintendent of the Lunatic Asylum at Staunton, ordering him to go to Charlestown and examine Brown. "If the prisoner is insane he ought to be cured," Wise wrote, "and if not insane the fact ought to be vouched in the most reliable form, now that it is questioned under oath and by counsel since conviction."[29] But Wise soon had second thoughts. He wrote "countermanded" on the back of the letter and did not send it.[30] Stribling was not summoned to Charlestown. Brown was not examined.

Brown had made his position clear during his trial. He did not want to rely on "the miserable artifice and pretext" of insanity to avoid responsibility for what he had done. He believed that what he did in Harper's Ferry was right; he was following God's law, not acting out some mad fantasy. Wise, too, had already expressed his opinion on Brown's mental condition.

"They are themselves mistaken who take him to be a madman," Wise stated after his first meeting with Brown. "He is a man of clear head, of courage, fortitude and simple ingenuousness. He is cool, collected, and indomitable."[31]

While efforts were being made to secure clemency for Brown, his attorneys were seeking judicial review of his sentence. They prepared a bill of exceptions and submitted it to Judge Parker for his signature. Chilton then assumed responsibility for petitioning the Supreme Court of Appeals, the highest appellate court of Virginia, for a writ of error. Since Chilton had important legal business in Washington, however, he secured the assistance of a Richmond attorney named William Green. The actual writing of the petition was primarily Green's work, although it bore the names of both attorneys.

The writ of error was the principal vehicle by which criminal judgments were appealed in Virginia. If a writ of error was granted, it issued from the appellate court to the inferior court, either reversing the judgment or ordering the inferior court to correct errors in it. Generally, any "mistake" in a judgment that prejudiced the accused person, or any cause that would have been sufficient to arrest the judgment, would justify issuance of the writ. This included such things as improperly refusing to postpone a trial, overruling or admitting challenges to the jury, admitting or rejecting witnesses or evidence, instructing the jury on questions of law, and refusing to give proper instructions.[32] Chilton and Green were under severe time constraints, as the date set for Brown's execution was fast approaching. They had to thoroughly research and analyze the applicable law, draft the petition and have it professionally printed, and file it with the clerk of the Supreme Court of Appeals in Richmond—all in time to give the five judges who constituted the court adequate opportunity to read it, reflect on it, and schedule oral arguments.

After all this was done, the attorneys held out hopes that the judges would issue the writ and a statement of their reasons for doing so.

The final petition, as filed in Richmond on November 18, was addressed to "the Honorable John J. Allen, President, and his associates, Judges of the Supreme Court of Appeals of Virginia." The associate judges were William Daniel, Richard C. L. Moncure, George Hay Lee, and William J. Robertson. It ran to sixteen tightly printed pages, beginning with the following words:

> Your petitioner, John Brown, humbly showeth, that in the record and proceedings, and in the giving of judgment, upon an indictment against him in the circuit court of the county of Jefferson, by which court, on the 2d day of November 1859, he was condemned and adjudged to be hanged by the neck until he be dead (a transcript of which said record accompanies this petition), manifest error hath intervened, to the great detriment of your petitioner: Wherefore he prays that a writ of error may be allowed him, to the end that the said record and proceedings may be reviewed by your honors; well hoping that for error therein the said judgment will be reversed.

The arguments of the petition focused primarily on issues related to treason. Citing treason prosecutions extending far back into the English common law, Chilton and Green argued that treason was an offense against allegiance, and that in a prosecution for treason the indictment had to allege facts showing a duty of allegiance. They quoted the words pronounced by John Marshall in *United States v. Wiltberger* (1820): "Treason is a breach of allegiance, and can be committed by him only who owes allegiance either perpetual or temporary."[33] But Brown owed no allegiance to Virginia, they argued, because he was not a citizen of that state, and the failure of the indictment to allege that he was a citizen completely removed this vital issue from the trial. No evidence was presented on the issue; the jury was not instructed on it; and the verdict contained nothing to indicate that the jury even considered it.[34]

The petition next argued that it was error for Judge Parker not to have required the prosecution to elect between the various counts of the indictment. It admitted that when an indictment included several counts, a general verdict of guilty would usually be upheld if any count was good, even if the others were "faulty."[35] But Brown's case was not usual, because treason was not an offense that was eligible for executive clemency, whereas the other alleged offenses were. Failing to require an election when one count alleged treason and failing to instruct the jury to disregard the count alleging treason put Brown "out of the reach of executive clemency." The jurors might believe him to be guilty of advising and conspiring with slaves to rebel, for example, but not of treason; but if they returned a general verdict of guilty, they would be finding him guilty of treason as well as advising and conspiring, thus removing the possibility of executive clemency. This was unjust. The applicable Virginia statute provided that the court "*may* instruct the jury to disregard any count that is faulty."[36] When a statute says that a court "*may* do what justice and right require," Chilton and Green argued, "it is the *duty* of the court so to act."[37]

The petition contained shorter arguments relating to the other offenses. The indictment and verdict were defective in their allegations of murder, it said, because they did not show whom Brown was supposed to have murdered or even if it was one or two or more persons. The indictment and verdict regarding "advising and conspiring" with slaves to rebel were similarly defective, the attorneys asserted. Who are these slaves he was supposed to have advised and conspired with?

It was a strong petition, especially in view of the fact that it was prepared in a short time, and it raised important issues. There was enough substance in it at least to bring forth a response from John Randolph Tucker, the attorney general of Virginia, who had the duty of representing the Commonwealth on criminal appeals.[38] But there was no written response to the petition; nor was there any oral argument.[39] The day after the petition was filed in Richmond, the Supreme Court of Appeals issued a short written statement denying it. The petition had been "maturely considered," the transcript of the record had been "seen and inspected," and the court was of the opinion that the judgment was "plainly right."[40] On November 19, Attorney General Tucker telegraphed Andrew Hunter from Richmond: "Brown's appeal unanimously refused."[41] The court issued no opinion, despite the mandate of the Virginia Constitution that "when a judgment or decree is reversed or affirmed by the Supreme Court of Appeals, the reasons therefor [*sic*] shall be stated in writing, and preserved with the record of the case."[42]

The denial of the writ of error left Henry Alexander Wise as Brown's last hope to evade the hangman's noose. Wise seemed to enjoy the attention that Brown's raid had focused on him and Virginia, and he was glad to answer the questions that were regularly put to him about Brown's fate. He left the door open just a crack to some gesture at clemency, although regularly denying that he had any intention of pardoning Brown or commuting his sentence. When he contemplated the prospect that Brown and the other men in the Charlestown jail now awaiting death might have to be buried in Jefferson County, he expressed displeasure. "Any who are hung ought not to have burial in Virginia," he grumbled. A few days later he wrote confidentially to Andrew Hunter that he would not reprieve or pardon any of the prisoners "after the letters I have received from the North." At the same time, his political organ, the *Richmond Enquirer,* told readers that Brown's fate "may be considered as sealed."[43] Just a few days later, however, the *New York Herald* reported that Wise was thinking of delaying Brown's execution long enough that he could be hanged on the same day as the other convicted men.[44] And on November 16 he wrote Andrew Hunter that Brown "ought to be hung between two Negroes & there oughtn't to be two days of excitement."[45]

Reports that Virginia's Senator Robert M. T. Hunter favored a commutation of Brown's sentence "as a good stroke of Southern policy" raised the possibility that Wise might waver. Both Hunter and Wise were in the race for the Democratic presidential nomination, and neither wanted to concede a political advantage to the other. "There is still a chance for Old Brown," the *Herald* commented, "when the two rival Virginia Presidential aspirants begin to quarrel over him, both looking to the North."[46] On November 21, the governor arrived in Charlestown to preside over a "grand military parade and review." After the show was finished, he went to the jail and spoke to Brown and the other prisoners. He urged them all "to prepare for death."[47] Brown replied that he was prepared. Afterward, Wise said that Coppoc was the only one of the prisoners he had ever thought of commuting, but he had now determined to hang them all. On his way back to Richmond, the governor paused in Harper's Ferry, where a man from Pennsylvania asked him if he intended to commute Brown's sentence. Brown had not asked for a pardon, Wise told the Pennsylvanian. When the Pennsylvanian retorted that he thought Brown was "a monomaniac on the subject of slavery," Wise answered that "men of that kind of insanity ought to be hanged."[48]

As the date set for Brown's execution drew near, a sense of anticipation mixed with fear fell over Jefferson County. There were frequent reports that Brown's sympathizers were gathering somewhere in the North—perhaps in Ohio, Pennsylvania, or Maryland—for a last-minute effort to rescue him.[49] Investigations failed to show any concrete evidence of such efforts, but the rumors persisted. Closer to home, there were disquieting signs that trouble might be afoot in the town and fields of the county. Barns, stables, and haystacks erupted in flames on the edges of Charlestown. Farm animals were mysteriously found dead in their pastures, as if they had been poisoned. Fields were set afire, raising an eerie glow in the night sky.[50] Authorities investigated the causes of the fires and reported that they were probably the work of abolitionists. The fact that some of the victims had served as jurors in Charlestown reinforced suspicions that Brown's supporters were behind them.[51] It is unlikely, however, that any substantial number of Northerners had been able to penetrate the line of troops and sentries that guarded the county's northern border. More likely the depredations were the work of black people in the county, some free, others slaves, who were outraged at the sentence handed down to Brown. They applauded his attack on slavery and wished that it had been successful. In the aftermath of the Harper's Ferry raid, white slaveholders went to great lengths to deny that any of their slaves had sympathized with Brown. The slaves had been dependably loyal and docile during the whole episode, they said. But this was all part of a myth that the whites sought to perpetuate. In fact, blacks in and around Harper's Ferry yearned mightily for freedom and an end to slavery, as they did elsewhere in the South. They supported Brown's goal of breaking their shackles, and were sorry that they could not have done more to help him achieve victory at Harper's Ferry. The fires that reddened the night skies around Charlestown and Harper's Ferry were probably the best they could do—at least for now.[52]

Even as they denied there was any sympathy for Brown in Jefferson County, the whites now adopted extraordinary measures to quell the "nonexistent" sympathy—and, at the same time, to make sure that surreptitious Brown supporters did not slip into Charlestown and wreak havoc. Governor Wise ordered volunteer militia units from neighboring counties—some from as far away as Richmond and Alexandria—to mass in Charlestown for Brown's execution, and he asked President Buchanan to send additional troops to Harper's Ferry, through which Northern invaders might try to enter Jefferson County. Obliging as usual, Buchanan ordered Colonel Robert E. Lee to return to the scene of his capture of Brown and guard the bridges. Lee came with more than two hundred federal artillerymen and took up positions at the entrances to the town.[53] Some volunteer militia units came in from Maryland, and towns scattered throughout Virginia sent expressions of support to Jefferson County. Men who expressed sympathy for Brown were ordered to recant and, if they refused to do so, were jailed or ordered to leave town. The *Baltimore Sun* reported that a white man in Madison County was required to give bail for "using seditious language" sympathizing with Brown and that a free black man in the same county was whipped for expressing his willingness to join his "brethren of the North" in their attack on slavery. A public meeting was convened in Rockingham County to order that a suspected Brown sympathizer leave that county immediately.[54] The town council in Lynchburg passed an ordinance establishing a curfew of 10 P.M.; anyone found on the streets later than that would be arrested, and any found in sympathy with Brown would be "committed to jail and taken care of."[55]

In Charlestown, Mayor Thomas C. Green, Brown's erstwhile defense counsel, issued a proclamation:

> *Whereas,* It is deemed prudent and right, by the Town Council of
> Charlestown, that there should no longer be permitted to remain
> in our town or county, any stranger, therefore, I, Thomas C.

Green, Mayor of Charlestown, do hereby proclaim, and make
known, that all such strangers must immediately leave the town
or county, and if they do not, any member of the Town Council,
the Town Sergeant, Col. [Lucius J.] Davis, Lawson Botts, E. M.
Asquith, Wells J. Hawks, are requested to make it their special
business to bring such strangers before the Mayor or some Justice of the Peace, to be dealt with according to law; and the authorities of Harper's Ferry, Bolivar, Shepherdstown, or Middle-
way, and all other authorities in the county are hereby requested
to take like action.

Nov. 12, 1859.

THOMAS C. GREEN

Mayor of Charlestown.[56]

Proclamation or not, visitors were still drawn to Jefferson
County. Some were Northerners who looked on the excitement
in the town with a mixture of contempt and amazement, and
others were Virginians or residents of neighboring states who
were thoroughly supportive of the local authorities and determined not to do anything to offend them.

One of the Northerners who came to Charlestown was
Edwin Brackett, a sculptor from Massachusetts who had devised
the rather bold plan of making a bust of John Brown. He di-
vulged his plan to George L. Stearns, one of Brown's financial
backers, who gave him enough money to make the train trip to
Charlestown and find a room in a local hotel. Brackett came
with letters of introduction to Andrew Hunter and Senator Mason. They greeted him courteously but made clear that they had
no intention of letting him into Brown's jail cell. They had received confidential information that Brackett was an abolitionist
and a spy, and they used every stratagem they could think of to
keep him away from Brown. The jailer, John Avis, followed
Hunter's and Mason's directives in refusing to let Brackett into

the jail. But Brackett approached the jail with Hiram Griswold while Avis was detained in the courthouse, and he persuaded an assistant jailer to let him go up to the door of Brown's cell. While Griswold went into the cell and took measurements of Brown's head and face, Brackett stood at the door and made sketches. If questioned later, Brackett could deny that he had ever been in Brown's cell. With the measurements and sketches he obtained in this way, supplemented by photographs taken elsewhere, Brackett was able to go back to Massachusetts and sculpt a marble bust that was widely admired—at least by abolitionists.[57]

Edmund Ruffin was one of the prominent Southerners who was inexorably drawn to Charlestown. A sixty-five-year-old agricultural reformer, editor, and political activist from Virginia's Prince George County, Ruffin boarded a train for Charlestown a few days before Brown's scheduled execution, eager to see for himself how the drama played out. A fervent supporter of slavery and an agitator for the cause of Southern independence, Ruffin hoped that the furor over Brown's raid and trial would lead to secession. He believed that this was almost sure to happen if Northerners overplayed their hand, mounted some kind of a military attack on Virginia, and attempted to rescue Brown. In such a case, he said, they would be "put to death like wolves," and the South would realize, as he did, that the "great mass of the people of the north . . . are more or less enemies of the South." In Charlestown, Ruffin walked the streets, his long, silvery hair hanging well below his shoulders, gathering information, stopping here and there to lecture passersby on the urgent need for the South to break its ties with the North. He found some of the pikes Brown had brought with him to Harper's Ferry. They had been looted from the Kennedy Farm after Brown was captured and were now items of curiosity. Ruffin labeled those that came into his possession with the ominous words: "Sample of the favors designed for us by our Northern Brethren." Supportive as he was of slavery, Ruffin regarded Wise as the South's "greatest demagogue" whose "inordinate vanity" had led him to a "crazy" desire for the presidency. But he instinctively condemned Brown's "diabolical" attack on Virginia and only grudging expressed admiration for his "undaunted courage." Through the agency of a friend, Ruffin managed to insinuate himself into a company of cadets from the Virginia Military Institute, ordered north from Lexington by Governor Wise to augment the formidable military establishment in Charlestown. Wise had decreed that no civilians would be allowed to witness Brown's execution, so Ruffin's "honorary" cadetship would give him temporary military status and an upfront view of the event.[58]

The Virginia Military Institute contingent at Charlestown was under the overall command of the institute's superintendent, Colonel Francis H. Smith, but it included a complement of twenty-one artillery cadets and two howitzers under Major Thomas J. Jackson, yet to be immortalized as the Confederate general "Stonewall" Jackson. Major J. T. L. Preston was detailed as quartermaster. A professor of natural and experimental philosophy at the Virginia Military Institute, Jackson was pleased by all the military activity in the town, for it had been eight years since his last service in the field.[59] When he reached his destination, he wrote his wife: "I am much more pleased than I expected to be; the people appear to be very kind. There are about one thousand troops here, and everything is quiet so far."[60]

The Richmond Grays, sometimes described as "the best drilled military company in Virginia," left for Charlestown a little before the Virginia Military Institute cadets left Lexington. A twenty-one-year-old actor named John Wilkes Booth was in Richmond at the time, preparing for a new role in the Marshall Theater. He had heard of the excitement in Charlestown and fervently sympathized with the South in its confrontation with John Brown. When he saw the Grays board a train opposite the theater, he went to the baggage car and asked to join them. He could not do so without a uniform, however, so two of the young soldiers gave him parts of theirs. When the Richmond soldiers reached Charlestown, they camped out in a field. It was an exciting time for the Grays, and for Booth, who enlivened their campfire gatherings with his brilliant histrionics.[61] The *Baltimore American* reported that the "military aspect of the town . . . was very gay, the weather being fine, and the troops availing themselves of the opportunity of making an exploration of the streets and alleys, many going beyond the suburbs." The Grays reminded the reporter of "uncaged birds, so wild and gleesome they appear." Among them was one "J. Wilkes Booth, a son of Junius Brutus Booth, who, though not a member, as soon as he heard the tap of the drum, threw down the sock and buskin, and shouldered his musket and marched with the Grays to the reported scene of deadly conflict."[62]

With all the troops in town, accommodations in hotels, boardinghouses, and private homes were at a premium, so the courthouse was hurriedly transformed from a temple of justice into a crowded barracks. Soldiers slept on the floors, stacked their arms against the walls, and set their cooking utensils on the tables and desks. The *American* reported: "The platform on which the Judge had his seat, together with all the space outside the bar occupied by the lawyers, is occupied by company F [of Richmond]. The inside of the bar is in possession of the Alexandria artillery; the large hall over the courtroom is held by the Alexandria riflemen, and the front of the upper portion of the courthouse is held by the Executive Guard. . . . You will observe by this that the courthouse is occupied by four military companies."[63] Judge Parker, whose "judicial dignity would not tolerate an armed man in Court," would not have been pleased.[64] But

Parker was busy with circuit court duties elsewhere in Virginia. He had never before seen a man hanged and was pleased that he would not see Brown meet that fate.[65]

Brown spent his last days in the Charlestown jail reading the Bible, writing letters to his family and friends, and meeting with the scores of curious men and women who came to Jefferson County to get a last glimpse of him. During all this time, he was treated with respect and kindness by the jailer, John Avis, for whom he developed affection and trust. Brown realized that if an attempt were made to rescue him, Avis and his family might get hurt or even killed, and he promised the jailer that he would make no attempt to get out. When Judge Thomas Russell of Boston came to Charlestown and asked Brown if he wanted his friends to mount a rescue attempt, Brown said he "would not walk out of jail if its doors were thrown open."[66]

On November 10, he wrote his wife, Mary Ann, expressing confidence that the sacrifices he and she had made "in behalf of the *cause we love* the *cause of God; & of humanity*" did not seem to him "at all too great." "I have been *whiped* [*sic*] as the saying *is;* but am sure I can recover all the lost capital occasioned by that disaster; by only hanging a few moments by the neck; & I feel quite determined to make the utmost possible out of a defeat."[67] On November 19, he wrote one of his cousins: "Whether I have any reason to 'be of good cheer' (or not) in view of my end; I can assure you that I *feel* so."[68] In a letter to his friend and supporter George L. Stearns, he said that he had asked "to be spared from having any *mock; or hypocritical prayers made over me,* when I am publicly murdered: & that my only *religious attendants* be *poor little, dirty, ragged, bare headed, & barefooted Slave boys; & Girls;* led by some old grey headed Slave Mother."[69] When a reporter for the Charlestown *Independent Democrat* asked him if he was ready to meet death "under the law," he answered that he was "entirely ready so far as I know."[70] When Samuel C. Pomeroy, one of his old friends from Kansas (and later a U.S. senator from that state), came to his cell, Brown greeted him with: "In prison ye came unto me." Pomeroy asked him if he wanted his friends to try to rescue him. Brown replied: "I am worth now infinitely more to die than to live."[71]

Mary Ann Brown tried to visit her husband in early November and even came as far south as Baltimore to do so, but he thought she should stay away. The scene in Charlestown would distress her too much, and she had to save her money to provide food and a home for herself and the children who still lived with her. As the execution drew nearer, however, she wrote Wise, asking that she be permitted to come to Charlestown to receive her husband's remains. The governor had earlier considered a request from a professor of anatomy in Richmond that Brown's skull and the skulls of the other condemned men be severed from their bodies and displayed in the museum of the Medical College of Virginia.[72] He now thought better of that suggestion and gave Mrs. Brown permission to come to Harper's Ferry and, from there, go to Charlestown for a last reunion with her husband, after which she would take his remains away. John and Mary Ann Brown's meeting in the jail lasted several hours. They concealed their emotions as best they could, but they were grateful for the opportunity to be together one last time.

On the day before his scheduled execution, Brown called Andrew Hunter to his cell and asked him to draft his will. Of all the attorneys in Charlestown, Hunter was the one Brown most respected, even though the prosecutor had fought hard to convict him.[73] The will that Hunter drew for Brown disposed of the condemned man's personal property in Virginia and Maryland (real property he owned in New York would have to be disposed of under the law of that state) and made special gifts to Sheriff

Campbell and John Avis—each was to receive a Sharps rifle, "or if no rifle can be had, then each a pistol."[74] Outside of his will, Brown gave a Bible to John Blessing, a Charlestown baker who had ministered to his needs (including dressing his wounds) and earned his special affection.[75]

On the morning of December 2, Brown said good-bye to his fellow prisoners and thanked Avis and Campbell for their kindness, then prepared to leave the jail for the last time. On his way out of the building, his arms bound behind his back, he kissed Avis's two-year-old son, Edward, as he was held in the arms of Mrs. Avis—not the black child he was later reported to have kissed (no blacks were allowed near the jail).[76] He also handed a note to Hiram O'Bannon, a jail guard. It read:

> I John Brown am now quite *certain* that the crimes of this *guilty land: will* never be purged *away;* but with Blood. I had as I now think: vainly flattered myself that without *very much* bloodshed: it might be done.[77]

He left the jail in an open wagon drawn by two white horses, sitting on top of a walnut coffin that had been prepared for him, with Avis and Campbell riding beside him. Three companies of soldiers marched ahead of the wagon, while others lined the route that led three blocks south and one block east to the open field in which the scaffold had been erected. In accordance with Governor Wise's orders, the fifteen hundred troops on duty formed two squares around the scaffold, one inside the other, so no civilians could get near enough to Brown to hear him if he attempted to make a last-minute speech.[78] Andrew Hunter's son, Henry, who had shot the helpless William Thompson to death during the closing hours of the Harper's Ferry raid, was stationed at the gate to the field, acting in his capacity as captain of a militia company.[79] The squares formed by the troops were lined with cavalrymen, and two cavalry officers, one on a black horse and the other on a "remarkable looking white horse," dashed to and fro inside the enclosure. Howitzers were placed at the sides of the gallows so as to sweep the field in the event of an attack. Outside the squares, soldiers were scattered here and there as rangers and scouts. It was, Major Preston said, "the greatest array of disciplined forces ever seen in Virginia."[80]

Brown climbed out of the wagon and ascended the steps to the top of the scaffold, wearing an ill-fitting suit and carpet slippers. The noose was fastened around his neck, and a hood slipped over his head. Major Preston, who stood nearby, watched Brown carefully to see if he could detect "any signs of shrinking or trembling in his person, but there was none."[81] Brown stood atop the trap door for twelve minutes while last-minute adjustments were made in the troop formations. The sheriff then asked him if he should give him a "private signal before the fatal moment." He answered that "it did not matter to him, if only they would not keep him too long waiting." Preston thought Brown's voice sounded "unnaturally natural—so composed was its tone, and so distinct its articulation."[82] At last, the sheriff swung the hatchet, severing the rope, and opening the trap door. Brown fell about three feet, and his neck snapped. A staff of surgeons was on hand to check his pulse. His heart continued to beat, at first vigorously, then more faintly, and finally not at all. When nearly forty minutes had passed, the surgeons pronounced him dead.[83]

To break the silence, Preston announced in solemn tones: "So perish all such enemies of Virginia! All such enemies of the Union! All such foes of the human race!"[84]

Edmund Ruffin witnessed the execution from about fifty yards away. During the time he waited for the trap door to open, Ruffin said that Brown "stood erect & as motionless as if he had been a statue."[85] Later, Ruffin confided to his diary that "the villain whose life has thus been forfeited, possessed but one virtue (if it should be so called,) or one quality that is more highly esteemed by the world than the most rare & perfect virtues. This is physical or animal courage, or the most complete fearlessness of & insensibility to danger & death. In this quality he seems to me to have had few equals."[86]

Major Jackson watched the execution from a distance of about forty yards. He thought the convicted man "behaved with unflinching firmness" and "ascended the scaffold with apparent cheerfulness." A religious man, Jackson offered a silent prayer for Brown's salvation and afterward wrote: "Awful was the thought that he might in a few moments receive the sentence 'Depart ye wicked into everlasting fire.' I hope that he was prepared to die, but I am very doubtful—he wouldn't have a minister with him."[87]

John Wilkes Booth stood somewhere in the vast military assembly, and later wrote: "I saw John Brown hung[.] And I blessed the justice of my country['']s laws. I may say I helped to hang John Brown and while I live, I shall think with joy upon the day when I saw the sun go down upon one trator [*sic*] less within our land."[88]

A few hours later, Preston reflected on the execution. "You may be inclined to ask, Was all this necessary? I have not time to enter upon this question now. Governor Wise thought it necessary, and he said he had reliable information. The responsibility of calling out the force rests with him. It only remained for those under his orders to dispose the force in the best manner."

"Yet the mystery was awful," Preston added. "To see the human form thus treated by men—to see life suddenly stopped in its current, and to ask one's self the question without answer, 'And what then?'"[89]

MARCHING ON

Abraham Lincoln was in Kansas on the day John Brown was executed, speaking to territorial settlers about the great issues then
facing the nation. Slavery, of course, was the greatest of these issues—Lincoln called it the "great and durable question of the
age"[1]—and he was not shy in speaking about it, or in referring
to Brown, whose name was then in the newspapers and on the
minds of Americans all over the country. Lincoln believed that
slavery was morally wrong; he had, in fact, condemned it as a
"monstrous injustice" that denied the "republican example of
its just influence in the world."[2] But he also believed that Brown
was wrong in attempting to deal with it by violent means.
Brown had shown "great courage, rare unselfishness," Lincoln
admitted. "But no man, North or South, can approve of violence or crime."[3] After news of Brown's hanging reached Kansas, Lincoln spoke in Leavenworth. "Old John Brown has just
been executed for treason against a state," he told his audience.
"We cannot object, even though he agreed with us in thinking
slavery wrong. That cannot excuse violence, bloodshed, and
treason."[4]

Lincoln elaborated on his views in a speech he gave at the
Cooper Union in New York City in February 1860. Like other
Republicans, he admitted that the federal government had no
power to interfere with slavery in the individual states; but it did
have the power to restrict its spread to the territories and to reg-
ulate it in the District of Columbia. He denied charges, then

current throughout the South, that Republicans were stirring up insurrections among the slaves. "John Brown!" Lincoln exclaimed. "John Brown was no Republican." His Harper's Ferry raid was "peculiar." "It was not a slave insurrection. It was an attempt by white men to get up a revolt among slaves, in which the slaves refused to participate. In fact, it was so absurd that the slaves, with all their ignorance, saw plainly enough it could not succeed."[5] (Lincoln had obviously accepted the slaveholders' myth that blacks had nothing to do with Brown at Harper's Ferry. In this he was mistaken, but his mistake was the same as that made by most white men in most states in most parts of the country in 1860.)

Senator William H. Seward of New York, the leading contender for the Republican presidential nomination in 1860, shared Lincoln's views on Brown. He condemned the Harper's Ferry raid as an "attempt to execute an unlawful purpose in Virginia by invasion," and he defended Brown's execution as "necessary and just."[6] Governor Salmon P. Chase of Ohio, another potential Republican presidential nominee, described Brown as a "poor old man" who was "sadly misled by his own imaginations." "How rash," Chase lamented, "how mad—how criminal then to stir up insurrection which if successful would deluge the land with blood and make void the fairest hopes of mankind!"[7] Reflecting the views of its prominent spokesmen, the Republican Party platform of 1860 pledged to respect "the right of each state to order and control its own domestic institutions" (meaning slavery) and denounced "the lawless invasion by armed force of the soil of any state or territory, no matter under what pretext" (meaning John Brown's raid on Harper's Ferry).[8]

But all these denials of sympathy for Brown fell on deaf ears in the South. A newspaper in Staunton, Virginia, reflected typical Southern views when it announced that Brown's attack on Virginia was "just a manifestation of the horrific and wrong-

headed doctrines of Black Republicanism," which should now
be called "Brown Republicanism after John Brown."[9] Speaking
on the floor of the Senate in December, Mississippi senator Jefferson Davis charged that Seward "knew of the Harper's Ferry
affair" and that he, like John Brown, deserved "the gallows for
his participation in it." "When the Government gets into the
hands of the Republican party," Davis continued, "the arm of
the General Government, we are told, will not be raised for the
protection of our slave property. . . . Then John Brown, and a
thousand John Browns, can invade us, and the Government will
not protect us."[10]

As Southern rhetoric grew more heated, abolitionists rallied
around Brown. Bells tolled and prayers were recited on the day
of his execution. As Mrs. Brown took his body in its coffin from
Charlestown to Harper's Ferry, then by train through Philadelphia, New York City, and the Hudson River Valley to its final
resting place in the Adirondacks, crowds formed to express their
respect for Brown, and speakers praised him. Wendell Phillips,
eminent orator of abolitionism, spoke at Brown's farm at New
Elba, where his body was interred, calling him a "marvelous old
man" and averring that "history will date Virginia Emancipation
from Harper's Ferry. True, the slave is still there. So, when the
tempest uproots a pine on your hills, it looks green for months
—a year or two. Still, it is timber not a tree. John Brown has
loosened the roots of the slave system; it only breathes,—it does
not live,—hereafter."[11]

Great literary men in the North extolled Brown. Emerson
called him "that new saint, than whom none purer or more
brave was ever led by love of men into conflict and death."[12]
Thoreau thought that Brown had not died on the Charlestown
gallows but had rather attained immortality. "He is not confined
to North Elba nor to Kansas," Thoreau wrote. "He is no longer

working in secret. He works in public, and in the clearest light that shines on this land."[13]

Six days after Brown was buried, the U.S. Senate authorized a special committee "to inquire into the facts attending the late invasion and seizure of the armory and arsenal of the United States at Harper's Ferry, in Virginia, by a band of armed men." The committee's stated purpose was to determine whether "any citizens of the United States not present" were implicated in the raid, "or accessory thereto, by contributions of money, arms, munitions, or otherwise." Virginia's senator James Mason was the chairman and guiding light of the five-man committee, which included Democratic senators Jefferson Davis of Mississippi and G. N. Fitch of Indiana and Republicans Jacob Collamer of Vermont and James R. Doolittle of Wisconsin. Mason took the lead in examining thirty-two witnesses, seeking to find some evidence that would implicate Northerners in the planning, instigation, or financing of Brown's raid on Harper's Ferry. None could be found. On June 15, 1860, the Democratic majority issued its report, which found no Northern conspiracy but gravely warned that if individual states did not guard against similar occurrences, "the committee can find no guarantee elsewhere for the security of peace between the States of the Union."[14]

As Civil War historian James M. McPherson has written, "John Brown's ghost stalked the South as the election year of 1860 opened."[15] In April, when Democrats assembled in Charleston, South Carolina, for their national convention, they were deeply divided along slavery lines. Illinois's senator Stephen Douglas, who struck a neutral posture in the moral debate over slavery, came into the convention the frontrunner for the party's presidential nomination, but he was bitterly opposed by Southern Democrats, who wanted the federal government to enact a slave code to protect the rights of slaveholders all over the country.

Henry Wise, now former governor of Virginia, was not a factor in the Charleston deliberations, for he had failed to win the support of his own state's Democrats in the delegate-picking process.[16] Douglas argued, as he had in Kansas, that the future of slavery in the territories should be decided according to the doctrine of popular sovereignty—that is, by the votes of the residents of the territories. When an impasse was reached, the convention adjourned to Baltimore, leaving Charleston to the raucous cheers of South Carolinians who wanted "an Independent Southern Republic." But the Democrats foundered again in Baltimore. Douglas won the nomination, but supporters of the slave code angrily withdrew to Richmond and nominated John C. Breckinridge of Kentucky as their candidate. Another candidacy, that of Tennessee's John Bell and the newly organized National Constitution Party, threatened to further splinter Democratic and Southern votes. After much vacillation, Wise endorsed Breckinridge.[17]

The Republicans met at Chicago in May. Senator Seward entered the convention as the favorite candidate for the presidential nomination, but his association with the rhetoric of an "irrepressible conflict" and Southern charges (unproved) that he sanctioned Brown's attack on Virginia bore him down. Votes for Seward, Governor Chase of Ohio, and Edward Bates of Missouri gradually dissolved in favor of Abraham Lincoln, who went on to a narrow election victory over Douglas, Breckinridge, and Bell in the November election. Lincoln won a comfortable majority of the electoral votes, but only 40 percent of the popular vote (54 percent in the North).[18]

While the campaign was under way, Southerners warned that they would not accept Lincoln's election, that they would never bow down to "Black Republicanism." One newspaper in Georgia argued that Lincoln's election would amount to "humiliation and degradation" for Southern states. A newspaper in New Orleans said that every Northern vote cast for Lincoln would be "a deliberate, cold-blooded insult and outrage" to Southern honor. John J. Crittenden, a senator from Kentucky, declared that if Lincoln was elected, the South "could not submit to the consequences, and therefore, to avoid her fate, will secede from the Union."[19] Now that Lincoln was elected, secession began. It started with South Carolina in December, and continued in 1861 until ten more Southern states had withdrawn. The Confederate States of America was organized and armed. In April, days after Lincoln was inaugurated, Fort Sumter was attacked by a Confederate army under the command of General P. G. T. Beauregard, as Edmund Ruffin, now an honorary Palmetto Guard, jerked the lanyard of a columbiad gun and let fly what was credited as "the first shot" of the Civil War. The secession of Virginia in turn led to the separation of western Virginia from the rest of the state, and to the ultimate admission of West Virginia as a pro-Union state. After a struggle between Confederates and Unionists, Jefferson County was torn from Virginia and tacked on to West Virginia, though it had much more support for the former than the latter.[20] So, just a year after John Brown was executed in Charlestown, the Union had been cracked, and less than four months later the war had begun in earnest. And at the root of it all was the festering sore that John Brown had tried to lance at Harper's Ferry: the American institution of chattel slavery.

It is ironic that military forces of the Commonwealth of Virginia moved so quickly after the state's secession to seize and occupy Harper's Ferry. Robert E. Lee, newly commissioned a major general of Virginia's military forces, and former Governor Wise, now a leader of the secessionist movement, recognized the strategic importance of the town and the federal arms stored there, just as John Brown had a little over a year earlier. On April 18, 1861, one day after Virginia adopted its ordinance of secession, troops of the Commonwealth advanced on the town.[21] The small contingent of federal forces that James Buchanan had ordered to the armory and arsenal after Brown's raid tried to set fire to the arms before they fell into Virginia's hands, but only a few were destroyed, and after the federal troops retreated into Maryland the rest were taken to state arsenals in Richmond and at Fayetteville, North Carolina.[22] Eight days later, Thomas J. Jackson, late of the Virginia Military Institute but now a colonel under Lee, was put in command of Harper's Ferry.[23] John Brown held Harper's Ferry for thirty-six hours, and paid for doing so with his life. Lee and Jackson and all of the other officers of the newly formed Confederate States of America held Harper's Ferry on and off for four bloody years and were rewarded for their efforts with monuments in public squares throughout the South. Brown was a traitor to Virginia. Lee and Jackson and the others who made war against the United States in the uniform of Confederate soldiers were heroes.[24]

Military operations in and around Harper's Ferry and neighboring Charlestown were so furious, with the Confederates in charge one day and Union troops the next, that local residents lost track of how many times the towns changed hands. The bridges leading into Harper's Ferry were burned; all of the armory buildings other than the engine house in which Brown took refuge were laid in ruins; and trains running between Harper's Ferry and Charlestown were stopped, passengers robbed, and cars set on fire. When Union soldiers reached Charlestown, they remembered that the jail there was the prison in which Brown had been held, and they tore bricks off its walls for souvenirs.[25] Union Major General David Hunter, a strong opponent of slavery, vented his anger at Brown's prosecutor Andrew

Hunter (who happened to be his first cousin) by putting the torch to his estate at the edge of town, destroying the house and its contents.[26] When Union soldiers reached the center of Charlestown, they quartered themselves in the courthouse, and the Confederates responded by unleashing a barrage of artillery against the building, damaging it badly.[27]

As the Union troops marched through Jefferson County, they took up the chant of "John Brown's Body," a song which had its origins among volunteer soldiers in Boston harbor in the early days of the war and gained popularity as Northern troops marched south.[28] It was sung to an evocative tune of murky origins, with its first words improvised by soldiers and subjected to countless variations as the war bore on. It was, however, well adapted to marching troops, and it soon became almost universal wherever the Union blue could be seen:

John Brown's body lies a-mouldering in the grave.
John Brown's body lies a-mouldering in the grave.
John Brown's body lies a-mouldering in the grave
    But his soul goes marching on!
Glory, Glory, Hallelujah!
Glory, Glory, Hallelujah!
    His soul goes marching on.
He's gone to be a soldier in the army of the Lord.
He's gone to be a soldier in the army of the Lord.
He's gone to be a soldier in the army of the Lord.
    But his soul goes marching on.
Etc.

In the spring of 1862, the song had a rebirth, when the *Atlantic Monthly* published a reworking of the "John Brown" tune by Julia Ward Howe, wife of John Brown's friend and abolitionist supporter Samuel Gridley Howe. In this version, it became

equally famous as the "Battle Hymn of the Republic" and a kind
of war anthem for the Union cause:

> Mine eyes have seen the glory of the coming of the Lord:
> He is trampling out the vintage where the grapes of wrath are
> stored;
> He hath loosed the fateful lightning of his terrible swift sword:
> His truth is marching on.[29]

On January 1, 1863, Abraham Lincoln issued his Emancipation Proclamation, declaring that all slaves held in any state or
part of a state then in rebellion against the United States "are,
and henceforward shall be free."[30] It was one of the many iro-
nies of that turbulent time that Lincoln, who had condemned
Brown's resort to violence at Harper's Ferry, ultimately accom-
plished the very goal for which Brown gave his life by resorting
to violence on a grand scale. In their hearts, both men hated
slavery. Lincoln insisted that slavery could be abolished only
through legal means, as provided in the U.S. Constitution, but
in the end he used a great war to end it. To be sure, he insisted
that the Emancipation Proclamation was a legal act, issued pursuant to his constitutional power as commander in chief of the
Army and Navy of the United States, and as a "fit and necessary
war measure" for suppressing the rebellion of the Confederate
states. The proclamation was required by "military necessity,"
Lincoln said, but was also "an act of justice."[31] Though it rested
on an entirely different constitutional foundation, of course,
Lincoln's act vindicated Brown's actions—if not legally, at least
morally.

Union infantrymen were camped near Charlestown on the
day that Lincoln issued the Emancipation Proclamation. When
they learned of it, they erupted in cheers and songs, first singing
the popular war chant "We are Coming Father Abraham, Three

hundred thousand more," and then "John Brown's Body." As soon as their commander, Brigadier General Robert Milroy, obtained the full text of the proclamation, he issued a handbill headed "Freedom to slaves," ordering his troops to comply with it. Milroy later wrote Lincoln that the "hand-bill order gave Freedom to the slaves through and around the region where Old John Brown was hung. I felt *then* that I was on *duty*, in the most righteous cause that man ever drew sword in."[32]

It may be true, as some historians have suggested, that John Brown's fame would not have been so bright or enduring if "John Brown's Body" had not become a phenomenally popular war song or, as Robert A. Ferguson has described it, "the most frequently voiced lyric in American history."[33] If that is the case, then his fame may have been something of a historical accident.[34] But it is equally true that "John Brown's Body" would not have become such a popular song if Brown had not lived. His life—and particularly his death—gave the song its substance, and supplied at least some of the raison d'être of the war itself. It symbolized a cause, and delineated a moral purpose for all the bloodshed. Without John Brown, without Harper's Ferry, without Charlestown, it is hard to imagine that American history would have played out exactly as it did, or that war between the North and South would have erupted as quickly as it did, or that slavery would have died so suddenly. Emerson reflected on this reality after the war was over, writing in his journal: "It has been impossible to keep the name & fame of John Brown out of the war from the first to the last."[35] The pro-Southern journalist and historian Charles Chauncey Burr described the war (disapprovingly) as "nothing but a stupendous John Brown raid."[36] And Alexander M. Stewart, chaplain of a regiment of Pennsylvania volunteers who fought in and around Charlestown during the war, wrote in his postwar memoir that when the true history of the great conflict was written, it would show that "Old John Brown threw the first bomb, discharged the first cannon, and thrust the first bayonet."[37]

As the fighting continued, it became more and more evident that it was as much about slavery as the preservation of the Union. Lincoln expressed this realization in his Second Inaugural Address, delivered on March 4, 1865, and sometimes acclaimed as his "greatest speech."[38] In it, he recalled that before the war started, the slaves "constituted a peculiar and powerful interest" and that "all knew that this interest was, somehow, the cause of the war." The object of the South was "to strengthen, perpetuate, and extend this interest," whereas that of the North was "to restrict the territorial enlargement of it." But the war progressed beyond the expectations of either side, eventually producing a result both "fundamental and astounding." "The Almighty has his own purposes," Lincoln declared. Then he continued:

> Fondly do we hope—fervently do we pray—that this mighty scourge of war may speedily pass away. Yet, if God wills that it continue, until all the wealth piled by the bondsman's two hundred and fifty years of unrequited toil shall be sunk, and until every drop of blood drawn with the lash shall be paid by another drawn with the sword, as was said three thousand years ago, so still it must be said "the judgments of the Lord, are true and righteous altogether."[39]

John Brown's speech, uttered in the courtroom of Judge Richard Parker in Charlestown on November 2, 1859, now seemed more relevant than ever:

> Now, if it is deemed necessary that I should forfeit my life for the furtherance of the ends of justice, and mingle my blood further with the blood of my children and with the blood of millions in

this slave country, whose rights are disregarded by wicked, cruel and unjust enactments, I say let it be done.

And the note he left with the jail guard at Charlestown on the day he was hanged seemed prophetic:

I John Brown am now quite *certain* that the crimes of this *guilty land: will* never be purged away; but with Blood.[40]

Before the war began, however, there was some unfinished business in Charlestown. Shields Green, John Copeland, Edwin Coppoc, and John Cook had been sentenced to die on the scaffold on December 16. There was no effort to obtain a writ of error for any of these men, for it was conceded that when the Supreme Court of Appeals denied Brown's petition without even an argument or an opinion, it sealed the other men's fate.[41] Green and Copeland, the black men, were hanged according to Judge Parker's sentence on December 16, in the morning. Coppoc and Cook ascended the same scaffold on the same date, but in the afternoon.[42] After much more vacillation than any accused man should be subject to, Aaron Stevens was finally brought back from the federal court to Charlestown, where he was tried on February 2, 1860, found guilty, and on March 16 hanged by the neck.[43] Albert Hazlett, one of Brown's men who originally escaped from Harper's Ferry, was captured in Pennsylvania, brought back to Charlestown, and condemned to the same death as Stevens. With the final hangings, the casualties of Brown's raid on Harper's Ferry could be tallied up. Of his original Provisional Army of twenty-two men, ten had been killed in action, five had escaped to the North (without being recaptured), and seven were hanged in Charlestown. Four townspeople, and one marine, were killed in and about the federal enclave. These were exact numbers. After Appomattox, the casualties of the war between the North and South could only be estimated. More than 620,000 soldiers (360,000 Northerners and 260,000 Confederates) were dead. And four million slaves—with all of their descendants forever—had been emancipated. The war John Brown helped to start had indeed been awful. But he had predicted that "the crimes of this *guilty land: will* never be purged *away;* but with Blood."

After the facts of John Brown's trial have all been recounted, after the effect the trial had on a nation bitterly divided between supporters and opponents of slavery has been described, after the legacy of the courtroom drama has been identified and, to some extent, explored, it is appropriate to ask one last question—and at least to suggest an answer to it: Was the trial *fair?*

As noted in the introduction, the concept of a fair trial is elusive. It is not easily pinned down to a single definition or limited by a prescribed list of essential conditions. More important, in the course of a hotly contested trial, with charges and countercharges flying wildly, claims and counterclaims advanced, prosecution theories and defense strategies proffered, opposed, and in some cases withdrawn, it is often difficult to discern the clear outlines of fairness and to determine whether, in sum, the trial was fair or unfair. A recent study of trial procedures around the world has concluded that the "standards against which a trial is to be measured in terms of fairness are numerous, complex, and evolving."[44] So it was in the United States in the middle of the nineteenth century. So it was in Jefferson County in the Commonwealth of Virginia in the epochal year of 1859, when John Brown was tried, found guilty, and executed.

Although essentially undefined, the concept of fairness was, as noted earlier, important to all those who participated in or were affected by Brown's trial. Virginia authorities repeatedly assured both Brown and the greater American public that his trial would be fair. At key points in the proceedings, Brown himself reminded the judge and the attorneys that he had been promised a "fair trial"; and, in the end, he declared that that was exactly what he received.[45] But Brown's declaration was not taken as the last word on the subject. By the time he delivered his final speech, he had decided to accept his punishment courageously and welcome the martyrdom that awaited him on the gallows. He would not quibble about denied requests for delay, arguments about jurisdiction, instructions to the jury, or the effectiveness of the assistance he received from counsel. He would meet his death, accepting all of the procedural steps that led up to it and, in his defense, indicting only the institution of slavery, which lay at the heart of the whole proceeding. It was because of slavery that he found himself in Charlestown on trial for his life. It was because of slavery that he would accept his penalty, in the confident hope that his death would help bring about its ultimate destruction.

The fairness of Brown's trial was publicly debated from the earliest days of the trial itself. Brown had not yet been hanged when the *Lawrence Republican* voiced the sentiments of many opponents of slavery. "We defy an instance to be shown in a civilized community," the Kansas newspaper editorialized on November 17, 1859, "where a prisoner has been forced to trial for his life, when so disabled by sickness or ghastly wounds as to be unable even to sit up during the proceedings, and compelled to be carried to the judgment hall upon a litter. . . . Such a proceeding shames the name of justice, and only finds a congenial place amid the records of the Bloody Inquisition."[46] The *Boston Transcript* went further, declaring: "Whatever may be his guilt or folly, a man convicted under such circumstances and, especially, a man executed after such a trial, will be the most terrible fruit that slavery has ever borne, and will excite the execration of the whole civilized world."[47] John Andrew, the Boston lawyer who helped Brown secure Samuel Chilton as his attorney in Virginia, was critical of the trial both because it seemed to have been rushed to judgment and because the Supreme Court of Appeals of Virginia refused to grant an oral argument or render an opinion before upholding the sentence as "plainly right."[48] Andrew (who was elected governor of Massachusetts in 1860) considered this refusal "a great blunder."[49]

The *New York Times* delivered a scathing critique of the trial while Brown was awaiting his execution. The newspaper reminded its readers that Brown had been promised a "full and fair trial," and that it was "above all things necessary to the honor and character of Virginia that the proceedings should result in a moral triumph of justice over vengeance, and equity over passion." The *Times* was no friend of Brown's: it had repeatedly and vehemently condemned his resort to violence in Harper's Ferry. But the paper worried that the unfairness of his Charlestown trial would actually work to his advantage. "If the result of this great State Trial shall simply be the hanging of four fanatics," the *Times* editorialized, "sure to carry with them to the scaffold the sympathies which the public always accords to those whom it believes to be the victims, however guilty, of haste and rage, it were far better for the South that Old Brown and his men had never been caught at all." The *Times* said that it was "a most unusual and uncalled-for thing to insist on the arraignment and trial of a wounded man, actually unable to stand upright in the dock." The haste with which the trial was conducted seemed to the *Times* objectionable, as did Judge Parker's failure to allow him sufficient time to obtain his own attorneys. "To allege that the Court had assigned him counsel, and that he ought to have been satisfied with the gentlemen so designated, is simply a cruel mockery, alike of law and of a dying man." The fact that his appointed attorneys had all been involved in the excitement in Harper's Ferry, some actually fighting against him, militated strongly against their ability to fairly represent him.

"How could he be asked to believe, after all that he heard in Court, that any Virginia lawyer, however capable or honorable, could so far divest himself of the passions by which his friends and neighbors were shaken, as to defend him, as a man in such a dreadful plight ought to be defended, with heart and soul, zealously, and even enthusiastically?"[50]

Contrary opinions, of course, were voiced. The *Richmond Enquirer* defended the trial against charges that it was conducted with "indecent haste." The *Enquirer* argued that "a speedy trial by an impartial jury" was "the great fundamental principle of criminal prosecutions" in the United States. A speedy trial was required by twenty-five states of the Union and was provided for in George Mason's universally esteemed draft for the Bill of Rights. The *Enquirer* grumbled that "fanatical love for the criminal" had come to equate a speedy trial with "indecent haste" and thus to "compromise the dignity and justice of Virginia with insinuations against her courts of justice." The Richmond editors may not have understood the difference between the right to a *speedy trial*, which protects accused criminals from languishing for long periods in jail without an opportunity to establish their innocence, and the distinct rights to the *effective assistance of counsel* and the opportunity to *adequately prepare a defense to criminal accusations*, both of which can be compromised by a trial conducted with "indecent haste." They did, however, understand the political connotations of Brown's trial and were not at all reluctant to underscore them. Attacks against the fairness of the Charlestown proceedings, the *Enquirer* argued, were "not calculated to allay the excited feelings of Virginia, or to temper justice with mercy; nor do such sentiments and conduct tend to reconcile an injured people with the Union."[51]

The *Baltimore Sun* was of much the same opinion as the *Enquirer*. If the Richmond newspaper seemed to confuse a speedy trial with a hasty trial, the Baltimore journal was eager to pin the blame for the haste in Charlestown on Brown himself. "It so happened that Brown selected a time for his demonstration immediately antecedent to the regular term of the court," the *Sun* opined (apparently with a straight editorial face). "And while such a thing as a postponement of the case until another term was out of the question, it followed, as a matter of course, that it must be tried at once. The same presiding judge was obliged to hold a court at Winchester on the tenth of November, and with several of the insurgents to try, delay was utterly impracticable."

The notion that Brown knew when Judge Parker would have to move on from Charlestown to Winchester, and that he factored that knowledge into his calculations of when he should attack Harper's Ferry, stretched the credulity even of the *Sun's* pro-Southern readers. There was, of course, no reason to believe that Brown thought he was going to be captured or tried in Charlestown at the end of October or at any other time; and the idea that he should have selected an attack date to meet the schedule of the circuit court was silly.

The *Sun* thought Brown was lucky he hadn't been tried by a court-martial and summarily executed. "We do not see how any man taking a rational and comprehensive view of the facts can for a moment complain of the treatment Brown and his party have received," the Baltimore paper concluded. "On the contrary, there has been an exhibition of leniency worthy of the State, and illustrative of the forbearance of civilization in Virginia."[52]

Daniel Voorhees, the Indiana lawyer who pleaded John Cook's case in Charlestown and later sought clemency from Governor Wise, thought Judge Parker's circuit court was "a model of judicial decorum, dignity and fairness." With the grandiloquence for which this "Tall Sycamore of the Wabash" was noted, Voorhees said that, if the court was "justly represented by the pen of the historian, it would pass into history as the most temperate and conservative judicial tribunal ever convened, when all the surrounding circumstances are considered."[53]

After the war, Bushrod C. Washington, a Jefferson County attorney and member of Charlestown's pioneer Washington family, appraised Brown's trial and found it satisfactory on all counts. For Washington, the fact that Lawson Botts and Thomas C. Green were appointed to represent Brown was in itself "an assurance that Brown would have a fair trial."[54]

A few years after Washington pronounced the trial fair, Marcus J. Wright, a Tennessee lawyer who became a brigadier general in the Confederate army, made an elaborate defense of the trial that hinged primarily on Governor Wise's promise that it would be fair and on the governor's refusal to subject Brown to "a drumhead court-martial."[55] Wright was also at pains to point out the virtues of Andrew Hunter. Brown's prosecutor was "a good, great, but unambitious man," Wright said. He was "a lawyer in every sense of the word, and therefore a good man, for no man can be a thorough and conscientious lawyer without being a good man."[56] In Wright's estimation, Hunter's virtues stamped the whole proceeding with fairness.

George E. Caskie of Lynchburg, Virginia, was another Southern lawyer who defended the fairness of Brown's trial. In August 1909, he read a comprehensive defense of the trial to the Virginia State Bar Association, then meeting in Hot Springs, Virginia. Caskie's speech was later printed in the *American Law Review*, where it reached a wide audience. After outlining the basic facts of the trial, Caskie concluded: "An able and impartial Judge presided at his trial, able lawyers looked to his defense. Every fact was proven in evidence. His guilt was absolutely established, and whatever divergent views may have existed upon the question of slavery, all fair and impartial minds must concede that the judgment was just and the penalty properly inflicted."[57]

But all "fair and impartial minds" were not of the same opinion. In the 1880s, Hermann von Holst, a German scholar who made a special study of American constitutional law, launched a vigorous attack on Brown's trial. Von Holst examined the trial in detail, attempting to place it in the context of the American legal tradition and the great sectional tensions that then tore at the national fabric, and concluded that the proceeding was infected by unfairness from beginning to end. Von Holst (whose early career was spent at the universities of Heidelberg, Strasbourg, and Freiburg but who finished up at the University of Chicago) thought the unfairness arose from the fact that the judge, the jurors, the prosecutors, and the court-appointed attorneys were all "born and bred under the poisonous breath of slavery." He also considered it an "outrage, under the existing circumstances," that Brown was denied his request for a short delay to secure attorneys of his own choosing.[58]

When Von Holst's harsh judgment reached Jefferson County, two surviving participants in the trial mounted a local response. Andrew Hunter, then in his eighties, was still living in Charlestown. In a specially prepared essay, the old prosecutor reviewed the circumstances that preceded and followed the trial and declared that the whole proceeding "was perfectly fair from beginning to end." He pointed out that the attorneys who came from outside the state to represent Brown were "courteously received" in Charlestown, that they were "introduced to the court and qualified as practitioners, and invited to the free use of my office and library during the whole time."[59] Judge Parker, then in his late seventies, was living in his home outside Winchester when he heard of Von Holst's judgment. In another paper prepared to vindicate the Charlestown proceedings, Parker recalled that Brown had not been denied "any presumption, benefit or right to which he was entitled; that no bias against him was exhibited by the jury or the Court; that he was defended by learned and zealous counsel who, without let or interruption, were granted all the time they were pleased to consume in the examination of witnesses, in discussing the various questions of law and fact which arose during the trial, in excepting to every opinion of the Court wherein they supposed there might be an error, and in arguing before the jury every matter which they deemed important or beneficial to the defense." In view of all this, Parker concluded that "John Brown had a fair and impartial trial, just such as should be granted to all persons so unfortunate as to be accused of crime."[60]

A few years after Hunter and Parker expressed their views, the black historian and philosopher W. E. B. Du Bois published a biography of Brown in which he wrote that the trial "was a difficult experience" in which Virginia "attempted to hold scales of even justice between mob violence and the world-wise sympathy of all good men." In the end, however, Du Bois concluded that the trial was "legally fair but pressed to a conclusion in unseemly haste."[61]

In 1924, a precocious young Kentuckian studying at Oxford University penned a provocative biography of Brown from the pro-Southern, proslavery viewpoint. Published in 1929, Robert Penn Warren's *John Brown: The Making of a Martyr* pictured a deceitful Brown who was motivated not by humanitarian impulses but by the crass instincts of a brigand. Warren, who was later celebrated as a Pulitzer Prize–winning novelist and poet and as the poet laureate of the United States, thought Brown's Charlestown trial was an inevitability that should not concern serious thinkers. "The trial, of course, was a mockery," he wrote, "not because it was unfair, but because the evidence was too sure. The mitigating circumstances had as little relevance as the dead languages. But the court respected the courage in that defiance."[62]

By the early 1950s, the weight of opinion was turning. In

1950, social critic Nathaniel Weyl published a study of treason prosecutions in the United States in which he described Brown's trial as "indecently hurried."[63] In 1952, New York historian Richard B. Morris condemned Brown's trial as "flagrantly unfair" because he was not given a "reasonable time to prepare" for it, because he was initially denied "the right to engage lawyers of his own choice," and because, when his own attorneys at last took over, "they were given no time to familiarize themselves with the case against their client." Morris, who was trained both as a lawyer and a historian, added as a fourth reason the fact that Brown was convicted of treason against Virginia, "a crime of which he could not conceivably have been guilty."[64] This was a point on which popular historian J. C. Furnas, otherwise a bitter critic of Brown's, agreed. In *The Road to Harper's Ferry* (1959), Furnas condemned Brown as a man who "made bad temper, poor judgment and eager self-deception feel righteous and valiant."[65] But Furnas admitted that it was "impossible" for Brown to have committed treason against Virginia, because "treason implies allegiance; allegiance implies at least some sort of domicile; and Old Brown had neither been born in Virginia nor had anything like a domicile there."[66] Apparently neither Morris nor Furnas gave much thought to Andrew Hunter's argument from the privileges and immunities clause, which led him and Judge Parker to the conclusion that Brown did indeed have a duty of allegiance to Virginia. Or if they thought about it, they did not seem to be much impressed by it.

In 1995, legal historian Paul Finkelman noted the haste with which Brown's trial was conducted, the judge's failure to delay the proceedings to allow Brown's own lawyers to arrive, and the fact that the trial was pushed forward, even though the wounded Brown had to be carried into court. All of this, in Finkelman's judgment, amounted to an "apparent lack of due process."[67] And in 2001, law professor Steven Lubet described

Brown's trial as a "trial in name only—the outcome never having been in doubt" and said that it was marked by "jurisdictional
blunders, professional misconduct, and conflicts of interest."[68]

It is easy to commend the authorities of Virginia for their decision to put Brown on trial in a regularly constituted civilian
court rather than condemn him by court-martial or, even worse,
turn him over to a lynch mob. The Commonwealth would rightly
have been subject to reproval if it had thus circumvented the judicial protections authorized in its constitution and statutes. But
the furor sparked by such a circumvention would have been
short-lived. When Brown was captured in Harper's Ferry, few
Americans understood his purposes or goals; they knew only
that he was a violent lawbreaker and, as such, subject to legal
punishment. If he had been hanged from the nearest tree, or
from a military gibbet, he could not have spoken out in his own
defense; he could not have delivered the eloquent statements he
later made in the circuit court in Charlestown. The outrage
would have quickly died.

By deciding to try Brown in Charlestown, however, the authorities of Virginia invited scrutiny. It is not enough to give an
accused man a trial if his trial is not fair and impartial. And if
a state chooses to try a man who could have been tried in federal court, as was the case with Brown, the state bears an even
greater burden, for it must show not only that he was tried according to the state's own laws, but that he was accorded the
same level of fairness he might have gotten in the federal tribunal. When Virginia elected to take custody of Brown and the
other men captured with him and not surrender them to federal
authorities, it accepted these double burdens. Given the excitement of the time, which was greatly exacerbated by the emotional responses of Governor Wise, it is not surprising that it did
not bear these burdens well.

Brown was clearly rushed to judgment. The requirement that

Judge Parker finish up his circuit court duties in Charlestown by November 10 was no excuse for conducting Brown's trial with such haste that fundamental standards of fairness had to be abandoned. Brown was indicted for treason, conspiring with slaves to rebel, murder, and aiding and abetting murder. For all those offenses, he stood to lose his life. Yet only four days of actual testimony and argument were devoted to his trial. He first faced his jury only eight days after his capture; he was found guilty five days later and sentenced to death two days after that. During most of the trial, he lay wounded and in pain on a cot brought into the courtroom. Though capable, the lawyers appointed to represent him were pillars of the local community, slaveholders themselves, and not attorneys of Brown's own choosing. Brown made clear from the outset that he wanted to secure his own attorneys, men who could be expected to support his cause with enthusiasm and conviction, but by the time his own attorneys arrived in Charlestown the trial was almost over. The new attorneys were placed at an enormous disadvantage when Judge Parker refused their request for a short delay so they could speak with their client, review notes of the testimony already taken, and analyze the law applicable to the case. With this ruling, the judge effectively foreclosed any chance Brown might have had for an acquittal on any of the charges against him. The right to counsel is essential to the fairness of any criminal trial. In Brown's case, he had attorneys, but his right to counsel was effectively denied because he did not have the *effective* assistance of any of the attorneys.

Hiram Griswold argued that the state should have been required to make an election among the four counts of the indictment and that requiring Brown to stand trial on all four put him at an unfair disadvantage. Three of the charged offenses were subject to the plenary clemency power of Governor Wise, but the fourth (the treason count) was not, because Virginia statutes provided that the governor could pardon or reprieve a person convicted of treason only with the consent of the General Assembly.[69] By failing to require the prosecution to elect which of the four counts it wished to pursue, the court put Brown to the general defense of four counts, only one of which required legislative concurrence for a pardon or commutation. The failure to require an election also raised the specter of unfairness because Brown was actually convicted of only three counts: treason, conspiring with slaves to rebel, and murder. What happened to the count charging that Brown aided and abetted the crime of murder? It seemed to have been lost in the jury's deliberations.

There were serious problems of proof in the trial. Where had Fontaine Beckham and Hayward Shepherd been killed? And were their killings committed within the jurisdiction of the Circuit Court of Jefferson County? At one point, Thomas Green suggested that the railroad trestle on which Beckham was standing when he was shot was actually in Maryland, for the line separating Virginia and Maryland followed the low water line on the Virginia side of the Potomac.[70] But Green was taken off the case before he could develop this argument, and it was not followed up by the other attorneys. In fact, Beckham may have been standing on federal land, for the armory grounds ran to the river's edge. Certainly the shot that killed him was fired from the engine house within the armory compound, where the federal government had jurisdiction. Shepherd was somewhere on the Potomac bridge at the time he was shot, but whether he was in Maryland or Virginia was never clearly established. Luke Quinn, the marine private who was shot when Lee ordered the storming of the engine house, was clearly killed on federal property, which would seem to have removed his murder from Virginia jurisdiction. Hunter argued that it had been the practice in the past to prosecute murders committed in the armory in the circuit court in Charlestown, but this hardly foreclosed further inquiry into the practice.[71] Surely an illegal practice does not become legal merely because it is repeated. Significantly, perhaps, there was no clear evidence as to how Quinn met his death. When John Allstadt testified, he stated that it was his "opinion" that Brown killed the marine. But on cross-examination, Allstadt admitted that he was "much confused and excited at the time" and could not "state certainly by what shot the marine was killed."[72] When Armistead Ball testified about the marines' attack on the engine house, he said he did not think he saw Brown fire his rifle at anyone.[73] But even if Brown did fire, did he do so with the malicious intent of killing his attackers, or merely in an effort to protect himself, his men, and his hostages from the marines' onslaught? He had repeatedly sent men outside the engine house under flags of truce, seeking to work out an agreement under which he and his men would be permitted to retreat into Maryland, and those men had repeatedly been fired upon. Some were killed. He might well have been held responsible for killings committed by some of his men because he was their leader, the instigator of the whole raid, and thus had aided and abetted the murders they committed. But the jury did not find him guilty of aiding and abetting. They found him guilty of murder, and they fixed the degree of that murder as first degree, thus requiring that he be hanged for the crime. In sum, there was a serious disconnect between the crimes charged and the crimes proved. The disconnect was a sign of the sloppiness with which the prosecution was conducted and the haste that animated the whole proceeding.

The fairness of a trial must be measured not only by the procedures followed but also by the law applied. The arguments advanced first by Hiram Griswold and Samuel Chilton, and later by Chilton and William Green in Brown's petition for a writ of error—that Brown could not be guilty of treason against Virginia because he owed no allegiance to Virginia or, as they stated it, because he was not a citizen of Virginia—were at least very provocative. It seemed almost incontrovertible that Brown had attacked Virginia from a neighboring state and passed over its sovereign territory for the briefest moments before finding himself pinned down in the federal enclave at Harper's Ferry. Andrew Hunter argued that Brown was a citizen of Harper's Ferry, and hence of Virginia, because he intended to "reside and hold the place permanently," but there had been no testimony on this point, and at best it was speculative. Hunter also argued that Brown should be treated as a citizen of Virginia because, like all American citizens, he enjoyed the benefits of the privileges and immunities clause of the U.S. Constitution. This was a strong argument, and it was ultimately accepted by Judge Parker, who observed laconically that "the Constitution did not give rights and immunities alone, but also imposed responsibilities." It was not, however, a conclusive argument, and Chilton and Griswold and Green all argued to the contrary. The failure of the Supreme Court of Appeals to issue a written opinion when it rejected Brown's petition for a writ of error left the issue, like all the other legal issues raised by the trial, ultimately unresolved.

The Supreme Court of Appeals's role in the Brown case was troubling, for the Virginia constitution required that the high judges state the reasons for their decision in writing and preserve it "with the record of the case."[74] The judges in Richmond certainly knew the high profile that Brown's case presented: it was one of the most sensational cases ever tried in Virginia, perhaps anywhere in the United States, and it had drawn enormous media attention. It had commanded the active attention of the governor of Virginia, at least one of Virginia's U.S. senators, and many other public officials inside and outside Virginia. A written statement of the reasons that the judges of the Supreme Court of Appeals deemed the decision in Brown's case "plainly right" would have been helpful, perhaps instructive—at the very least reassuring. The statement might have dampened Northern criticism of the Charlestown proceeding and foreclosed the possibility that the fairness of his trial would be subject to repeated questions. Why did the judges decline to state the reasons for their quick decision? Was it because there was not enough time? Was it because the reasons were so plain that they needed no statement? Or was it perhaps because the reasons were actually weak? John Andrew thought the Supreme Court of Appeals committed a "great blunder." It is not easy to argue that he was mistaken.

Brown's trial was not, as Robert Penn Warren declared, a "mockery." For all its faults, it was a serious proceeding, conducted with the full panoply of judicial attributes traditionally associated with criminal trials. There was a calm and experienced judge, skilled attorneys both for the prosecution and the defense, and an indictment duly arrived at according to time-honored rituals passed down from England to the United States. There were twelve jurors, witnesses sworn to tell the truth, and jury deliberations—albeit painfully short. There was a sentencing hearing, an opportunity for the accused to make a statement to the court, a judgment, and an appeal to a higher court—although the appeal was strangely truncated. Yet when all of these attributes are tallied up, they fall short of the conclusion that the trial was fair. Rather, they establish that it was conducted with regard for the dignity and decorum required by Virginia law and practice. But *dignity* and *decorum* do not translate to fairness when the accused is rushed to judgment and denied the effective assistance of counsel, when the proof does not sustain the verdict, when important legal issues are left unresolved, and when the appeal is dismissed almost as if it were an annoyance.

In the final analysis, however, it does not really matter whether the trial was fair or merely dignified and decorous. Nobody seriously questioned that Brown had broken the laws of Virginia or that he had done so in a very serious way. There was ample evidence of his guilt and little doubt that he would be convicted, if not of all the charges brought against him, at least of some of them. The real question in the trial was not whether Brown had committed crimes, but what would happen after he was convicted of those crimes. Viewed in the long lens of history, it is clear that John Brown was not really on trial in Charlestown. Slavery was. Through his impassioned manipulation of the proceeding, Brown turned the accusation against him into an accusation against slavery. He was hanged in Charlestown thirty days after Judge Parker pronounced his sentence. But slavery itself died its own death barely five years later, thanks in large part to what happened in the Circuit Court of Jefferson County. Brown delivered a sharp and ultimately fatal blow to an institution that had persisted for hundreds of years and was finally recognized as a travesty. John Brown died a martyr. But for generations to come, thanks in large part to Charlestown, his soul kept marching on.

NOTES

INTRODUCTION

1. It was Harper's Ferry, Virginia, in 1859, but is Harpers Ferry, West Virginia, today. The historic spelling and state designation are used in this book.

2. Major biographical treatments of Brown began in 1860 with the publication of James Redpath's *The Public Life of Capt. John Brown* (1860) and continued with Franklin B. Sanborn's *Life and Letters of John Brown* (1885) and Richard J. Hinton's *John Brown and His Men* (1894). The parade of twentieth-century biographies began in 1909 with W. E. B. Du Bois's *John Brown* (1909) and Oswald Garrison Villard's *John Brown, 1800–1859* (1910). These were followed by Hill Peebles Wilson's *John Brown, Soldier of Fortune* (1913), Robert Penn Warren's *John Brown: The Making of a Martyr* (1929), James C. Malin's *John Brown and the Legend of Fifty-six* (1942), Stephen B. Oates's *To Purge This Land with Blood* (1970), Jules Abel's *Man on Fire* (1971), Richard O. Boyer's *The Legend of John Brown* (1973), and Truman Nelson's *The Old Man* (1973). David S. Reynolds's *John Brown, Abolitionist* was published in 2005, and Evan Carton's *Patriotic Treason* in 2006. Poetry about John Brown has been written by John Greenleaf Whittier, Henry Wadsworth Longfellow, William Dean Howells, Louisa May Alcott, Herman Melville, Walt Whitman, Oliver Wendell Holmes, Edgar Lee Masters, Edwin Arlington Robinson, Muriel Rukeyser, and many others. Stephen Vincent Benét's epic *John Brown's Body* (1929) was one of the best-selling volumes of poetry ever published in the United States. Novels about or featuring John Brown have included *God's Angry Man* (1932), by Leonard Ehrlich; *The Surveyor* (1960), by Truman Nelson; *Raising Holy Hell* (1995), by Bruce

13. See Stutler, "The Hanging of John Brown," 5.

14. *New York Herald*, Nov. 10, 1859 (line extended from Harper's Ferry to Charlestown).

15. *New York Times*, Oct. 25, 1859.

16. Ferguson, *The Trial in American Life*, 117, 118; Stutler, "The Hanging of John Brown," 5.

17. *New York Herald*, Oct. 26, 1859.

18. Ibid., Nov. 3, 1859.

19. Reynolds, *John Brown, Abolitionist*, 334, argues that, if Brown had been killed, "the affair would have gotten momentary attention but then have disappeared from view."

20. See Ferguson, *The Trial in American Life*, 118.

21. See Potter, *The Impending Crisis*, 358 (Brown's "ultimate triumphant failure was built upon the accident of his survival to face trial after Harpers Ferry").

22. *Ferguson v. Georgia*, 365 U.S. 570 (1961).

23. U.S. Const., amend. V (no person shall be compelled in any criminal case to be a witness against himself).

24. The first statute that permitted criminal defendants to give sworn evidence was apparently enacted in Maine in 1859; it made defendants competent witnesses, but only in the prosecution of a few crimes. Maine enacted a general competency statute in 1864. This was apparently the first such statute in the English-speaking world. A federal statute was adopted in 1878. By the end of the nineteenth century, every state except Georgia had abolished the disqualification. Georgia's disqualification was held to be unconstitutional by the U.S. Supreme Court in 1961. *Ferguson v. Georgia*, 365 U.S. 570 (1961).

25. As early as 1689, it was recognized that the court's failure to ask the defendant if he had anything to say before sentence was imposed required reversal. *Green v. United States*, 365 U.S. 301, 304 (1961), citing Anonymous, 3 Mod. 265, 266, 87 Eng. Rep. 175 (K. B.). When the judgment is reversed, the appellate court will remand the case to the trial court for resentencing. At the resentencing, the trial court must ask the prisoner if he or she has anything to say before sentence is passed, and the prisoner must be given the opportunity to respond in

his or her own words. See *State v. Lundberg,* 2009-Ohio 1641, a decision of the Court of Appeals for Montgomery County, Ohio, in which the right of allocution was improperly denied.

26. Emerson, *Complete Works of Ralph Waldo Emerson,* 8:125.

27. Ferguson, "Story and Transcription in the Trial of John Brown," 39; McPherson, *Battle Cry of Freedom,* 208.

28. *New York Herald,* Nov. 3, 1859.

29. See discussion in chap. 3.

30. See Story, *Commentaries on the Constitution of the United States,* §1791 ("highest crime, which can be committed in civil society"); and John Wise, *A Treatise on American Citizenship,* 77 ("greatest crime known to the law").

31. *U.S. v. Wiltberger,* 18 U.S. (5 Wheat.), 76, 96 (1820) ("Treason is a breach of allegiance, and can be committed by him only who owes allegiance either perpetual or temporary"); Leek, "Treason and the Constitution, 604 ("Treason may be briefly and generally defined as a breach of allegiance"). See Carso, *"Whom Can We Trust Now?"* 8, 11, 34, and 37.

32. See U.S. Const., art. I, §8, cl. 17 (enclave clause); see also discussion in chap. 3.

33. There were previous prosecutions for treason against a state, but none that resulted in execution. In 1814, residents of New York were charged in state court with treason against New York for supplying provisions to British warships during the war between Great Britain and the United States. They were discharged on the ground that supplying provisions to British ships during that war might be treason against the United States but not New York. *People v. Lynch,* 11 John R. 549 N.Y. (1814). In 1844, Thomas Wilson Dorr, a resident of Rhode Island, was charged with treason against Rhode Island for having established a government in opposition to the existing government and taken the office of governor in it. He was convicted and sentenced to life in prison, but later he was granted amnesty by the state legislature. See Pitman, *Report of the Trial of Thomas Wilson Dorr.*

34. The arguments advanced in defense of slavery are summarized, with pertinent examples, in Finkelman, *Defending Slavery.*

35. In his Second Inaugural Address, Lincoln noted that the slaves of the South "constituted a peculiar and powerful interest. All knew that this interest was, somehow, the cause of the war." Basler, *Collected Works of Abraham Lincoln*, 8:332. McPherson, *This Mighty Scourge*, 3–13, discusses the centrality of the slavery issue in the tensions between North and South, and how those tensions culminated in the Sumter crisis. In *What Caused the Civil War?* Ayers writes: "What caused the Civil War? If you have to offer a one-word answer, go ahead and just say slavery" (142).

36. Samuel Longfellow, *Life of Henry Wadsworth Longfellow*, 2:396.

37. Melville, *Battle Pieces and Aspects of the War*, 11.

38. Reynolds, *John Brown, Abolitionist*, x, 56; McPherson, *This Mighty Scourge*, 29, 39.

39. Lubet, *Nothing But the Truth*, 51, argues that Brown's trial might well be "the most significant, or perhaps we should say consequential, trial in U.S. history. . . . The trial of John Brown, in some ways more than the Harpers Ferry raid itself, did much to hasten, and perhaps even make inevitable, the onset of the Civil War."

1. TO FREE THE SLAVES

1. Jefferson, *Notes on the State of Virginia*, 17, 18.

2. Geffert (with Libby), "Regional Black Involvement in John Brown's Raid on Harpers Ferry," 165, estimates the total black population of Harper's Ferry at about 200, equally divided between free blacks and slaves. National Park Service History Series, *John Brown's Raid*, 15, states that there were 150 slaves and 150 free blacks in the town.

3. J. B. to Henry L. Stearns, July 15, 1857, in Ruchames, *John Brown, The Making of a Revolutionary*, 44.

4. Although the Potomac here forms the boundary between Maryland and Virginia (now West Virginia), the dividing line is not the center of the river, but the low-water mark on the Virginia side. This somewhat unusual result came about through a curious history. The royal charters for both Virginia (1612) and Maryland (1632) purported to

include the river bed, thus creating a conflict, but since the Maryland charter came later it was accepted as controlling.

5. *Report of the Select Committee of the Senate,* 27.

6. Ibid., 22.

7. Chap. 24, Acts of the General Assembly of Virginia, Nov. 28, 1794.

8. J. B. to Henry L. Stearns, July 15, 1857, in Ruchames, *John Brown, The Making of an Abolitionist,* 16.

9. Sanborn, *Life and Letters of John Brown,* 38–39.

10. Ibid., 16.

11. Villard, *John Brown,* 21.

12. Stutler, "John Brown and the Oberlin Lands," 183–199.

13. Matthew 7:12.

14. Sanborn, *Life and Letters of John Brown,* 122.

15. Job 29:17.

16. Sanborn, *Life and Letters of John Brown,* 327.

17. Boyer, The *Legend of John Brown,* 314.

18. Act of Sept. 18, 1850, chap. 60, 9 Stat. 462.

19. Judges 7:3.

20. Dana, "How We Met John Brown," 6–7.

21. Act of May 30, 1854, Chapter 59, 10 Stat. 277.

22. Sanborn, *Life and Letters of John Brown,* 269 n. 1.

23. Villard, *John Brown,* 218.

24. Ibid., 283–284.

25. Ibid., 248.

2. CARRYING THE WAR INTO AFRICA

1. See Geffert, "They Heard His Call," and Geffert (with Libby), "Regional Black Involvement in John Brown's Raid on Harper's Ferry," for evidence that Brown expected substantial black help when he decided to raid Harper's Ferry.

2. *Provisional Constitution and Ordinances for the People of the United States, by John Brown,* 1, 3, 15.

3. See Boyd B. Stutler, "Preface" to *Provisional Constitution and Ordinances for the People of the United States, by John Brown*, 3.

4. Redpath, *Public Life of Capt. John Brown*, 239.

5. Villard, *John Brown*, 389–390.

6. Ibid., 413; Ruchames, *John Brown, The Making of a Revolutionary*, 297.

7. Sanborn, *Life and Letters*, 526–527.

8. Villard, *John Brown*, 679.

9. Ibid., 684.

10. Anderson, *A Voice from Harper's Ferry*, 28–29.

11. Ibid., 35.

12. *Report of the Select Committee of the Senate*, 40–44.

13. Anderson, *Voice from Harper's Ferry*, 39.

14. Ibid., 36–37, stating that "of the many colored men living in the neighborhood, who had assembled in the town, a number were armed for the work." Geffert, "They Heard His Call," 30–31, and Geffert (with Libby), "Regional Black Involvement in John Brown's Raid on Harper's Ferry," 173, state that during the initial phase of the raid, Brown's men armed twenty-five to fifty slaves.

15. Boteler, "Recollections of the John Brown Raid," 406. Zittle, *A Correct History*, says that Newby's wound was "gaping open quite large enough to admit the fore part of an ordinary sized foot."

16. Barry, *The Strange Story of Harper's Ferry*, 82.

17. Ibid., 59–60; Villard, *John Brown*, 442–443; *New York Tribune*, Oct. 29, 1859; *New York Herald*, Oct. 31, 1859.

18. Thomas, "The Greatest Service I Rendered the State," 345–346.

19. *Report of the Select Committee of the Senate*, 41.

20. Ibid., 43–44.

21. Thomas, "The Greatest Service I Rendered the State," 355.

22. Green, "The Capture of John Brown," 566.

23. Ibid., 566; Thomas, "The Greatest Service I Rendered the State," 356.

24. J. B. to Mary Ann Brown, Oct. 31, 1859, Boyd B. Stutler Collection; J. B. to Thomas Russell, Oct. 21, 1859, in Ruchames, *John Brown, The Making of a Revolutionary*, 135.

25. Thomas, "The Greatest Service I Rendered the State," 356.

26. Boteler, "Recollections of the John Brown Raid," 410.

27. *Report of the Select Committee of the Senate*, 59.

28. Ibid., 60.

29. *New York Herald*, Oct. 21, 1859.

30. *New York Times*, Oct. 26, 1859.

31. *New York Herald*, October 21, 1859. Byrne, *The News from Harper's Ferry*, 95–99, and Zittle, *A Correct History*, 101–102, point out that Wise initially had two conversations with Brown, one on Tuesday afternoon, October 18, and another on Wednesday morning, October 19. Brown's biographers have erroneously telescoped these two meetings into the subsequent interrogation of Brown led by Mason and Vallandigham.

32. *New York Herald*, Oct. 21, 1859.

3. FRAMING THE CHARGES

1. *New York Herald*, Oct. 21, 1859.

2. Ibid., Oct. 26, 1859.

3. *Black's Law Dictionary*, 8th ed. (St. Paul, MN: Thomson West, 1999), 996.

4. See Ex Parte Milligan, 71 U.S. 2, 21 (1866).

5. Va. Const. (1851), art V, § 5.

6. *Report of the Select Committee of the Senate*, 37; Barton H. Wise, *Life of Henry A. Wise*, 243.

7. John Wise, *End of an Era*, 119. The *Richmond Enquirer* (semiweekly edition), Oct. 21, 1859, reported that Brown expected "assistance of from 3,000 to 5,000 men."

8. John Wise, *End of an Era*, 119.

9. Ibid., 119, 120, 124.

10. *Richmond Enquirer* (semiweekly edition), Oct. 25, 1859.

11. Villard, *John Brown*, 503.

12. *Richmond Enquirer* (semiweekly edition), Oct. 21, 1859.

13. *New York Herald*, Nov. 1, 1859.

14. *Richmond Enquirer* (semiweekly edition), Oct. 25, 1859, 2.

15. Ibid., Oct. 26, 1859, 1.

16. Ibid., Dec. 6, 1859, 2.

17. Barton H. Wise, *Life of Henry A. Wise*, 38.

18. Simpson, *A Good Southerner*, 66.

19. Ibid., 81.

20. Ibid., 224.

21. Rosengarten, "John Brown's Raid," 716.

22. Redpath, *Public Life of Capt. John Brown*, 286–287.

23. Va. Const. (1851), art. VI, §§2 (XIII), 7.

24. See Code of Va. (1849), chap. 158, §1.

25. A question later arose as to whether Beckham was on federal land or Maryland territory at the time he was shot, as the line between Maryland and Virginia followed the low-water mark on the Virginia side of the Potomac.

26. *New York Herald*, Oct. 21, 1859.

27. U.S. Const., art. I, §8, cl. 17.

28. Engdahl, "State and Federal Power over Federal Property," 290; see *S.R.A., Inc. v. Minnesota*, 327 U.S. 558, 562 (1946).

29. *Reily v. Lamar*, 6 U.S. (2 Cranch) 344, 356–357 (1805) (Marshall as to District of Columbia); *United States v. Cornell*, 25 Fed. Cases 650, 650 (Cir. Court of Rhode Island, 1820) (Story as to Rhode Island); see *Fort Leavenworth R. Co. v. Lowe*, 114 U.S. 525, 526 (1885).

30. Act to provide for the erecting and repairing of Arsenals and Magazines, and for other purposes, April 2, 1794, Chap. 14, 1 Stat. 352.

31. *Cultural Landscape Report: Lower Town, Harper's Ferry National Historical Park*, 3–7.

32. Act of Nov. 28, 1794, Chap. 24, Acts of the General Assembly of Virginia (Richmond, 1795).

33. *Cultural Landscape Report: Lower Town, Harper's Ferry National Historical Park*, 3–8; Smith, *Harper's Ferry Armory and the New Technology*, 41. For full texts of the deeds, see Noffsinger, *Harper's Ferry, West Virginia: Contributions toward a Physical History*, 70–78.

34. The Virginia enactment provided simply that "it shall and may be lawful for the President of the United States, or any person appointed by him for that purpose, to purchase within the limits of this State a

quantity of land, not exceeding six hundred and forty acres, for the use of the United States, for the purpose of erecting a magazine and arsenal thereon." Act of Nov. 28, 1794, chap. 24, Acts of the General Assembly of Virginia (Richmond, 1795). The deeds were grant deeds, reciting that the described land was "granted bargained and sold" to "the said George Washington president of the United States & his successors forever." Noffsinger, *Harper's Ferry, West Virginia: Contributions toward a Physical History*, 70–78.

35. Code of Va. (1849), chap. 2, §1 (places purchased by United States for forts and other buildings). The code here clearly acknowledged that, by the Act of 1794, Virginia had given its consent to the federal purchase at Harper's Ferry.

36. Grace "Federal-State 'Negotiations' over Federal Enclaves in the Early Republic," 559–569.

37. Cushing, "Extraterritoriality of Military Sites Occupied by the United States," 577–582. *Commonwealth v. Clary*, 8 Massachusetts Reports 72.

38. *Montana Wilderness Ass'n v. United States Forest Serv.*, 496 F. Supp. 880, 884 (D. Mont. 1980); *American Jurisprudence*, 2d ed. (2007), "Attorney General," Section 10.

39. See Engdahl, "State and Federal Power over Federal Property," 288–300.

40. Story, *Commentaries on the Constitution of the United States*, §1219.

41. *Fort Leavenworth R. Co. v. Lowe*, 114 U.S. 525, 526 (1885). The law relating to federal installations acquired under the enclave clause remained constant throughout the nineteenth century. The jurisdiction of the United States was "exclusive," and any attempt by a state to qualify that jurisdiction, either by attaching conditions to its consent or reserving any kind of "concurrent jurisdiction," was void. Beginning in 1937, however, the U.S. Supreme Court began to treat enclave property in the same way as other property acquired by the United States. Under Article IV, §3, cl. 2, of the Constitution, Congress has "power to dispose of and make all needful rules and regulations respecting the territory or other property belonging to the United States." Under this

power, Congress may acquire property for some purpose other than those listed in the enclave clause and enter into negotiations with states to share jurisdiction over the property. In *James v. Drago Contracting Co.*, 302 U.S. 134 (1937), the Supreme Court held that a state's consent under the enclave clause could be qualified in the same way as a cession of territory under Article IV. Thereafter, the law relating to federal jurisdiction over federal enclaves was driven more by policy considerations than strict constitutional doctrine. It was recognized that it was often good policy for the federal government to allow some exercise of state jurisdiction in federal enclaves, so long as the state jurisdiction did not interfere with the federal functions. See Engdahl, "State and Federal Power over Federal Property," 321–384.

42. Act of April 30, 1790, "An Act for the Punishment of certain Crimes against the United States," 1 Stat. 112–119.

43. Act of March 3, 1825, chap. 65, §3, 4 Stat. 115.

44. *United States v. Prejean*, 494 F.2d 495, 496 (Court of Appeals, 5th Cir., 1974).

45. Story, *Commentaries on the Constitution of the United States,* §1791.

46. The Federalist No. 43, *The Federalist, or the New Constitution,* 200.

47. Story, *Commentaries on the Constitution of the United States,* §1791.

48. Wilson, "Of Crimes Immediately against the Community, Lectures on Law," 437.

49. Act of April 30, 1790, "An Act for the Punishment of Certain Crimes against the United States," 1 Stat. 112–119, §1. (emphasis added).

50. Hurst, *The Law of Treason in the United States,* 144 (the word "treason" expresses "the central concept of betrayal of allegiance"); Sir Michael Foster, "Discourse on High Treason" (1762), 410 ("High Treason being an Offence committed against the Duty of Allegiance"); Leek, "Treason and the Constitution," 604 (treason "may be briefly and generally defined as a breach of allegiance").

51. *United States v. Wiltberger*, 18 U.S. (5 Wheat.) 76, 97 (1820) (emphasis added).

52. *Black's Law Dictionary*, 8th ed. (2004).

53. Blackstone, "Commentaries," 423–424.

54. Ibid., 424.

55. Leek, "Treason and the Constitution, 607; see *Radich v. Hutchins*, 95 U.S. 210, 211 (1877) (subject of Russian emperor owed allegiance to United States while domiciled in Texas during Civil War); Larson, "The Forgotten Constitutional Law of Treason and the Enemy Combatant Problem," 867–868 ("under American law, allegiance is owed to the United States by any person present within its borders other than those persons accompanying an invading military force").

56. Code of Va. (1849), chap. 191, §§1 and 2; chap. 209, §9.

57. Ibid., chap. 191, §§1, 3.

58. Ibid., chap. 200, §§1–9 ("Offences by Negroes").

59. Ibid., chap. 190, §1.

60. Ibid., chap. 190, §1; chap. 209, §9.

61. *New York Herald*, Oct. 26, 1859.

62. *Richmond Enquirer* (semiweekly edition), Oct. 21, 1859.

63. *New York Times*, Oct. 19, 1859.

64. *New York Herald*, Oct. 21, 1859.

65. *New York Times*, Oct. 19, 1859.

66. James Buchanan to Andrew Hunter, Dec. 17, 1859, in *Proceedings of Massachusetts Historical Society*, 46 (Dec. 1912): 245.

67. *New York Herald*, Oct. 26, 1859.

68. U.S. Const., art. IV, §2, cl. 2.

69. U.S. Const., art. VI, cl. 2.

70. Richard Parker to Andrew Hunter, Dec. 26, 1859, in *Proceedings of the Massachusetts Historical Society* 46 (Dec. 1912): 245–246.

71. U.S. Const., art. II, §2; Code of Virginia (1849), chap. 17, §18; see Va. Const. (1851), art. V, §5 (power to grant reprieves and pardons except as otherwise provided by law).

72. *New York Herald*, Oct. 26, 1859.

73. Ibid.

74. Code of Va. (1849), chap. 208, §2.

75. Copy of record of examining court, *Commonwealth of Virginia vs. John Brown,* Aaron C. Stephens, and Edwin Coppoc, white men, and Shields Green and John Copeland, negroes, Oct. 20 and Oct. 25, 1859, John Brown Papers, Jefferson County Circuit Clerk's Office, Charles Town, West Virginia.

76. *Richmond Enquirer* (semiweekly edition), Oct. 25, 1859.

77. Ibid.

78. Code of Va. (1849), chap. 205, §6.

79. Ibid., §4.

80. Ibid., chap. 206, §§2, 7.

81. Ibid., §7.

82. Parker's physical appearance was described in "John Brown's Invasion," *New York Weekly Tribune,* Nov. 12, 1859.

83. Stutler, "Judge Richard Parker," 27–33.

84. Ibid., 28, 35.

85. *New York Herald,* Oct. 22, 1859; *Richmond Enquirer* (semiweekly edition), Oct. 25, 1859; see Washington, "The Trial of John Brown," 170–171.

4. THE INDICTMENT

1. Bushong, *History of Jefferson County,* 67, 84.

2. In 1888, Judge Parker recollected that in 1859 there was "a long, narrow passage between two dead walls of brick on either side, without any light, except what came through the single door opening toward the street, or what might reach it from the door of the court room when it chanced to be opened." Richard Parker, "Trial of John Brown," manuscript in John Brown Papers, Library of Congress, printed in "John Brown's Raid," *St. Louis Globe-Democrat,* April 8, 1888, 26.

3. *New York Herald,* Nov. 10, 1859.

4. Bushong, *History of Jefferson County,* 17.

5. Villard, *John Brown,* 472–474.

6. See Finkelman, *Defending Slavery,* 29–33.

7. Ibid., 19–20, 15–16, 37–39.

8. Basler, *Collected Works*, 2:461.

9. Bushong, *History of Jefferson County*, 67 (built in 1806).

10. *New York Daily Tribune*, Nov. 5, 1859.

11. *Report of the Select Committee of the Senate*, 66.

12. Sanborn, *Life and Letters of John Brown*, 578–579.

13. Affidavit of John Avis, April 25, 1882, in *Southern Historical Society Papers* 13 (1885): 340.

14. *New York Herald*, Oct. 22, 1859.

15. Ibid., Oct. 27, 1859.

16. Ibid., Oct. 26, 1859.

17. 1860 U.S. Federal Census, Slave Schedules, Jefferson County, Virginia.

18. *New York Herald*, Nov. 10, 1859.

19. Ibid., Oct. 26, 1859.

20. Pulliam, *Constitutional Conventions of Virginia*, 107; Morrison, *College of Hampden Sidney Dictionary of Biography 1776–1825*, 229–230; Norris, *History of the Lower Shenandoah Valley Counties of Frederick, Berkeley, Jefferson, and Clarke*, 634–635.

21. *Report of the Select Committee of the Senate*, 64.

22. Villard, *John Brown*, 485 n. 53.

23. Hunter to Wise, Oct. 22, 1859, in Executive Papers of Governor Henry A. Wise, Library of Virginia, Richmond.

24. *New York Herald*, Oct. 26, 1859.

25. 1860 U.S. Federal Census, Slave Schedules, Jefferson County, Virginia.

26. Ibid., Slave Inhabitants, Berkeley County, Virginia.

27. *New York Times*, Nov. 12, 1859.

28. *New York Herald*, Oct. 26, 1859.

29. Ibid.

30. Ibid.

31. Ibid.

32. Ibid.

33. Ibid.

34. *Baltimore Sun*, Oct. 26, 1859.

35. *New York Herald,* Oct. 26, 1859.

36. Ibid.

37. Copy of record of examining court, *Commonwealth v. John Brown et al.,* John Brown Records, Circuit Court of Jefferson County.

38. *New York Herald,* Oct. 26, 1859.

39. Ibid.

40. "Informal Recollections," *St. Louis Globe-Democrat,* April 8, 1888, 26.

41. Indictment, Oct. 26, 1859, in John Brown Papers, Jefferson County Circuit Clerk's Office, Charles Town, West Virginia.

42. Copy of record of examining court, *Commonwealth of Virginia vs. John Brown, Aaron C. Stephens, and Edwin Coppoc, white men, and Shields Green and John Copeland, negroes,* Oct. 20 and Oct. 25, 1859, in John Brown Papers, Jefferson County Clerk's Office, Charles Town, West Virginia.

43. Story, *Commentaries on the Constitution of the United States,* §1791. In §1296 of the same volume, Story writes that a state could not "take cognizance [of], or punish the offence" of treason against the United States, "whatever it may do in relation to the offence of treason, committed exclusively against itself," thus allowing the possibility of prosecutions for treason against a state. Story expresses doubt, however, whether "any case can, under the constitution, exist, which is not at the same time treason against the United States."

44. *Richmond Enquirer* (semiweekly edition), Oct. 25, 1859.

45. Boyd B. Stutler to Barrie Stavis, Jan. 19, 1968, Boyd B. Stutler Collection.

46. U.S. Const., art. IV, §2, cl. 2 (emphasis added).

47. In New York in 1814, defendants charged with treason were acquitted. See *People v. Lynch,* 11 John R. 549 N.Y. (1814). In Rhode Island in 1844, Thomas William Dorr was convicted of treason against Rhode Island, but he was later granted amnesty by the state legislature. See Pitman, *Report of the Trial of Thomas Wilson Dorr.*

48. See Blackstone, "Commentaries," 423–424; Larson, "The Forgotten Constitutional Law of Treason and the Enemy Combatant Problem," 885–890 (allegiance and the John Brown trial); and Carso,

"Whom Can We Trust Now?" 8, 11, 34, and 37. See also my discussion of allegiance in chap. 3.

5. THE JURY IS SUMMONED

1. *New York Times,* Nov. 12, 1859.
2. 1860 U.S. Federal Census, Slave Schedules, Jefferson County, Virginia.
3. Villard, *John Brown,* 484.
4. *New York Herald,* Oct. 27, 1859.
5. *Harper's Weekly,* Nov. 5, 1859, 710.
6. Matthews, *Digest of the Laws of Virginia of a Criminal Nature* (1861), 236 n. 1.
7. Strother, *Lecture on John Brown in Cleveland, 1868.*
8. Matthews, *Digest of the Laws of Virginia of a Criminal Nature* (1861), 261 n. 24.
9. *New York Herald,* Oct. 27, 1859.
10. *Baltimore Sun,* Oct. 28, 1859, 1.
11. *New York Herald,* Oct. 28, 1859, 1.
12. Strother, *Lecture on John Brown in Cleveland, 1868.*
13. *New York Herald,* Nov. 10, 1859.
14. Code of Va. (1849), chap. 162, §9.
15. Ibid., chap. 208, §4. A "freehold" is an estate in land held in fee simple, in fee tail, or for a term of life. The term may also refer to a real property interest that is or may become possessory. A freeholder is a person who holds a freehold. *Black's Law Dictionary,* 8th ed. (1999). Generally, this excludes persons who are mere renters of real property or who have the right to the use of the property for some period less than a lifetime.
16. Order of Oct. 25, 1859, *Commonwealth v. John Brown et al.,* Circuit Court of Jefferson County.
17. Virginia Acts 1852–1853, chap. 27, §1; Matthews, *Digest of the Laws of Virginia of a Criminal Nature* (1861), 238 n. 7.
18. Code of Va. (1849), chap. 208, §8.
19. Ibid., chap. 208, §9.

20. *New York Herald*, Oct. 28, 1859.

21. *Baltimore Sun*, Oct. 28, 1859.

22. *Record of the Trial of John Brown by Judge Richard Parker*, University of Virginia Library, Charlottesville.

23. U.S. Census schedules for the State of Virginia, County of Jefferson, 1860, show the following jurors owned slaves, in the numbers indicated: Joseph Myers (twelve), Thomas Osbourn (ten), John C. Wiltshire (ten), Richard Timberlake (seven), Isaac Dust (seven), John C. McClure (four), Thomas Watson Jr. (four). No slave records were found for the other jurors.

24. *Baltimore Sun*, Oct. 28, 1859; *New York Herald*, Oct. 28, 1859.

25. *Baltimore Sun*, Oct. 28, 1859.

26. Redpath, *Public Life of Capt. John Brown*, 324–325.

27. *Baltimore Sun*, Oct. 28, 1859; *New York Herald*, Oct. 28, 1859.

28. *Baltimore Sun*, Oct. 28, 1859.

6. THE TESTIMONY BEGINS

1. *New York Herald*, Oct. 28, 1859.

2. Ibid.

3. *Report of the Select Committee of the Senate*, 42; *New York Herald*, Oct. 28, 1859, 4.

4. *New York Herald*, Oct. 20, 1859.

5. *Louisville Journal*, as quoted in *New York Times*, Oct. 25, 1859.

6. Code of Va. (1849), chap. 208, §16 (no person shall be tried for criminal offense while insane); §17 (if jury finds person insane at time of offense, court may dismiss prosecution and either discharge prisoner or order him removed to lunatic asylum).

7. Ray, *Treatise on the Medical Jurisprudence of Insanity* (1853), 2.

8. Code of Va. (1849), chap. 16, §17, *Fifth*.

9. Ibid., chap. 208, §17.

10. Ibid., 386, editor's note.

11. Ray, *Treatise on the Medical Jurisprudence of Insanity* (1853), 2.

12. M'Naghten's [*sic*] Case, 10 Clark and Finnelly's Reports, House of Lords, 200 (1843).

13. *New York Herald*, Oct. 28, 1859.

14. Hill, *Decisive Battles of the Law*, 87.

15. *New York Herald*, Oct. 28, 1859.

16. The newspaper reports here confused "Mr. Lewis" with "Mr. Tilden." Hunter was clearly referring to the latter.

17. See Code of Va. (1849), chap. 190, §1.

18. Matthews, *Digest of the Laws of Virginia of a Criminal Nature* (1861), 253 n. 14.

19. Ibid.

20. Evidence assembled by Hannah Geffert and Jean Libby shows that during the initial phase of the raid, twenty to fifty black men were armed with Brown's pikes. "Eyewitness accounts tell of considerable local black activity. . . . The hillsides became congested with frightened people seeking refuge, and for a time, armed Africans were seen in some numbers." When the engine house was under siege, blacks participated in the fighting on Brown's side. See Geffert (with Libby), "Regional Black Involvement in John Brown's Raid on Harper's Ferry," 173–174. See also Geffert, "They Heard His Call."

21. Young, *Senator James Murray Mason*, xiii, 35–36, 38.

22. Villard, *John Brown*, 485, 645 n. 54.

23. See Cushing, "Extraterritoriality of Military Sites Occupied by the United States," 577–582, and my discussion in chap. 3 of this book.

24. Maryland's claim was well rooted in colonial history, for in the royal charter creating Maryland (1632) King Charles I granted Lord Baltimore title to the land north of the "River of Pattowmack . . . unto the farther Bank of the said River." Virginia expressed formal acceptance of Maryland's claim in its constitution of 1776. See Barry, *Strange Story of Harper's Ferry*, 173 ("The State of Maryland has always laid claim to jurisdiction over the Potomac, as far as the ordinary water mark on the Virginia shore").

25. Although there had been previous prosecutions for treason against a state, none ended with the execution of the defendant. See discussion in chap. 4.

26. Code of Va. (1849), chap. 190, §1.

27. Ibid.

28. *New York Herald*, Oct. 28, 1859.

29. Barry, *The Strange Story of Harper's Ferry*, 25–26; Merritt R. Smith, *Harper's Ferry Armory and the New Technology*, 256; Bushong, *History of Jefferson County*, 78; Washington, "The Trial of John Brown," 173.

30. *New York Herald*, Oct. 28, 1859.

31. The usual form for administering an oath to a witness in Virginia was: "You do swear, upon the Holy Bible, that the evidence you shall give in the matter now pending before me, shall be the truth, the whole truth, and nothing but the truth. So help you God." A witness who was a nonbeliever or objected to taking an oath could substitute the words "solemnly affirm" in place of "swear, upon the Holy Bible" and omit the reference to God. Mayo, *A Guide to Magistrates*, 250.

32. *New York Herald*, Oct. 28, 1859.

33. Ibid.

34. Ibid.

35. Matthews, *Digest of the Laws of Virginia of a Criminal Nature* (1861), 256 n. 18.

36. Ibid., 256–259; Virginia Acts, 1850–1851, 34, §18.

7. The Name and the Shadow of a Fair Trial

1. *New York Daily Tribune*, Nov. 7, 1859, quoting *Independent Democrat* and *Free Press*.

2. Hinton, *John Brown and His Men*, 365–366 n. 1.

3. *New York Herald*, Oct. 29, 1859.

4. *Baltimore Sun*, Oct. 29, 1859.

5. *New York Daily Tribune*, Nov. 7, 1859, quoting the *Democrat*.

6. *New York Herald*, Oct. 29, 1859.

7. Ibid.

8. Ibid.

9. Ibid.

10. Ibid.

11. Ibid.
12. Ibid.
13. Ibid.
14. Ibid.
15. Ibid.
16. Ibid.
17. Ibid.
18. Ibid.
19. *New York Herald,* Oct. 31, 1859.
20. Ibid.
21. Ibid.
22. Ibid.
23. Virginia Bill of Rights, §8.
24. Code of Va. (1849), chap. 176, §§20, 22, 23; chap. 211, §2.
25. Ibid., chap. 176, §19: "A negro or Indian shall be a competent witness in a case of the Commonwealth for or against a negro or Indian, or in a civil case to which only negroes or Indians are parties, *but not in any other case*" (emphasis added).
26. *New York Herald,* Oct. 29, 1859.
27. Ibid.
28. Ibid.
29. Ibid.
30. Ibid.
31. Ibid.

8. THE QUIET WAS DECEPTIVE

1. *New York Daily Tribune,* Nov. 5, 1859.
2. Bushong, *History of Jefferson County,* 68–69.
3. *New York Daily Tribune,* Nov. 5, 1859.
4. *New York Daily Tribune,* Nov. 8, 1859 (Harding sleeps in court); *New York Daily Tribune,* Nov. 10, 1859 (Harding "a little notorious for his bibulous weaknesses").
5. *New York Herald,* Nov. 10, 1859.

6. Extracts from Hoyt's letters, enclosed in Thomas Wentworth Higginson to friends, Nov. 4, 1859; original in Worcester, Massachusetts; copy in Boyd B. Stutler Collection.

7. Ibid.

8. John Andrew to George L. Stearns, Nov. 3, 1859, Boyd B. Stutler Collection.

9. Extracts from Hoyt's letters, enclosed in Thomas Wentworth Higginson to friends, Nov. 4, 1859; copy in Boyd B. Stutler Collection.

10. Riddle, *Recollections of War Times,* 3 n. 1.

11. Griswold to editors of Cleveland newspapers, Nov. 15, 1859, in *New York Times,* Nov. 19, 1859.

12. Cleon Moore to David H. Strother, Nov. 4, 1859, copy in Boyd B. Stutler Collection.

13. *Baltimore Sun,* Oct. 31, 1859.

14. Ibid.

15. Ibid.

16. *New York Herald,* Oct. 31, 1859.

17. "A brief history of John Brown, otherwise (old B) and his family: *as connected With Kansas;* By one who knows." See Villard *John Brown* 87, 597 n. 17.

18. See Federal Rules of Evidence, Rule 801.

19. *New York Herald,* Oct. 31, 1859.

20. Ibid.

21. Ibid.

22. Ibid.

23. Ibid.

24. Ibid.

25. Ibid.

26. Ibid.

27. Ibid.

28. Ibid.

29. Ibid.

30. Ibid.

31. *Baltimore Sun,* Oct. 31, 1859.

32. Ibid.

33. Ibid.

34. *New York Herald,* Oct. 31, 1859.

35. Although the newspapers did not report this inflammatory statement as part of Harding's argument, it was later attributed to him in the argument made by Hiram Griswold. For a summary of that argument, see chap. 9.

9. THE VERDICT

1. Ruchames, *John Brown, the Making of a Revolutionary,* 154.

2. J. B. to Mary Ann Brown, Oct. 31, 1859, copy in Boyd B. Stutler Collection.

3. Extracts from Hoyt's letters, enclosed in Thomas Wentworth Higginson to friends, Nov. 4, 1859; original in Worcester, Massachusetts; copy in Boyd B. Stutler Collection.

4. *The Life, Trial, and Execution of Captain John Brown,* 84.

5. Ibid., 85.

6. Ibid., 86.

7. Ibid.

8. Ibid., 87.

9. Ibid., 88.

10. Under the common-law felony murder rule, any killing committed in the course of a felony was murder. If more than one person participated in the felony, a killing by any one of the participants would make the others guilty of the murder. This was the case even when the felony was not inherently dangerous or likely to result in death. The rule was widely followed in the United States, although some of its harshness was relieved by requiring that the felony involve an act of violence or that death be its natural and probable consequence. In modern years, many jurisdictions have limited the rule in other ways. See LaFave, *Criminal Law,* 4th ed., §14.5.

11. *The Life, Trial, and Execution of Captain John Brown,* 88.

12. Ibid., 89.

13. Ibid., 89–90.

14. *New York Herald,* Nov. 7, 1859.

15. Ibid.

16. Ibid.

17. Ibid.

18. Ibid.

19. Ibid.

20. Ibid.

21. *New York Herald*, Nov. 1, 1859.

22. Ibid.

23. Ibid.

24. Code of Va. (1849), chap. 3, §1. In *Gassies v. Ballou*, 6 Pet. 761 (1832), Chief Justice Marshall had laid down the rule that a citizen of the United States residing in any state of the Union was a citizen of the state.

25. *Report of the Select Committee of the Senate*, 60.

26. *New York Herald*, Nov. 1, 1859.

27. U.S. Const., art. IV, §2, cl. 1. This clause is sometimes called the comity clause. Another privileges and immunities clause became part of the Constitution when the Fourteenth Amendment was adopted after the Civil War. U.S. Const., amend. XIV, §1. Since this was not ratified until July 9, 1868, however, it had no application to Brown's trial.

28. Amar, *America's Constitution*, 253; Bogen, *Privileges and Immunities*, xviii, 23–24. In *Corfield v. Coryel*, 6 Fed. Case 546 (C.C.E.D. Pa. 1832), Supreme Court Justice Bushrod Washington stated that this clause protected "privileges and immunities which are, in their nature, fundamental; which belong, of right, to the citizens of all free governments; and which have, at all times, been enjoyed by the citizens of the several states which compose this Union, from the time of their becoming free, independent, and sovereign." According to Washington, these included "protection by the government; the enjoyment of life and liberty, with the right to acquire and possess property of every kind, and to pursue and obtain happiness and safety; subject nevertheless to such restraints as the government may justly prescribe for the general good of the whole."

29. Story, *Commentaries on the Constitution of the United States*, §1800.

30. The Federalist No. 80, *The Federalist, or the New Constitution*, 366.

31. See "Can the Crime of Treason Be Committed against One of the United States?" *American Law Magazine* 4 (1845), 318–350.

32. Larson, "The Forgotten Constitutional Law of Treason and the Enemy Combatant Problem," 887, 889, characterizes Hunter's privileges and immunities argument as "convoluted" and notes that Brown "did not receive, and clearly did not want to receive, any protection whatsoever from the government of Virginia." Yet under the privileges and immunities clause he was legally entitled to that protection whether he wanted it or not, and, at least arguably, he was legally obligated to be loyal to the government of Virginia and obey Virginia's laws whether he wanted to or not. Larson poses a challenging hypothetical, in which a group of Virginians "gathered with arms and marched on Richmond in attempt to overthrow the state government." He says that that would "seem to clearly constitute treason by levying war against the State of Virginia." If, however, a group of armed North Carolinians crossed over the border and marched to Richmond for the same purpose, it would seem "peculiar that they could not be punished for the same crime" (889).

33. Although Hunter's argument was not laid out in detail, some case decisions lend it support. See, e.g., *Dunham v. Lamphere*, 69 Mass. (3 Gray) 268, 275 (1855), in which the court stated, "And surely those inhabitants of other states, who come within the territorial limits of this state, and thereby owe a temporary allegiance, and become amenable to its laws, have no just reason to complain, if . . . they are bound to conform to a salutary law, necessary for their common good." In *Heridia v. Ayres*, 29 Mass. (12 Pick.) 334, 345 (1832), the court wrote, "Every stranger . . . coming within [Massachusetts's] jurisdiction, owes a temporary allegiance and is bound by its laws." In *Bissell v. Briggs*, 9 Mass. (8 Tyng.) 462, 470 (1813), the court said, "An inhabitant of one state may, without changing his domicile, go into another; . . . and while there he owes a temporary allegiance and is bound by its laws."

34. Brian S. Carso Jr. has written: "Virtually any theory by which Brown and his men would owe loyalty to Virginia would have to be

grounded in a concept of national allegiance, which in turn would put the Virginia treason law on shaky ground" (*"Whom Can We Trust Now?"* 196). Rather that put the Virginia treason law on "shaky ground," however, Brown's national allegiance would seem to provide a constitutionally sound basis for charging him with treason against Virginia.

35. *New York Herald,* Nov. 1, 1859. For an interesting summary and analysis of Hunter's arguments, see Larson, "The Forgotten Constitutional Law of Treason and the Enemy Combatant Problem," 886–890.

36. *New York Herald,* Nov. 1, 1859.

37. Ibid.

38. Ibid.

39. Ibid.

10. The Sentence

1. Story, *Commentaries on the Constitution,* §1296.

2. The official court records kept in Charles Town today do not include the written verdict. Records were removed from the courthouse during the Civil War. When they were returned, some were missing.

3. *New York Herald,* Nov. 2, 1859.

4. Code of Va. (1849), chap. 190, §1 (treason defined).

5. Wise to Andrew Hunter, Nov. 6, 1859, in *Proceedings of the Massachusetts Historical Society,* 3rd series, 1 (February 1908): 329.

6. *Baltimore Sun,* Oct. 31, 1859.

7. Ibid., Nov. 3, 1859.

8. *New York Herald,* Nov. 10, 1859.

9. *New York Daily Tribune,* Nov. 5, 1859.

10. *New York Herald,* Nov. 3, 1859.

11. *St. Louis Globe-Democrat,* April 8, 1888.

12. *New York Daily Tribune,* Nov. 5, 1859.

13. Ibid.

14. *Baltimore Sun,* Nov. 3, 1859.

15. Villard, *John Brown,* 498.

16. Printed versions of Brown's speech vary slightly, mostly in punctuation. This version follows the text in the *New York Herald*, Nov. 3, 1859, except that paragraph breaks have been added.

17. Robert Penn Warren charged that "every reference to fact in that oration was a lie." See Warren, *John Brown: The Making of a Martyr*, 412.

18. *Report of the Select Committee of the Senate*, 62–63.

19. Ibid., 67–68.

20. Matthews, *Digest of the Laws of Virginia of a Criminal Nature* (1861), 266 n. 32.

21. Code of Va. (1849), chap. 210, §8.

22. Villard, *John Brown*, 499.

23. Typescript of sentence delivered Nov. 2, 1859, in Boyd B. Stutler Collection. The death warrant of the same date is in the John Brown Papers, Jefferson County Circuit Clerk's Office, Charles Town, West Virginia.

24. *New York Daily Tribune*, Nov. 5, 1859.

25. Villard, *John Brown*, 647 n. 83.

26. Ibid., 500.

11. THE EXECUTION

1. Villard, *John Brown*, 413; Ruchames, *John Brown, The Making of a Revolutionary*, 297.

2. Villard, *John Brown*, 687; Anderson, *A Voice from Harper's Ferry*, 45.

3. *Dred Scott v. Sandford*, 19 How. (60 U.S.) 393 (1857), 407.

4. See discussion in chap. 9.

5. *New York Daily Tribune*, Nov. 8, 1859; see Death Sentence of Shields Green, Nov. 10, 1859, in John Brown Papers, Circuit Clerk's Office, Charles Town, West Virginia.

6. *New York Daily Tribune*, Nov. 9, 1859, quoting from *The Spirit of Jefferson* (Charlestown).

7. *New York Daily Tribune*, Nov. 9, 1859.

8. Ibid.; *New York Herald,* Nov. 9, 1859, 4. Jury verdict (no date) and death sentence (Nov. 10, 1859) of John Copeland, Circuit Court of Jefferson County, Charlestown.

9. Letter from Wise to Hunter, Nov. 16, 1859, in *Proceedings of Massachusetts Historical Society,* 3rd series, 1 (May 1907): 94.

10. Wise to Hunter, endorsement on letter of A. Jones to H. A. Wise, in *Proceedings of Massachusetts Historical Society,* 1 (June 1908): 513.

11. *New York Daily Tribune,* Nov. 9, 1859.

12. *New York Herald,* Nov. 9, 1859.

13. *New York Daily Tribune,* Nov. 10, 1859.

14. Indictment, Nov. 7, 1859, *Commonwealth v. John E. Cooke* [*sic*], in John Brown Papers, Jefferson County Circuit Clerk's Office, Charles Town, West Virginia.

15. *New York Daily Tribune,* Nov. 10, 1859.

16. Voorhees, "Defense of John E. Cook," 379–402.

17. Jury verdict, Nov. 9, 1859, *Commonwealth v. John E. Cooke* [*sic*], in John Brown Papers, Jefferson County Circuit Clerk's Office, Charles Town, West Virginia.

18. Death sentence (warrant) for John Copeland; death sentence for Shields Green; death sentence for John E. Cook; Nov. 10, 1859, in John Brown Papers, Jefferson County Circuit Clerk's Office, Charles Town, West Virginia; *New York Herald,* Dec. 12, 1859, 1.

19. Voluminous files of these letters are preserved in the Executive Papers of Governor Henry A. Wise in the Library of Virginia and in the Henry Alexander Wise and Family Collection in the Library of Congress.

20. Villard, *John Brown,* 502.

21. *New York Daily Tribune,* Nov. 9, 1859.

22. Code of Virginia (1849), chap. 17, §18; see Va. Const. (1851), art. V, §5 (power to grant reprieves and pardons except as otherwise provided by law). For further discussion, see chap. 3.

23. Code of Virginia (1849), chap. 17, §18.

24. *Baltimore Sun,* Nov. 8, 1859.

25. See chap. 6.

26. Villard, *John Brown,* 507–508 n. 97.

27. Oates, *To Purge This Land with Blood,* 329.

28. These affidavits are in the John Brown Papers in the Library of Congress. Their contents are summarized in Oates, *To Purge This Land with Blood,* 329–331, 410–412 nn. 38 and 39.

29. Villard, *John Brown,* 508.

30. Wise to Stribling, November 10, 1859, Henry Alexander Wise and Family Collection, Library of Congress.

31. *Richmond Enquirer* (semiweekly edition), Oct. 25, 1859.

32. Matthews, *Digest of the Laws of Virginia of a Criminal Nature* (1861), 276–279.

33. *U.S. v. Wiltberger,* 18 U.S. (5 Wheat.) 76, 97 (1820).

34. *Commonwealth v. Brown. To the Honorable John J. Allen, President, and his associates, Judges of the Supreme Court of Appeals of Virginia. Petition of John Brown for writ of error, by his counsel Samuel Chilton and William Green,* 11.

35. Code of Virginia (1849), chap. 208, §34.

36. Ibid.

37. *Commonwealth v. Brown. To the Honorable John J. Allen, President, and his associates, Judges of the Supreme Court of Appeals of Virginia. Petition of John Brown for writ of error, by his counsel Samuel Chilton and William Green,* 11.

38. Code of Va. (1849), chap. 165, §2.

39. See *New York Daily Tribune,* Nov. 23, 1859 (Brown's counsel "were not allowed to be heard").

40. Entry for November 19, 1859, in Order Book No. 20, Supreme Court of Appeals, Richmond Session, Library of Virginia; denial of writ of error to Supreme Court of Appeals, Richmond, for John Brown, Nov. 19, 1859, in Jefferson County Circuit Clerk's Office, Charles Town, West Virginia; see *New York Herald,* Nov. 20, 1859; *New York Daily Tribune,* Nov. 23, 1859.

41. Tucker to Hunter, Nov. 19, 1859, in *Proceedings of Massachusetts Historical Society,* 3rd series, 1 (June 1908): 514.

42. Va. Const. (1851), art. VI, §13.

43. *Richmond Enquirer,* as reported in *Baltimore Sun,* Nov. 7, 1859.

44. *New York Herald,* Nov. 11, 1859.

45. Wise to Hunter, Nov. 16, 1859, in *Proceedings of Massachusetts Historical Society*, 3rd series, 1 (May 1907): 93.

46. *New York Herald*, Nov. 18, 1859.

47. *Ibid.*, Nov. 23, 1859.

48. *Baltimore Sun*, Nov. 30, 1859.

49. Bushong, *History of Jefferson County*, 132.

50. See *New York Times*, Nov. 17, 1859 (three large fires, the last consuming more than twelve hundred bushels of wheat); "John Brown's Raid[:] Recollections of Prosecuting Attorney Andrew Hunter," Huntington Library, 12, ("fires were being lighted up all over the county and barns burned").

51. Bushong, *History of Jefferson County*, 131.

52. On Nov. 19, Col. J. Lucius Davis, commander of the Virginia troops in Charlestown, wired Governor Wise that Negroes were setting the fires. See Geffert, "They Heard His Call," 36. For fires and other property damage committed by blacks in Jefferson and Berkeley Counties, see Geffert (with Libby), "Regional Black Involvement in John Brown's Raid on Harper's Ferry," 175.

53. Villard, *John Brown*, 523.

54. *Baltimore Sun*, Nov. 29, 1859.

55. Ibid., Nov. 30, 1859.

56. *New York Times*, Nov. 15, 1859.

57. Katherine Mayo, "Sculptor's Visit to John Brown," clipping (1909) from unidentified newspaper, in Boyd B. Stutler Collection.

58. Ruffin, *Diary of Edmund Ruffin*, 367–368.

59. Robertson, *Stonewall Jackson*, 198.

60. Ibid.

61. Tucker, "John Wilkes Booth at the John Brown Hanging," 10.

62. As reported in *New York Herald*, Dec. 1, 1859.

63. Ibid.; see also *New York Herald*, Dec. 3, 1859.

64. Strother, *Lecture on John Brown in Cleveland, 1868;* see chap. 5.

65. "Informal Recollections," *St. Louis Globe-Democrat*, April 8, 1888, 26.

66. Villard, *John Brown*, 546.

67. Ibid., 540.

68. Ibid., 543.

69. Ibid., 551.

70. *Independent Democrat,* Nov. 22, 1859, as quoted in Villard, *John Brown,* 545.

71. Villard, *John Brown,* 546.

72. Wise to Andrew Hunter, Nov. 2, 1859, in *Proceedings of the Massachusetts Historical Society,* 3rd series, 1 (Feb. 1908): 329.

73. "John Brown's Raid[:] Recollections of Prosecuting Attorney Andrew Hunter," Huntington Library, 7 8; *Report of the Select Committee of the Senate,* 60. A will was executed on December 1 and a codicil on December 2, the morning of the execution.

74. John Brown's Will and Codicil, Book 16, p. 143, Jefferson County Court Records, Charles Town, West Virginia; also in Villard, *John Brown,* 669.

75. Villard, *John Brown,* 653 n. 122.

76. The myth that Brown kissed a black child in the arms of its mother was thoroughly demolished by John Avis in an affidavit made in 1882. See "Refutation of Several Romances about the Execution of John Brown," 341. The interesting story of the myth, with the additional information that John Avis's son, Edward Spaw Avis, was probably kissed by Brown is in Eby, "John Brown's Kiss," 42–47.

77. *Harper's Weekly,* December 24, 1859, 823; Stutler, "John Brown's Letter," 16 n. 13.

78. Villard, *John Brown,* 523.

79. General Order No. 25, Major General William B. Taliaferro, November 30, 1859, in Military Order Book, 1859–1860, John Brown's Raid, Department of Military Affairs, Commonwealth of Virginia, Library of Virginia, Richmond.

80. Preston, "The Execution of John Brown," 187–188.

81. Ibid., 188.

82. Ibid.

83. Ruffin, *The Diary of Edmund Ruffin,* 370.

84. Preston, "The Execution of John Brown," 189.

85. Ruffin, *Diary of Edmund Ruffin,* 370.

86. Ibid., 371.

87. Robertson, *Stonewall Jackson*, 199.

88. Booth, *"Right or Wrong, God Judge Me,"* 60. Booth received $64.58 from the state for his nineteen days of service. Auditor of Public Accounts, entry 145, Harper's Ferry Fund, Accounts and Vouchers, 1860, Library of Virginia, Richmond.

89. Preston, "The Execution of John Brown," 189.

12. MARCHING ON

1. Basler, *Collected Works*, 3:339.

2. Ibid., 2:255.

3. Ibid., 3:496.

4. Ibid., 3:502.

5. Ibid., 3:538, 541.

6. Villard, *John Brown*, 564–565.

7. Chase to Joseph H. Barrett, Oct. 29, 1859, Boyd B. Stutler Collection.

8. Henry Steele Commager, ed., *Documents of American History*, 8th ed. (New York, 1968), 363–365.

9. *Staunton Republican Vindicator*, Nov. 18, 1859, quoted in Reynolds, *John Brown, Abolitionist*, 359.

10. Congressional Globe, 36th Cong., 1st sess., 1859, 69.

11. Ruchames, *John Brown, The Making of a Revolutionary*, 266–267.

12. Emerson, *Complete Works of Ralph Waldo Emerson*, 7:427.

13. Ruchames, *John Brown, The Making of a Revolutionary*, 277.

14. *Report of the Select Committee of the Senate*, 18.

15. McPherson, *Battle Cry of Freedom*, 212.

16. Simpson, *A Good Southerner*, 232–236.

17. Ibid., 236.

18. McPherson, *Battle Cry of Freedom*, 232.

19. Ibid., 230–231.

20. Bushong, *History of Jefferson County*, 190–200; Barry, *Strange Story of Harper's Ferry*, 141 ("ninety-nine in every hundred of the in-

habitants of the county had been in active sympathy with the rebellion").

21. Bushong, *History of Jefferson County*, 145–146; Stutler, *West Virginia in the Civil War*, v, 16–18.

22. Ibid., 19.

23. Ibid., 20; Bushong, *History of Jefferson County*, 147–148.

24. Hammond, "John Brown as Founder," 74, contrasts Brown with Lee, asking· "Which of the two acted on the higher principle, which violated the greater law, which one carried more blood on his hands, and who between them is a more genuinely American hero?"

25. *John Brown's Raid[:] Recollections of Prosecuting Attorney Andrew Hunter*, 21, Huntington Library.

26. Douglas, *I Rode with Stonewall*, 297; Taylor, *With Sheridan up the Shenandoah Valley in 1864*, 39, 53.

27. Ibid., 59, 242; Bushong, *History of Jefferson County*, 146, 148, 150, 153, 154, 160, 164, 167, 172–173, 201.

28. Taylor, *With Sheridan up the Shenandoah Valley in 1864*, 264 (sung in front of Charlestown courthouse on Aug. 23, 1864); see Rhodes, *All for the Union*, 178; Fisk, *Hard Marching Every Day*, 253.

29. "Battle Hymn of the Republic," *Atlantic Monthly* 9 (February 1862), 10.

30. Basler, *Collected Works*, 6:29–30.

31. Ibid., 6:30.

32. Milroy to Lincoln, Jan. 1, 1864, Abraham Lincoln Papers, Library of Congress.

33. Ferguson, *The Trial in American Life*, 150.

34. J. C. Furnas, one of Brown's most strident critics, called the song "a miraculous accident" and sarcastically stated that "being sung about is the perfect way to become a folk hero." Furnas, *The Road to Harpers Ferry*, 46–47.

35. Emerson, *Journals and Miscellaneous Notebooks of Ralph Waldo Emerson*, 15:468.

36. Burr, "War Democrats—Their Crimes," 201.

37. Stewart, *Camp, March and Battle-field*, 24–25.

38. See White, *Lincoln's Greatest Speech*.

39. Basler, *Collected Works*, 8:332–333.

40. Ruchames, *John Brown, The Making of a Revolutionary*, 167. Carton, *Patriotic Treason*, 340, states that Brown's "last written words predicted both the suffering and the redemption that Lincoln's oratory would later struggle to sanctify."

41. George H. Hoyt to John Brown, Nov. 22, 1859, Boyd B. Stutler Collection (advising Brown that the Supreme Court of Appeals had denied a writ of error in his case and that the attorneys have "deemed it futile to ask for one on account of the other prisoners").

42. Hinton, *John Brown and His Men*, 508–512; Villard, *John Brown*, 570, 681, 682, 684. Death sentence (warrant) for John Copeland; death sentence for Shields Green; death sentence for John E. Cook; Nov. 10, 1859, in John Brown Papers, Jefferson County Circuit Clerk's Office, Charles Town, West Virginia; *New York Herald*, Dec. 12, 1859, 1.

43. Hinton, *John Brown and His Men*, 500; Villard, *John Brown*, 580.

44. *What Is a Fair Trial? A Basic Guide to Legal Standards and Practice*, 2.

45. See discussion in chap. 10.

46. *Lawrence (Kansas) Republican*, Nov. 17, 1859, as quoted in Villard, *John Brown*, 480.

47. Villard, *John Brown*, 481.

48. *New York Herald*, Nov. 20, 1859.

49. Andrew, "Letter from Gov. Andrew," 211.

50. *New York Times*, Nov. 1, 1859.

51. *Richmond Enquirer* (semiweekly edition), Nov. 8, 1859.

52. *Baltimore Sun*, Nov. 5, 1859.

53. Wright, "Trial of John Brown," 361.

54. Washington, "The Trial of John Brown," 171.

55. Wright, "Trial of John Brown," 358.

56. Ibid., 359.

57. Caskie, "The Trial of John Brown," 425.

58. Von Holst, *John Brown*, 150.

59. Andrew Hunter, *John Brown's Raid*, 2, Huntington Library, San Marino, California.

60. Richard Parker, "Trial of John Brown," manuscript in John Brown Papers, Library of Congress; printed in "John Brown's Raid," *St. Louis Globe-Democrat*, April 8, 1888, 26–27.

61. Du Bois, *John Brown*, 214.

62. Warren, *John Brown: The Making of a Martyr*, 397–398.

63. Weyl, *Treason*, 260.

64. Morris, *Fair Trial*, 259.

65. Furnas, *The Road to Harper's Ferry*, 5.

66. Ibid., 42–43.

67. Finkelman, *His Soul Goes Marching On*, 8.

68. Lubet, *Nothing but the Truth*, 51–52.

69. U.S. Const., art. II, §2; Code of Va. (1849), chap. 17, §18; see Va. Const. (1851), art. V, §5 (power to grant reprieves and pardons except as otherwise provided by law).

70. See discussion in chap. 6.

71. See discussion in chap. 6.

72. *New York Herald*, Oct. 26, 1859; Oct. 29, 1859.

73. *Ibid.*, Oct. 29, 1859.

74. Va. Const. (1851), art. VI, §13.

BIBLIOGRAPHY

ARCHIVES AND MANUSCRIPTS

Harpers Ferry National Historical Park

Noffsinger, James P. *Harpers Ferry, West Virginia: Contributions towards a Physical History.* Typescript prepared November 1958 for the U.S. Department of the Interior, National Park Service, Eastern Office of Design and Construction, Philadelphia.

Henry E. Huntington Library and Art Gallery,
San Marino, California

John Brown's Raid[:] Recollections of Prosecuting Attorney Andrew Hunter. Typescript of twenty-four pages prepared about 1887, with Hunter's recollections of the John Brown raid and trial. In Robert Alonzo Brock Collection.

The Trial of John Brown by Gen'l Marcus J. Wright, Richmond, Va[.], *1889.* Typescript of four pages introducing *John Brown's Raid[:] Recollections of Prosecuting Attorney Andrew Hunter.* In Robert Alonzo Brock Collection.

Jefferson County Circuit Clerk's Office, Charles Town, West Virginia
John Brown Papers.

Library of Congress, Washington, D.C.
Henry Alexander Wise and Family Collection.
John Brown Collection.

The Library of Virginia, Richmond
Executive Papers of Governor Henry A. Wise.

University of Virginia Library, Charlottesville
Record of the Trial of John Brown by Judge Richard Parker.
Commonwealth v. Brown. To the Honorable John J. Allen, President, and
his associates, Judges of the Supreme Court of Appeals of Virginia. Petition of John Brown for writ of error, by his counsel Samuel Chilton
and William Green. Court of Appeals of Virginia, Richmond, 1859.

West Virginia State Archives, Charleston
Boyd B. Stutler Collection.

West Virginia University Libraries, Morgantown
David Hunter Strother (Porte Crayon). *Lecture on John Brown in
Cleveland, 1868.*

BOOKS AND ARTICLES

Abels, Jules. *Man on Fire: John Brown and the Cause of Liberty.* New
York: Macmillan, 1971.
Amar, Akhil Reed. *America's Constitution: A Biography.* New York:
Random House, 2005.
Anderson, Osborne P. *A Voice from Harper's Ferry: A Narrative of
Events at Harper's Ferry; With Incidents Prior and Subsequent to Its
Capture by Captain Brown and His Men.* Boston: Printed for the
author, 1861.
Andrew, John. "Letter from Gov. Andrew." *Old and New,* February
1871, 211–212.
Ayers, Edward L. *What Caused the Civil War?: Reflections on the South
and Southern History.* New York: W. W. Norton, 2005.
Barry, Joseph. *The Strange Story of Harper's Ferry, with Legends of the*

Surrounding Country. Martinsburg, WV: Thompson Brothers, 1903.

Basler, Roy P., ed. *The Collected Works of Abraham Lincoln*. New Brunswick, NJ: Rutgers University Press, 1952–1955.

Blackstone, William. "Commentaries." In *The Founders' Constitution*, Vol. 4, edited by Philip B. Kurland and Ralph Lerner, 423–429. Chicago: University of Chicago Press, 1987.

Bodenhamer, David J. *Fair Trial: Rights of the Accused in American History*. New York: Oxford University Press, 1992.

Bogen, David Skillen. *Privileges and Immunities: A Reference Guide to the United States Constitution*. Westport, CT: Praeger, 2003.

Booth, John Wilkes. *"Right or Wrong, God Judge Me": The Writings of John Wilkes Booth*. Edited by John Rhodehamel and Louise Taper. Chicago: University of Illinois Press, 1997.

Borchard, Gregory. "*The New York Tribune* at Harper's Ferry: 'Horace Greeley on Trial.'" *American Journalism* 20, no. 1 (Winter 2003): 13–31.

Boteler, Alexander R. "Recollections of the John Brown Raid." *Century Magazine* 26, no. 3 (1883): 399–411.

Boyer, Richard O. *The Legend of John Brown: A Biography and a History*. New York: Alfred A. Knopf, 1973.

Brown, John. *Testimonies of Capt. John Brown at Harper's Ferry, with His Address to the Court*. New York: American Anti-Slavery Society, 1860.

Burr, Charles Chauncey. "War Democrats—Their Crimes." *Old Guard* 1 (1863): 200–204.

Bushong, Millard Kessler. *A History of Jefferson County, West Virginia*. Charles Town, WV: Jefferson Publishing, 1941.

Byrne, John Edward. *The News from Harper's Ferry: The Press as Lens and Prism for John Brown's Raid*. Ph.D. dissertation, George Washington University, 1987.

Campbell, Douglas S. *Free Press v. Fair Trial: Supreme Court Decisions since 1807*. Westport, CT: Praeger, 1994.

"Can the Crime of Treason Be Committed against One of the United

Bibliography

States?" *American Law Magazine* [Philadelphia] 4 (1845): 318–350.

Carso, Brian F., Jr. *"Whom Can We Trust Now?": The Meaning of Treason in the United States, from the Revolution through the Civil War.* Lanham, MD: Lexington Books, 2006.

Carton, Evan. *Patriotic Treason: John Brown and the Soul of America.* New York: Free Press, 2006.

Caskie, George E. "The Trial of John Brown." *American Law Review* 44 (1910): 405–425.

Chapin, Bradley. The *American Law of Treason: Revolutionary and Early National Origins.* Seattle: University of Washington Press, 1964.

Chowder, Ken. "Father of American Terrorism." *American Heritage* 33 (February/March 2000): 81–91.

Christianson, Stephen G. "John Brown Trial: 1859." In *Great American Trials,* edited by Edward W. Knappman. Detroit: Visible Ink Press, 1994.

Cook, John E. *Confession of John E. Cooke* [*sic*], *Brother-in-law of Governor A. P. Willard of Indiana, and One of the Participants in the Harper's Ferry Invasion.* Charlestown, VA: D. S. Eichelberger, 1859.

Cultural Landscape Report: Lower Town, Harper's Ferry National Historical Park. Harpers Ferry, WV: National Park Service, Department of the Interior, Harpers Ferry National Historical Park, 1993.

Curtis, Michael Kent. *No State Shall Abridge: The Fourteenth Amendment and the Bill of Rights.* Durham, NC: Duke University Press, 1986.

Cushing, Caleb. "Extraterritoriality of Military Sites Occupied by the United States." In *Opinions of the Attorney General of the United States.* Washington, D.C.: Robert Farnham, 1856.

Dana, Richard Henry, Jr. "How We Met John Brown." *Atlantic Monthly* 28, no. 165 (July 1871): 1–9.

Davidson, James West, and Mark Hamilton Lytle. *After the Fact: The Art of Historical Detection.* New York: Alfred A. Knopf, 1982.

Davis, Julia. *The Shenandoah.* Rivers of America Series. New York: Farrar and Rinehart, 1945.

Dershowitz, Alan M. *America on Trial: Inside the Legal Battles That Transformed Our Nation.* New York: Warner Books, 2004.

DeVillers, David. *The John Brown Slavery Revolt Trial.* Berkeley Heights, NJ: Enslow, 2000.

Douglas, Henry Kyd. *I Rode with Stonewall.* Chapel Hill: University of North Carolina Press, 1940.

Draper, Daniel C. "Legal Phases of the Trial of John Brown." *West Virginia History* 1 (January 1940): 87–103.

[Drew, Thomas.] *The John Brown Invasion[:] An Authentic History of the Harper's Ferry Tragedy, with Full Details of the Capture, Trial and Execution of the Invaders, and of All the Incidents connected Therewith.* Boston: James Campbell, 1860.

Du Bois, W. E. B. *John Brown.* Edited and with an introduction by David Roediger. New York: Modern Library, 2001.

[Dunphy, Thomas.] "Captain John Brown." In *Remarkable Trials of All Countries; with the Evidence and Speeches of Counsel, Court Scenes, Incidents, &c. Compiled from Official Sources.* Vol. 2, 37–122. New York: S. S. Peloubet, 1882.

Eby, Cecil D. "John Brown's Kiss." *Virginia Cavalcade* 11 (Autumn 1961): 42–47.

Emerson, Ralph Waldo. *Complete Works of Ralph Waldo Emerson.* 12 vols. Boston: Houghton Mifflin, 1903–1904.

———. *The Journals and Miscellaneous Notebooks of Ralph Waldo Emerson.* Vol. 15 (1860–1866). Edited by Linda Allardt, David W. Hill, and Ruth H. Bennett. Cambridge, MA: Harvard University Press, 1982.

Engdahl, David E. "State and Federal Power over Federal Property." *Arizona Law Review* 18 (1976): 283–384.

The Federalist, or the New Constitution, Written in 1788, by Mr. Hamilton, Mr. Madison, and Mr. Jay. Hallowell, ME: Glazier, Masters, and Smith, 1842.

Ferguson, Robert A. "Story and Transcription in the Trial of John Brown." *Yale Journal of Law and the Humanities* 6 (1994): 37–73.

———. *The Trial in American Life*. Chicago: University of Chicago Press, 2007.

Finkelman, Paul, ed. *Defending Slavery: Proslavery Thought in the Old South, A Brief History with Documents*. Boston: Bedford/St. Martin's, 2003.

———. *His Soul Goes Marching On: Responses to John Brown and the Harpers Ferry Raid*. Charlottesville: University Press of Virginia, 1995.

Fisk, Wilbur. *Hard Marching Every Day: The Civil War Letters of Private Wilbur Fisk, 1861–1865*. Edited by Emil and Ruth Rosenblatt. Lawrence: University Press of Kansas, 1992.

Fleming, Thomas J. "The Trial of John Brown." *American Heritage* 18, no. 4 (August 1967): 28–33, 92–100.

Foster, Sir Michael. "Discourse on High Treason" (1762). In *The Founders' Constitution*, Vol. 4, edited by Philip B. Kurland and Ralph Lerner, 410–423. Chicago: University of Chicago Press, 1987.

Freedman, Warren. *The Constitutional Right to a Speedy and Fair Criminal Trial*. New York: Quorum Books, 1989.

Furnas, J. C. *The Road to Harpers Ferry*. New York: William Sloane Associates, 1959.

Geffert, Hannah. "They Heard His Call: The Local Black Community's Involvement in the Raid on Harpers Ferry." In *Terrible Swift Sword: The Legacy of John Brown*, edited by Peggy A. Russo and Paul Finkelman, 23–45. Athens: Ohio University Press, 2005.

Geffert, Hannah (with Jean Libby). "Regional Black Involvement in John Brown's Raid on Harpers Ferry." In *Prophets of Protest: Reconsidering the History of American Abolitionism*, edited by Timothy Patrick McCarthy and John Stauffer, 165–179. New York: New Press, 2006.

Gilbert, James N. "A Behavioral Analysis of John Brown: Martyr or Terrorist? In *Terrible Swift Sword: The Legacy of John Brown*, edited by Peggy A. Russo and Paul Finkelman, 107–117. Athens: Ohio University Press, 2005.

Grace, Adam S. "Federal-State 'Negotiations' over Federal Enclaves in the Early Republic: Finding Solutions to Constitutional Problems at the Birth of the Lighthouse System." *Mississippi Law Journal* 75 (2006): 545–582.

Green, Israel. "The Capture of John Brown." *North American Review* 141 (December 1885): 564–569.

Gridley, Karl. "'Willing to Die for the Cause of Freedom in Kansas': Free State Emigration, John Brown, and the Rise of Militant Abolitionism in the Kansas Territory." In *Prophets of Protest: Reconsidering the History of American Abolitionism,* edited by Timothy Patrick McCarthy and John Stauffer, 147–164. New York: New Press, 2006.

Hammond, Scott John. "John Brown as Founder." In *Terrible Swift Sword: The Legacy of John Brown,* edited by Peggy A. Russo and Paul Finkelman, 61–76. Athens: Ohio University Press, 2005.

Hill, Frederick Trevor. "The Commonwealth vs. Brown—The Prelude to the Civil War." *Harper's Magazine* 113 (July 1906): 264–279.

———. *Decisive Battles of the Law: Narrative Studies of Eight Legal Contests Affecting the History of the United States between the Years 1800 and 1886.* New York: Harper and Brothers, 1907.

Hinton, Richard J. *John Brown and His Men: With Some Account of the Roads They Traveled to Reach Harper's Ferry.* Rev. ed. New York: Funk and Wagnalls, 1894.

Hurst, James Willard. *The Law of Treason in the United States: Collected Essays.* Westport, CT: Greenwood, 1971.

Jefferson, Thomas. *Notes on the State of Virginia.* Boston: Lilly and Wait, 1832.

Keller, Allan. *Thunder at Harper's Ferry.* Englewood Cliffs, NJ: Prentice-Hall, 1958.

Kurland, Philip B., and Ralph Lerner, eds. *The Founders' Constitution.* 5 vols. Chicago: University of Chicago Press, 1987.

LaFave, Wayne R. *Criminal Law.* 4th ed. St. Paul, MN: Thompson West, 2003.

Larson, Carlton F. W. "The Forgotten Constitutional Law of Treason and the Enemy Combatant Problem." *University of Pennsylvania Law Review* 154 (2006): 863–926.

Lawson, John D., ed. *American State Trials: A Collection of the Important and Interesting Criminals Trials which have taken place in the United States, from the Beginning of Our Government to the Present Day.* Vol. 6, 700–805. St. Louis: F. H. Thomas Law, 1916.

"Lee and Stuart at Harper's Ferry." *Southern Historical Society Papers* 38 (1910): 372–378.

Leek, J. H. "Treason and the Constitution." *Journal of Politics* 13 (1951): 604–622.

The Life, Trial and Execution of Captain John Brown, Known as Old Brown of Ossawatomie, with a Full Account of the Attempted Insurrection at Harper's Ferry, Compiled from Official and Authentic Sources, Including Cooke's Confession, and all the Incidents of the Execution. New York: Robert M. De Witt, 1859.

Longfellow, Samuel. *Life of Henry Wadsworth Longfellow, with Extracts from His Journals and Correspondence.* Vol. 2. Boston: Houghton Mifflin, 1891.

Lubet, Steven. "John Brown's Trial. *Alabama Law Review* 52 (2001): 425–466.

———. *Nothing But the Truth.* New York: New York University Press, 2002.

———. "So Perish All Enemies of the Union." *Litigation* 28 (Winter 2002): 2, 51–66.

Matthews, James M. *Digest of the Laws of Virginia of a Criminal Nature, Illustrated by Judicial Decisions.* Richmond, VA: West and Johnson, 1861.

Mayo, Joseph. *A Guide to Magistrates: with Practical Forms for the Dishcarge of their Duties out of Court, to Which Are Added Precedents for the Use of Prosecutors, Sheriffs, Coroners, Constables, Escheators, Clerks, &c., Adapted to the New Code of Virginia.* Richmond, VA: Colin, Baptist, and Nowlan, 1850.

McCarthy, Timothy Patrick, and John Stauffer, eds. *Prophets of Protest: Reconsidering the History of American Abolitionism.* New York: New Press, 2006.

McKivigan, John R., and Stanley Harrold, eds. *Antislavery Violence:*

Sectional, Racial, and Cultural Conflict in Antebellum America. Knoxville: University of Tennessee Press, 1999.

Mcpherson, James M. *Battle Cry of Freedom: The Civil War Era.* New York: Oxford University Press, 1988.

———. *This Mighty Scourge: Perspectives on the Civil War.* New York: Oxford University Press, 2007.

Melville, Herman. *Battle Pieces and Aspects of the War.* New York: Harper and Brothers, 1866.

Moore, Cleon. *Epitome of the Life of "Ossawatomie" John Brown, Including the Story of His Attack on Harpers Ferry and His Capture, Trial and Execution, as Related by Cleon Moore, Esq., of Charles Town, W. Va.* Point Pleasant, WV: Mrs. Livia Simpson Poffenbarger, 1904.

Morris, Richard B. *Fair Trial: Fourteen Who Stood Accused from Anne Hutchinson to Alger Hiss.* Rev. ed. New York: Harper Torchbooks, 1967.

Morrison, A. J. *College of Hampden Sidney Dictionary of Biography 1776–1825.* Hampden Sidney, VA: Hampden Sidney College, 1921.

National Park Service History Series. *John Brown's Raid.* Washington, D.C.: National Park Service, 1973.

Nelson, William. *The Fourteenth Amendment from Political Principle to Judicial Doctrine.* Cambridge, MA: Harvard University Press, 1988.

Norris, J. E. *History of the Lower Shenandoah Valley Counties of Frederick, Berkeley, Jefferson, and Clarke.* Chicago: H. Warner, 1890.

Oates, Stephen B. *To Purge This Land with Blood: A Biography of John Brown.* 2nd ed. Amherst: University of Massachusetts Press, 1984.

Peterson, Merrill D. *John Brown: The Legend Revisited.* Charlottesville: University of Virginia Press, 2002.

Pitman, Joseph S. *Report of the Trial of Thomas Wilson Dorr.* Boston: Tappan and Dennet, 1844.

Potter, David M. *The Impending Crisis, 1848–1861.* New York: Harper and Row, 1976.

————. *The South and the Sectional Conflict*. Baton Rouge: Louisiana State University Press, 1968.

Preston, J. T. L. "The Execution of John Brown." *Southern Bivouac*, August 1886, 187–189.

Provisional Constitution and Ordinances for the People of the United States, by John Brown. Preface by Boyd B. Stutler. Weston, MA: M and S Press, 1969.

Pulliam, David L. *The Constitutional Conventions of Virginia from the Foundation of the Commonwealth to the Present Time*. Richmond: John T. West, 1901.

Quarles, Garland E. *Some Worthy Lives: Mini-Biographies, Winchester and Frederick County*. Winchester, VA: Winchester–Frederick County Historical Society, 1988.

Ray, Isaac, M.D. *A Treatise on the Medical Jurisprudence of Insanity*. 3rd ed. Boston: Little, Brown, 1853.

Redpath, James. *Echoes of Harper's Ferry*. Boston: Thayer and Eldridge, 1860.

————. *The Public Life of Capt. John Brown by James Redpath, with an Auto-Biography of his Childhood and Youth*. Boston: Thayer and Eldridge, 1860.

"Refutation of Several Romances about the Execution of John Brown." *Southern Historical Society Papers* 13 (1885): 336–342.

Renehan, Edward J., Jr. *The Secret Six: The True Tale of the Men Who Conspired with John Brown*. Columbia: University of South Carolina Press, 1997.

Report of the Select Committee of the Senate Appointed to Inquire into the Late Invasion and Seizure of the Public Property at Harper's Ferry. 36th Congress, 1st Session. June 1860.

Reynolds, David S. *John Brown, Abolitionist: The Man Who Killed Slavery, Sparked the Civil War, and Seeded Civil Rights*. New York: Alfred A. Knopf, 2005.

Rhodes, Elisha Hunt. *All for the Union: The Civil War Diary and Letters of Elisha Hunt Rhodes*. Edited by Robert Hunt Rhodes. New York: Orion Books, 1991.

Riddle, Albert Gallatin. *Recollections of War Times: Reminiscences of*

Men and Events in Washington, 1860–1865. New York: G. P. Putnam's Sons, 1895.

Robertson, James I., Jr. *Stonewall Jackson: The Man, the Soldier, the Legend.* New York: Macmillan, 1997.

Ronda, Bruce A. *Reading the Old Man: John Brown in American Culture.* Knoxville: University of Tennessee Press, 2008.

Rosengarten, Joseph. "John Brown's Raid." *Atlantic Monthly* 15 (1865): 711–718.

Ruchames, Louis, ed. *John Brown, The Making of a Revolutionary: The Story of John Brown in His Own Words and in the Words of Those Who Knew Him.* New York: Universal Library, Grosset and Dunlap, 1969.

Ruffin, Edmund. *The Diary of Edmund Ruffin.* Vol. 1: *Toward Independence, October 1856–April 1861.* Edited by William Kauffman Scarborough. Baton Rouge: Louisiana State University Press, 1972.

Russo, Peggy A., and Paul Finkelman, eds. *Terrible Swift Sword: The Legacy of John Brown.* Athens: Ohio University Press, 2005.

Sanborn, Franklin B. *The Life and Letters of John Brown, Liberator of Kansas, and Martyr of Virginia.* Boston: Roberts Brothers, 1891.

Siebert, Fred S., Walter Wilcox, and George Hough III. *Free Press and Fair Trial: Some Dimensions of the Problem.* Edited by Chilton R. Bush. Athens: University of Georgia Press, 1970.

Simpson, Craig. *A Good Southerner: The Life of Henry A. Wise of Virginia.* Chapel Hill: University of North Carolina Press, 1985.

———. "John Brown and Governor Wise: A New Perspective on Harpers Ferry." *Biography* 1, no. 1 (1974): 15–38.

Smith, Kenneth L. "Edmund Ruffin and the Raid on Harper's Ferry." *Virginia Cavalcade* 22, no. 2 (Autumn 1972): 28–37.

Smith, Merritt Roe. *Harpers Ferry Armory and the New Technology.* Ithaca, NY: Cornell University Press, 1977.

Stauffer, John. *The Black Hearts of Men: Radical Abolitionists and the Transformation of Race.* Cambridge, MA: Harvard University Press, 2002.

Stavis, Barrie. *John Brown: The Sword and the Word.* South Brunswick, NJ: A. S. Barnes, 1970.

Stewart, A. M. *Camp, March and Battle-field; or Three Years and a Half with the Army of the Potomac.* Philadelphia: Jas. B. Rodgers, 1865.

Stone, Edward, ed. *Incident at Harper's Ferry.* Englewood Cliffs, NJ: Prentice-Hall, 1956.

Story, Joseph. *Commentaries on the Constitution of the United States.* 3 vols. Boston: Hilliard, Gray, 1833.

————. *A Familiar Exposition of the Constitution of the United States: Containing a Brief Commentary on Every Clause, Explaining the True Nature, Reasons, and Objects Thereof; Designed for the Use of School Libraries and General Readers.* New York: Harper and Brothers, 1847.

Strother, David H. "The Last Hours of the John Brown Raid," edited by Cecil D. Eby. *Virginia Magazine of History and Biography* 73 (1965): 169–177.

Stutler, Boyd B. "Abraham Lincoln and John Brown—A Parallel." *Civil War History* 8 (1962): 290–299.

————. "The Hanging of John Brown." *American Heritage* 6, no. 2 (February 1955): 4–9.

————. "John Brown and the Oberlin Lands." *West Virginia History* 12, no. 3 (April 1951): 183–199.

————. "John Brown's Constitution." *Lincoln Herald* (December 1948–February 1949): 17–25.

————. "John Brown's Letter." *West Virginia History* 9, no. 1 (October 1947): 1–25.

————. "Judge Richard Parker–He Tried John Brown." *Magazine of the Jefferson County Historical Society* 19 (December 1953): 27–37.

————. *West Virginia in the Civil War.* 2nd ed. Charleston, WV: Education Foundation, 1966.

Sutherland, Keith A. "The Senate Investigates Harpers Ferry." *Prologue: The Journal of the National Archives* 8, no. 4 (1976): 193–207.

Tackach, James. *The Trial of John Brown: Radical Abolitionist.* San Diego: Lucent Books, 1998.

Taylor, James E. *With Sheridan up the Shenandoah Valley in 1864.* Cleveland, OH: Western Reserve Historical Society, 1989.

Thomas, Emory E., ed. "'The Greatest Service I Rendered the State': J. E. B. Stuart's Account of the Capture of John Brown." *Virginia Magazine of History and Biography* 94, no. 3 (July 1986): 345–357.

Toledo, Gregory. *The Hanging of Old Brown: A Story of Slaves, Statesmen, and Redemption.* Westport, CT: Praeger, 2002.

Tripp, Bernell. "The Case of John Brown (1859). 'John Brown still lives.'" In *The Press on Trial: Crimes and Trials as Media Events,* edited by Lloyd Chiasson Jr., 25–36. Westport, CT: Greenwood, 1997.

Trodd, Zoe, and John Stauffer, eds. *Meteor of War: The John Brown Story.* Maplecrest, NY: Brandywine Press, 2004.

Tucker, Glenn. "John Wilkes Booth at the John Brown Hanging." *Lincoln Herald* 78, no. 1 (Spring 1978): 3–11.

Villard, Oswald Garrison. *John Brown, 1800–1859. A Biography Fifty Years After.* Rev. ed. New York: Alfred A. Knopf, 1943.

Von Holst, Hermann. *John Brown.* Edited by Frank Preston Stearns. Boston: Cupples and Heard, 1888.

Voorhees, Daniel Wolsey, "Defense of John E. Cook." In *Daniel Wolsey Voorhees: Lectures, Addresses and Speeches,* edited by Harriet Cecilia Voorhees. Indianapolis: Bobbs-Merrill, 1897.

Warch, Richard, and Jonathan F. Fanton, eds. *John Brown.* Englewood Cliffs, NJ: Prentice-Hall, 1973.

Warren, Robert Penn. *John Brown: The Making of a Martyr* With an introduction by C. Vann Woodward. Nashville: J. S. Sanders, 1993.

Washington, Bushrod C. "The Trial of John Brown." *Green Bag* 11 (1899): 164–175.

Weiner, Mark S. *Black Trials: Citizenship from the Beginnings of Slavery to the End of Caste.* New York: Alfred A. Knopf, 2004.

Weyl, Nathaniel. *Treason: The Story of Disloyalty and Betrayal in American History.* Washington, D.C.: Public Affairs Press, 1950.

What Is a Fair Trial? A Basic Guide to Legal Standards and Practice. New York: Lawyers Committee for Human Rights, 2000.

White, Charles. "John Brown's Raid at Harpers Ferry: An Eyewitness Account by Charles White," edited by Rayburn S. Moore. *Virginia Magazine of History and Biography* 67, no. 4 (October 1959): 387–395.

White, Ronald C., Jr. *Lincoln's Greatest Speech: The Second Inaugural.* New York: Simon and Schuster, 2002.

Wilson, James. "Of Crimes Immediately against the Community, Lectures on Law." In *The Founders' Constitution*, Vol. 4, edited by Philip B. Kurland and Ralph Lerner, 436–439. Chicago: University of Chicago Press, 1987.

———. *The Works of the Honourable James Wilson, L.L.D.* Vol. 3. Philadelphia: Lorenzo Press, 1804.

Wise, Barton H. *The Life of Henry A. Wise of Virginia, 1806–1876.* New York: Macmillan, 1899.

Wise, John S. *End of an Era.* Edited and annotated by Curtis Carroll Davis. New York: Thomas Yoseloff, 1965.

———. *A Treatise on American Citizenship.* Northrop, Long Island, NY: Edward Thompson, 1906.

Wright, Marcus J. "Trial of John Brown: Its Impartiality and Decorum Vindicated." *Southern Historical Society Papers* 16 (1888): 357–365.

Young, Robert W. *Senator James Murray Mason: Defender of the Old South.* Knoxville: University of Tennessee Press, 1998.

Zittle, John Henry. *A Correct History of the John Brown Invasion at Harper's Ferry, West Va., Oct. 17, 1859.* Hagerstown, MD: Mail Publishing, 1905.

INDEX